P9-CFU-571

THE INVINCIBLE
IRON MAN
UNFIXABLE

WRITER: **MATT FRACTION**
ARTIST: **SALVADOR LARROCA**
COLORS: **FRANK D'ARMATA**
LETTERS: **VC'S JOE CARAMAGNA**
COVER ART: **SALVADOR LARROCA** & **FRANK D'ARMATA**
EDITOR: **ALEJANDRO ARBONA**
SENIOR EDITOR: **STEPHEN WACKER**

FREE COMIC BOOK DAY 2010: IRON MAN/THOR
WRITER: **MATT FRACTION**
PENCILER: **JOHN ROMITA JR.**
INKER: **KLAUS JANSON**
COLORIST: **DEAN WHITE**
LETTERS: **VC'S JOE SABINO**
COVER ART: **JOHN ROMITA JR., KLAUS JANSON** & **DEAN WHITE**
ASSISTANT EDITOR: **ALEJANDRO ARBONA**
EDITOR: **RALPH MACCHIO**

RESCUE #1
WRITER: **KELLY SUE DECONNICK**
ARTIST: **ANDREA MUTTI**
COLORIST: **JOSE VILLARRUBIA**
LETTERS: **CLAYTON COWLES**
COVER ART: **TRAVEL FOREMAN** & **JUNE CHUNG**
ASSISTANT EDITOR: **ALEJANDRO ARBONA**
EDITOR: **RALPH MACCHIO**

Collection Editor: Jennifer Grünwald • Editorial Assistants: James Emmett & Joe Hochstein
Assistant Editors: Alex Starbuck & Nelson Ribeiro • Editor, Special Projects: Mark D. Beazley
Senior Editor, Special Projects: Jeff Youngquist • Senior Vice Presidet of Sales: David Gabriel
SVP of Brand Planning & Communications: Michael Pasciullo

Editor in Chief: Axel Alonso • Chief Creative Officer: Joe Quesada • Publisher: Dan Buckley • Executive Producer: Alan Fine

INVINCIBLE IRON MAN VOL. 8: UNFIXABLE. Contains material originally published in magazine form as FREE COMIC BOOK DAY 2010 (IRON MAN/THOR), RESCUE #1 and IRON MAN #501-503. First printing 2011. Hardcover ISBN# 978-0-7851-5322-1. Softcover ISBN# 978-0-7851-5323-8. Published by MARVEL WORLDWIDE, INC., a subsidiary of MARVEL ENTERTAINMENT, LLC. OFFICE OF PUBLICATION: 135 West 50th Street, New York, NY 10020. Copyright © 2010, 2011 and 2012 Marvel Characters, Inc. All rights reserved. Hardcover: $19.99 per copy in the U.S. and $21.99 in Canada (GST #R127032852). Softcover: $15.99 per copy in the U.S. and $17.99 in Canada (GST #R127032852). Canadian Agreement #40668537. All characters featured in this issue and the distinctive names and likenesses thereof, and all related indicia are trademarks of Marvel Characters, Inc. No similarity between any of the names, characters, persons, and/or institutions in this magazine with those of any living or dead person or institution is intended, and any such similarity which may exist is purely coincidental. **Printed in the U.S.A.** ALAN FINE, EVP - Office of the President, Marvel Worldwide, Inc. and EVP & CMO Marvel Characters B.V.; DAN BUCKLEY, Publisher & President - Print, Animation & Digital Divisions; JOE QUESADA, Chief Creative Officer; JIM SOKOLOWSKI, Chief Operating Officer; DAVID BOGART, SVP of Business Affairs & Talent Management; TOM BREVOORT, SVP of Publishing; C.B. CEBULSKI, SVP of Creator & Content Development; DAVID GABRIEL, SVP of Publishing Sales & Circulation; MICHAEL PASCIULLO, SVP of Brand Planning & Communications; JIM O'KEEFE, VP of Operations & Logistics; DAN CARR, Executive Director of Publishing Technology; SUSAN CRESPI, Editorial Operations Manager; ALEX MORALES, Publishing Operations Manager; STAN LEE, Chairman Emeritus. For information regarding advertising in Marvel Comics or on Marvel.com, please contact John Dokes, SVP Integrated Sales and Marketing, at jdokes@marvel.com. For Marvel subscription inquiries, please call 800-217-9158. **Manufactured between 7/18/2011 and 8/15/2011 (hardcover), and 7/18/2011 and 2/13/2012 (softcover), by R.R. DONNELLEY, INC., SALEM, VA, USA.**

10 9 8 7 6 5 4 3 2 1

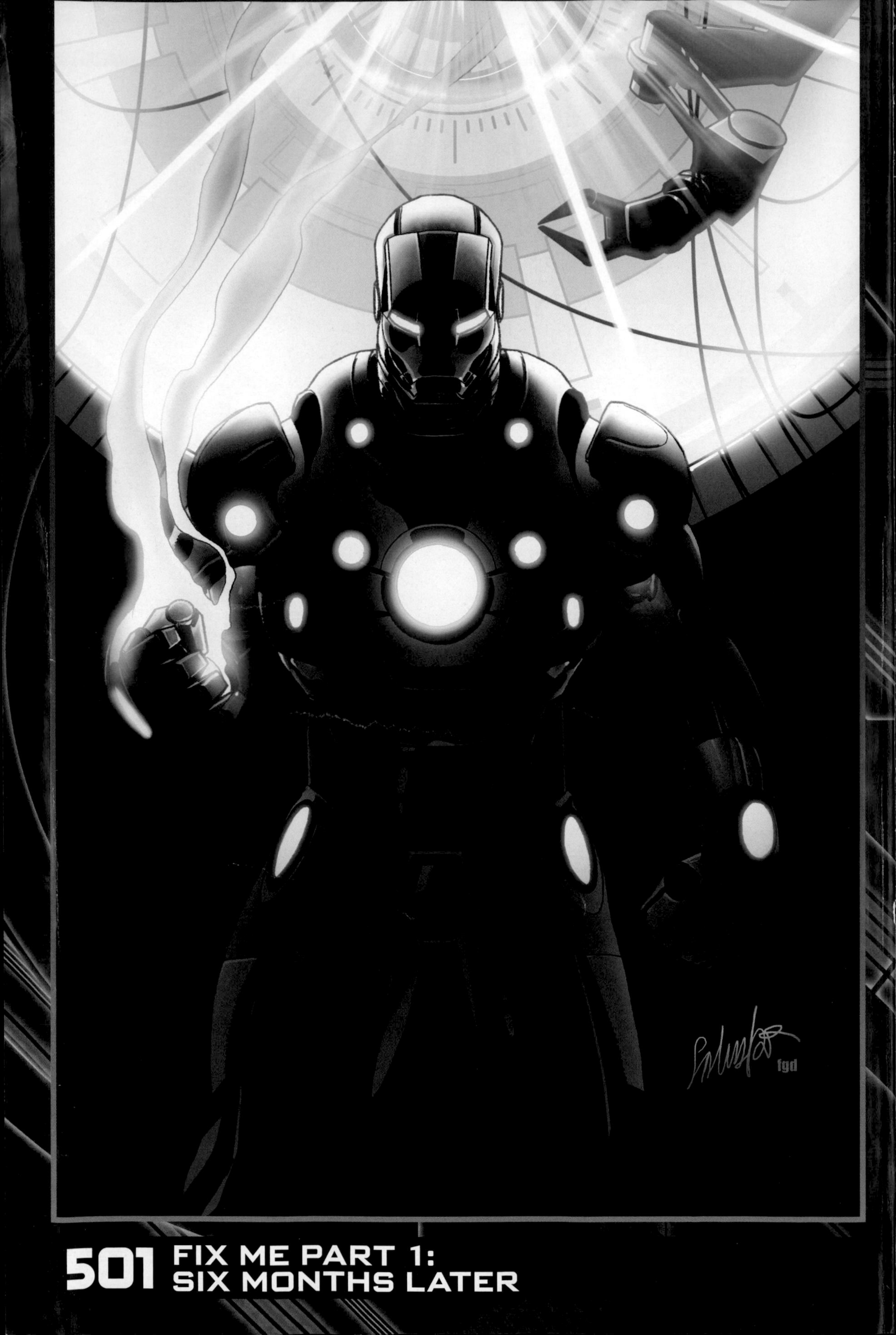

501 FIX ME PART 1: SIX MONTHS LATER

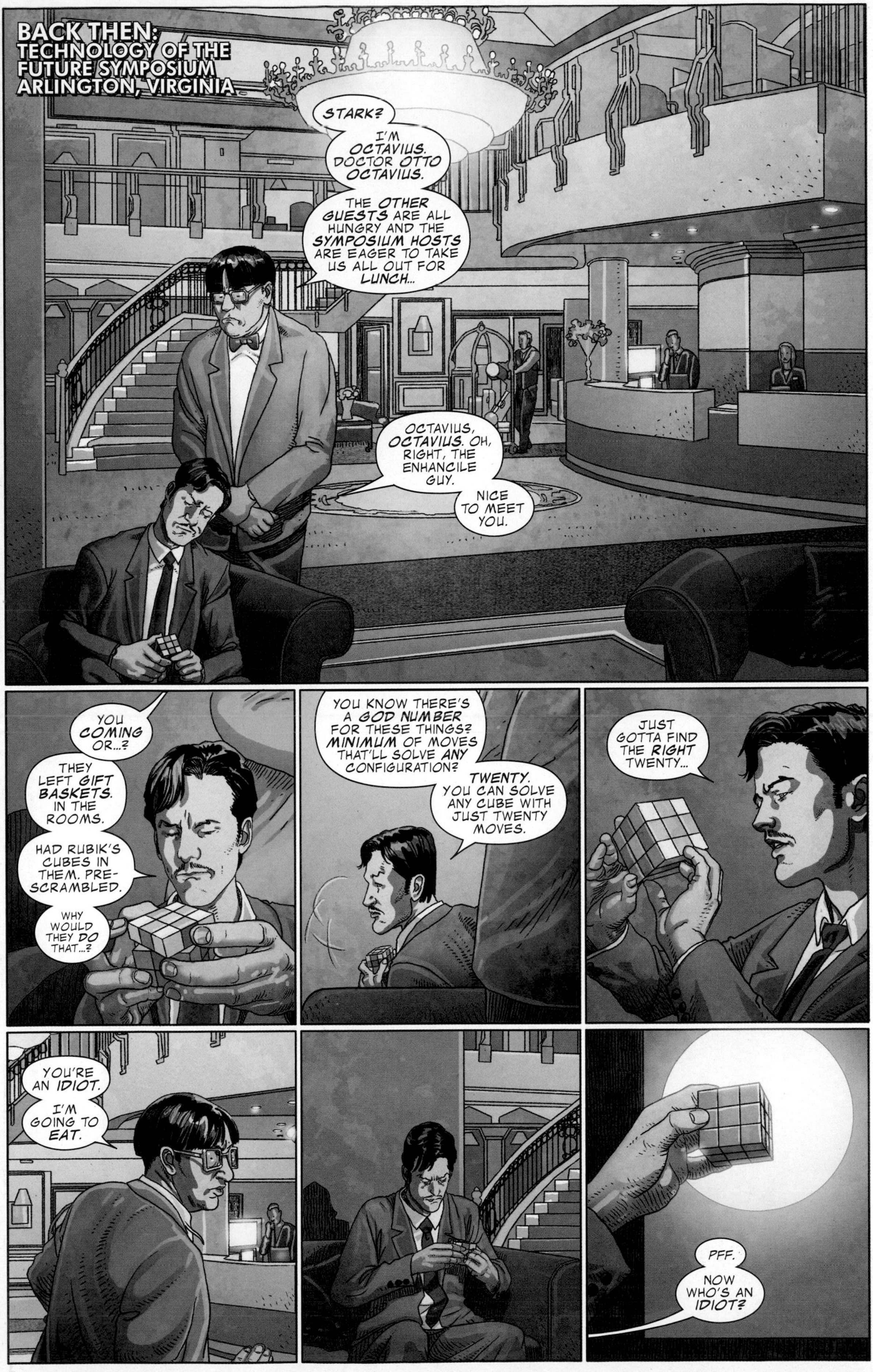
BACK THEN:
TECHNOLOGY OF THE FUTURE SYMPOSIUM
ARLINGTON, VIRGINIA
STARK?
I'M OCTAVIUS. DOCTOR OTTO OCTAVIUS.
THE OTHER GUESTS ARE ALL HUNGRY AND THE SYMPOSIUM HOSTS ARE EAGER TO TAKE US ALL OUT FOR LUNCH...
OCTAVIUS, OCTAVIUS. OH, RIGHT, THE ENHANCILE GUY.
NICE TO MEET YOU.
YOU COMING OR...?
THEY LEFT GIFT BASKETS. IN THE ROOMS.
HAD RUBIK'S CUBES IN THEM. PRE-SCRAMBLED.
WHY WOULD THEY DO THAT...?
YOU KNOW THERE'S A GOD NUMBER FOR THESE THINGS? MINIMUM OF MOVES THAT'LL SOLVE ANY CONFIGURATION?
TWENTY. YOU CAN SOLVE ANY CUBE WITH JUST TWENTY MOVES.
JUST GOTTA FIND THE RIGHT TWENTY...
YOU'RE AN IDIOT.
I'M GOING TO EAT.
PFF.
NOW WHO'S AN IDIOT?

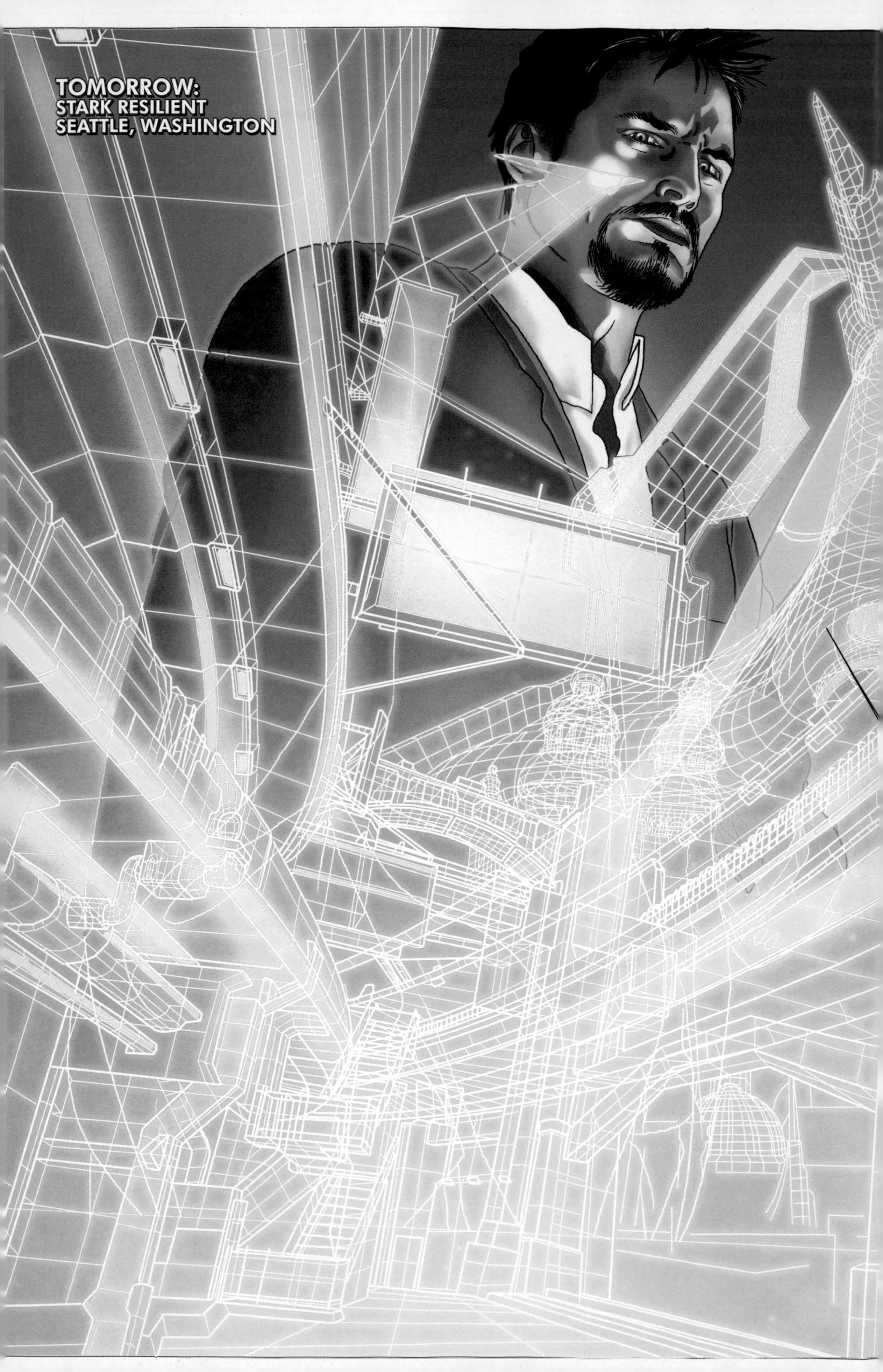
TOMORROW:
STARK RESILIENT
SEATTLE, WASHINGTON

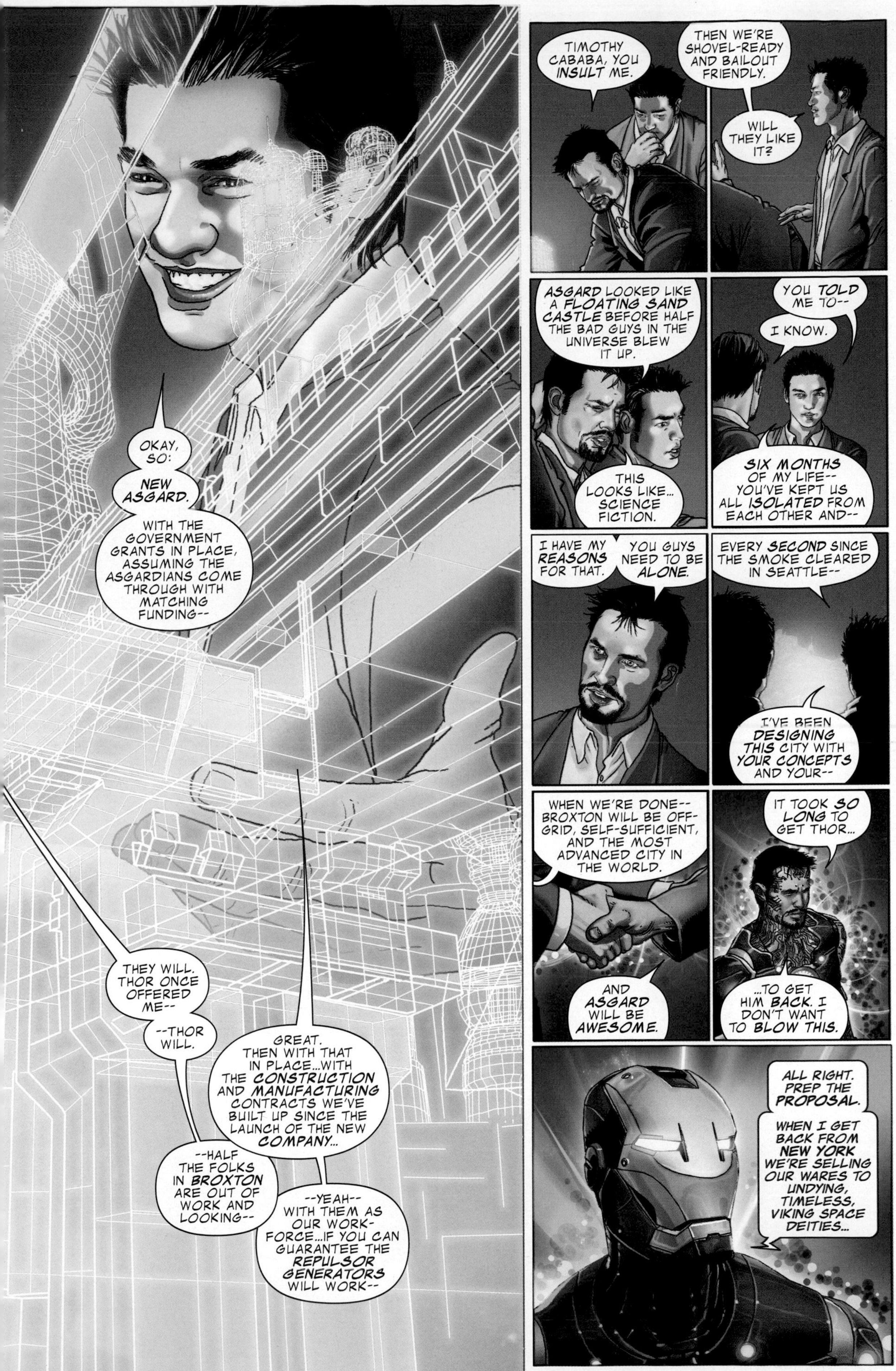

OKAY, SO:
NEW ASGARD.
WITH THE GOVERNMENT GRANTS IN PLACE, ASSUMING THE ASGARDIANS COME THROUGH WITH MATCHING FUNDING--
THEY WILL. THOR ONCE OFFERED ME--
--THOR WILL.
GREAT. THEN WITH THAT IN PLACE...WITH THE CONSTRUCTION AND MANUFACTURING CONTRACTS WE'VE BUILT UP SINCE THE LAUNCH OF THE NEW COMPANY...
--HALF THE FOLKS IN BROXTON ARE OUT OF WORK AND LOOKING--
--YEAH-- WITH THEM AS OUR WORK-FORCE...IF YOU CAN GUARANTEE THE REPULSOR GENERATORS WILL WORK--
TIMOTHY CABABA, YOU INSULT ME.
THEN WE'RE SHOVEL-READY AND BAILOUT FRIENDLY.
WILL THEY LIKE IT?
ASGARD LOOKED LIKE A FLOATING SAND CASTLE BEFORE HALF THE BAD GUYS IN THE UNIVERSE BLEW IT UP.
THIS LOOKS LIKE... SCIENCE FICTION.
YOU TOLD ME TO--
I KNOW.
SIX MONTHS OF MY LIFE-- YOU'VE KEPT US ALL ISOLATED FROM EACH OTHER AND--
I HAVE MY REASONS FOR THAT.
YOU GUYS NEED TO BE ALONE.
EVERY SECOND SINCE THE SMOKE CLEARED IN SEATTLE--
I'VE BEEN DESIGNING THIS CITY WITH YOUR CONCEPTS AND YOUR--
WHEN WE'RE DONE-- BROXTON WILL BE OFF-GRID, SELF-SUFFICIENT, AND THE MOST ADVANCED CITY IN THE WORLD.
AND ASGARD WILL BE AWESOME.
IT TOOK SO LONG TO GET THOR...
...TO GET HIM BACK. I DON'T WANT TO BLOW THIS.
ALL RIGHT. PREP THE PROPOSAL.
WHEN I GET BACK FROM NEW YORK WE'RE SELLING OUR WARES TO UNDYING, TIMELESS, VIKING SPACE DEITIES...

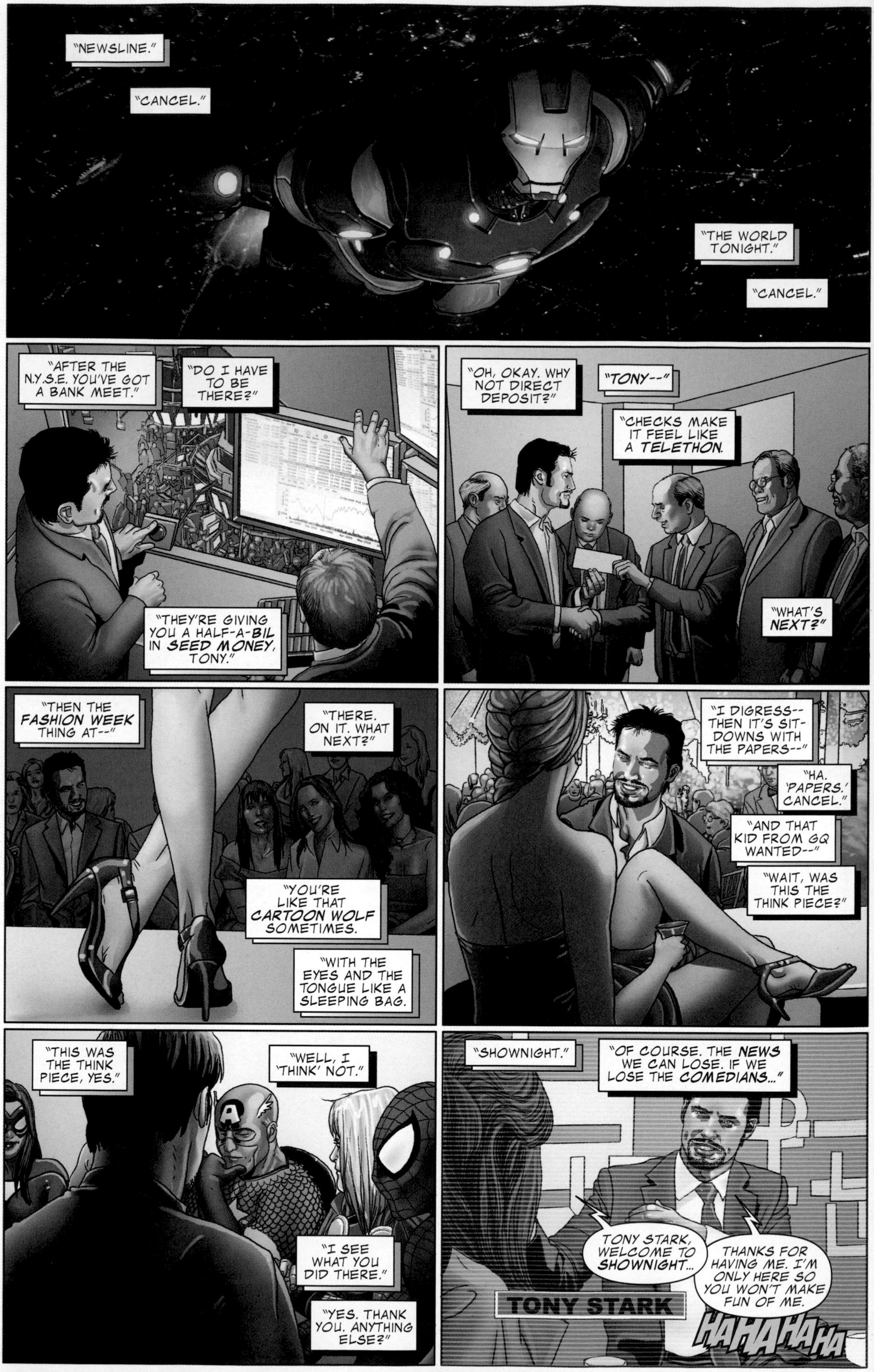
"NEWSLINE."
"CANCEL."
"THE WORLD TONIGHT."
"CANCEL."
"AFTER THE N.Y.S.E. YOU'VE GOT A BANK MEET."
"DO I HAVE TO BE THERE?"
"THEY'RE GIVING YOU A HALF-A-BIL IN SEED MONEY, TONY."
"OH, OKAY. WHY NOT DIRECT DEPOSIT?"
"TONY--"
"CHECKS MAKE IT FEEL LIKE A TELETHON.
"WHAT'S NEXT?"
"THEN THE FASHION WEEK THING AT--"
"THERE. ON IT. WHAT NEXT?"
"YOU'RE LIKE THAT CARTOON WOLF SOMETIMES.
"WITH THE EYES AND THE TONGUE LIKE A SLEEPING BAG.
"I DIGRESS-- THEN IT'S SIT-DOWNS WITH THE PAPERS--"
"HA. 'PAPERS.' CANCEL."
"AND THAT KID FROM GQ WANTED--"
"WAIT, WAS THIS THE THINK PIECE?"
"THIS WAS THE THINK PIECE, YES."
"WELL, I 'THINK' NOT."
"I SEE WHAT YOU DID THERE."
"YES. THANK YOU. ANYTHING ELSE?"
"SHOWNIGHT."
"OF COURSE. THE NEWS WE CAN LOSE. IF WE LOSE THE COMEDIANS..."
TONY STARK, WELCOME TO SHOWNIGHT...
THANKS FOR HAVING ME. I'M ONLY HERE SO YOU WON'T MAKE FUN OF ME.
TONY STARK
HAHAHAHAHA

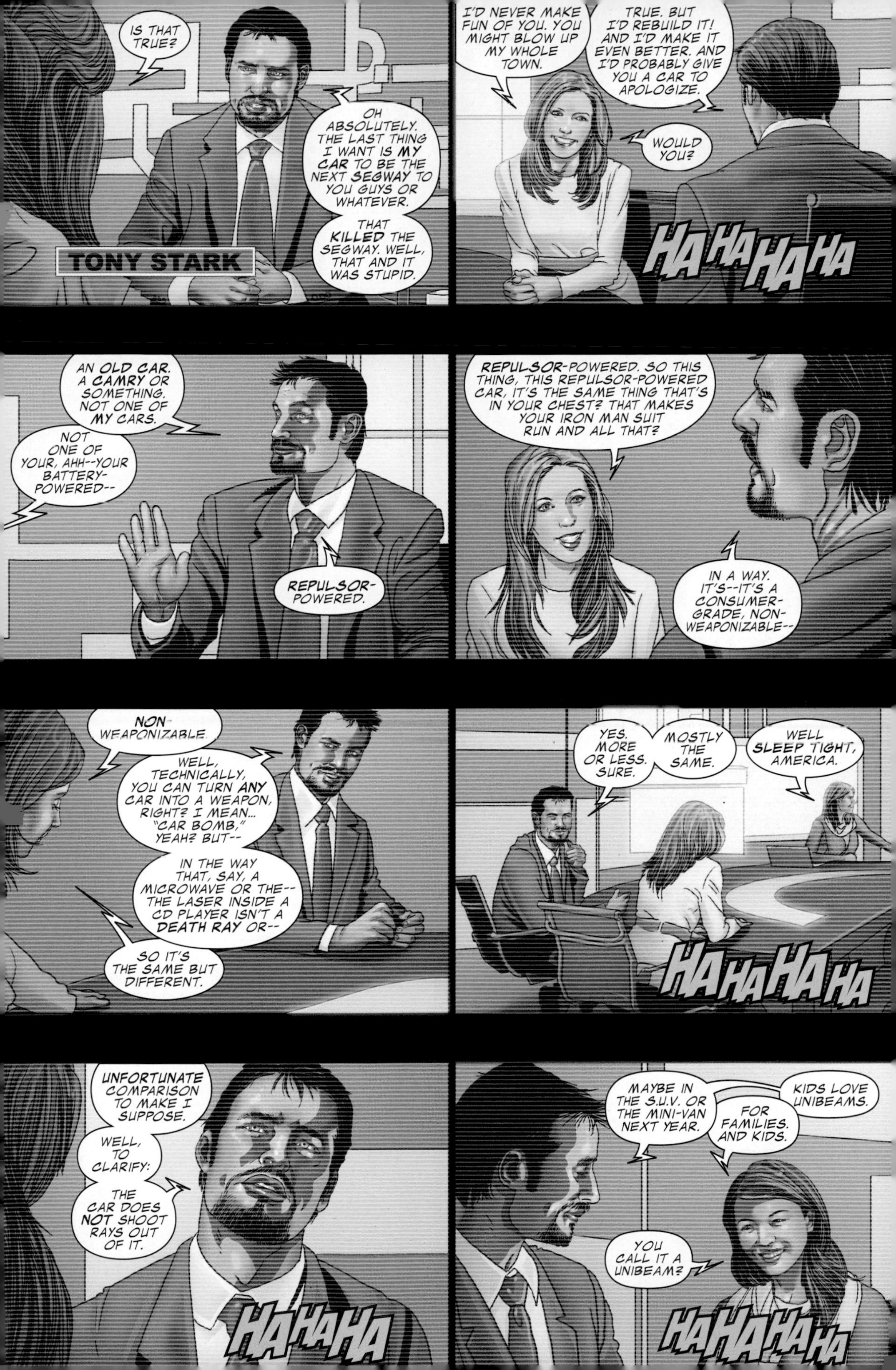
IS THAT TRUE?
OH ABSOLUTELY. THE LAST THING I WANT IS MY CAR TO BE THE NEXT SEGWAY TO YOU GUYS OR WHATEVER.
THAT KILLED THE SEGWAY. WELL, THAT AND IT WAS STUPID.
TONY STARK
I'D NEVER MAKE FUN OF YOU. YOU MIGHT BLOW UP MY WHOLE TOWN.
TRUE. BUT I'D REBUILD IT! AND I'D MAKE IT EVEN BETTER. AND I'D PROBABLY GIVE YOU A CAR TO APOLOGIZE.
WOULD YOU?
HA HA HA HA
AN OLD CAR. A CAMRY OR SOMETHING. NOT ONE OF MY CARS.
NOT ONE OF YOUR, AHH--YOUR BATTERY-POWERED--
REPULSOR-POWERED.
REPULSOR-POWERED. SO THIS THING, THIS REPULSOR-POWERED CAR, IT'S THE SAME THING THAT'S IN YOUR CHEST? THAT MAKES YOUR IRON MAN SUIT RUN AND ALL THAT?
IN A WAY. IT'S--IT'S A CONSUMER-GRADE, NON-WEAPONIZABLE--
NON-WEAPONIZABLE.
WELL, TECHNICALLY, YOU CAN TURN ANY CAR INTO A WEAPON, RIGHT? I MEAN... "CAR BOMB," YEAH? BUT--
IN THE WAY THAT, SAY, A MICROWAVE OR THE-- THE LASER INSIDE A CD PLAYER ISN'T A DEATH RAY OR--
SO IT'S THE SAME BUT DIFFERENT.
YES. MORE OR LESS. SURE.
MOSTLY THE SAME.
WELL SLEEP TIGHT, AMERICA.
HA HA HA HA HA
UNFORTUNATE COMPARISON TO MAKE I SUPPOSE.
WELL, TO CLARIFY:
THE CAR DOES NOT SHOOT RAYS OUT OF IT.
HA HA HA
MAYBE IN THE S.U.V. OR THE MINI-VAN NEXT YEAR.
KIDS LOVE UNIBEAMS.
FOR FAMILIES. AND KIDS.
YOU CALL IT A UNIBEAM?
HA HA HA HA HA

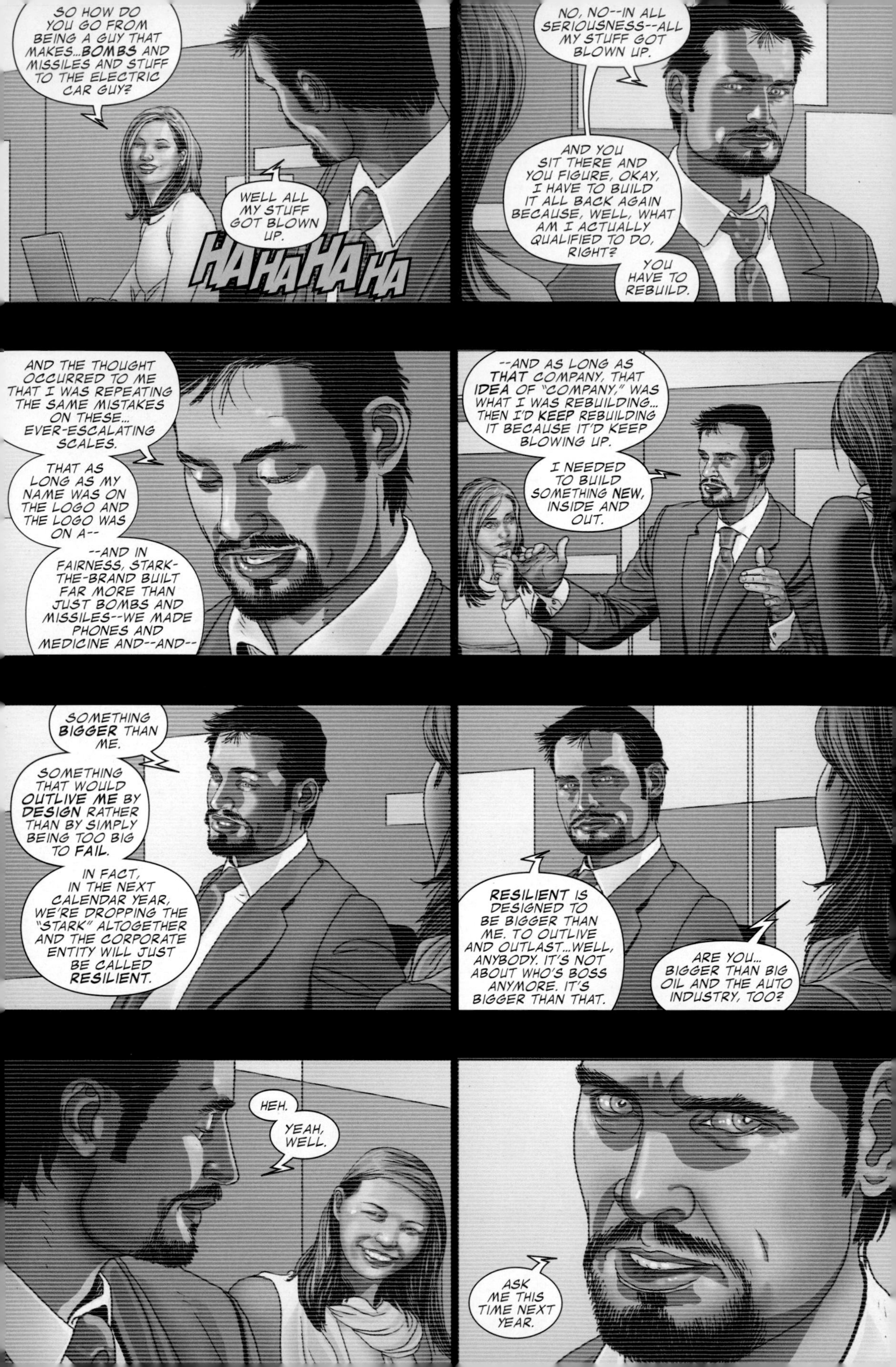
SO HOW DO YOU GO FROM BEING A GUY THAT MAKES...BOMBS AND MISSILES AND STUFF TO THE ELECTRIC CAR GUY?
WELL ALL MY STUFF GOT BLOWN UP.
HAHAHAHAHA
NO, NO--IN ALL SERIOUSNESS--ALL MY STUFF GOT BLOWN UP.
AND YOU SIT THERE AND YOU FIGURE, OKAY, I HAVE TO BUILD IT ALL BACK AGAIN BECAUSE, WELL, WHAT AM I ACTUALLY QUALIFIED TO DO, RIGHT?
YOU HAVE TO REBUILD.
AND THE THOUGHT OCCURRED TO ME THAT I WAS REPEATING THE SAME MISTAKES ON THESE... EVER-ESCALATING SCALES.
THAT AS LONG AS MY NAME WAS ON THE LOGO AND THE LOGO WAS ON A--
--AND IN FAIRNESS, STARK-THE-BRAND BUILT FAR MORE THAN JUST BOMBS AND MISSILES--WE MADE PHONES AND MEDICINE AND--AND--
--AND AS LONG AS THAT COMPANY, THAT IDEA OF "COMPANY," WAS WHAT I WAS REBUILDING... THEN I'D KEEP REBUILDING IT BECAUSE IT'D KEEP BLOWING UP.
I NEEDED TO BUILD SOMETHING NEW, INSIDE AND OUT.
SOMETHING BIGGER THAN ME.
SOMETHING THAT WOULD OUTLIVE ME BY DESIGN RATHER THAN BY SIMPLY BEING TOO BIG TO FAIL.
IN FACT, IN THE NEXT CALENDAR YEAR, WE'RE DROPPING THE "STARK" ALTOGETHER AND THE CORPORATE ENTITY WILL JUST BE CALLED RESILIENT.
RESILIENT IS DESIGNED TO BE BIGGER THAN ME. TO OUTLIVE AND OUTLAST...WELL, ANYBODY. IT'S NOT ABOUT WHO'S BOSS ANYMORE. IT'S BIGGER THAN THAT.
ARE YOU... BIGGER THAN BIG OIL AND THE AUTO INDUSTRY, TOO?
HEH.
YEAH, WELL.
ASK ME THIS TIME NEXT YEAR.

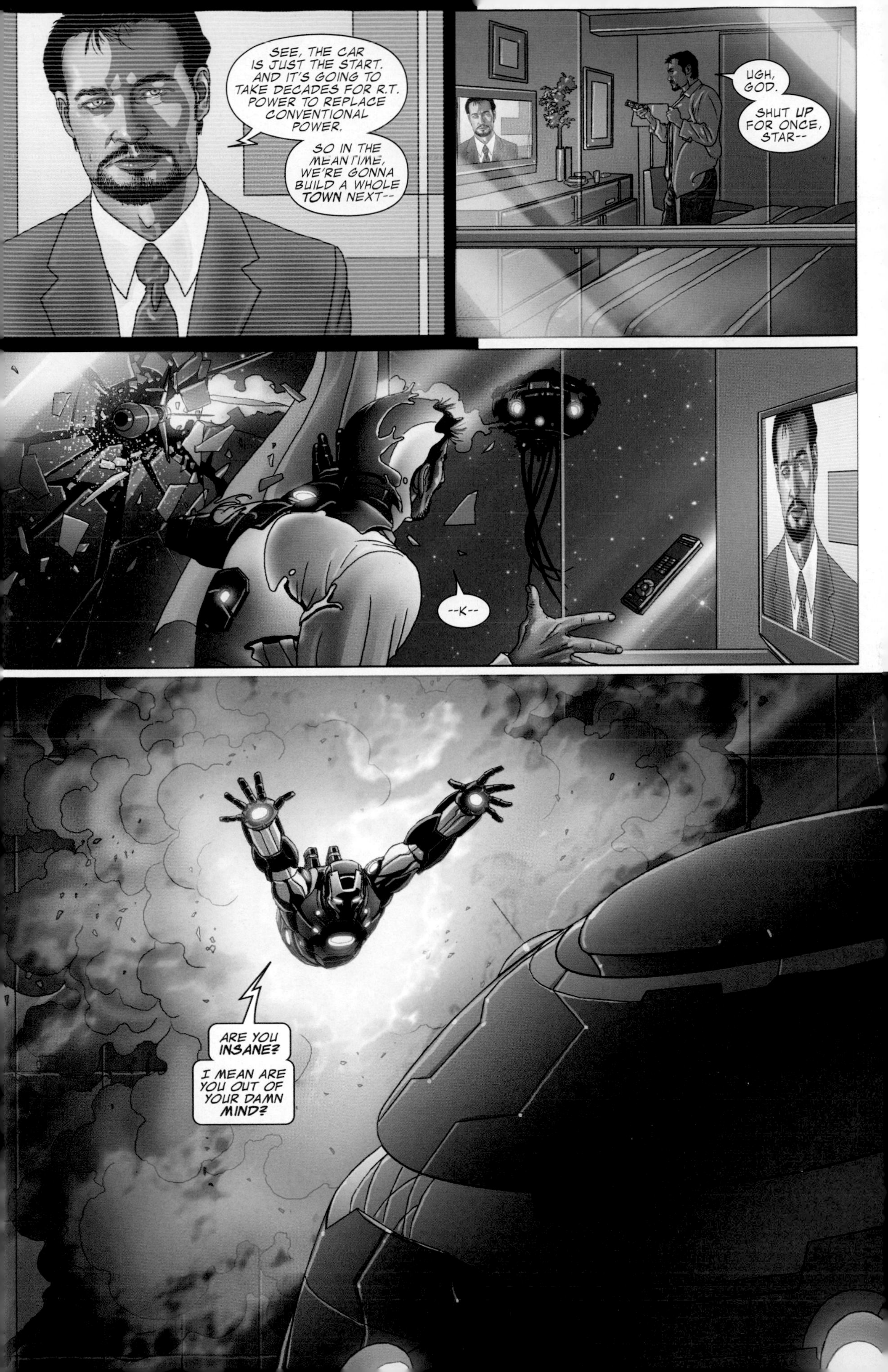
SEE, THE CAR IS JUST THE START. AND IT'S GOING TO TAKE DECADES FOR R.T. POWER TO REPLACE CONVENTIONAL POWER.
SO IN THE MEANTIME, WE'RE GONNA BUILD A WHOLE TOWN NEXT--
UGH, GOD.
SHUT UP FOR ONCE, STAR--
--K--
ARE YOU INSANE?
I MEAN ARE YOU OUT OF YOUR DAMN MIND?

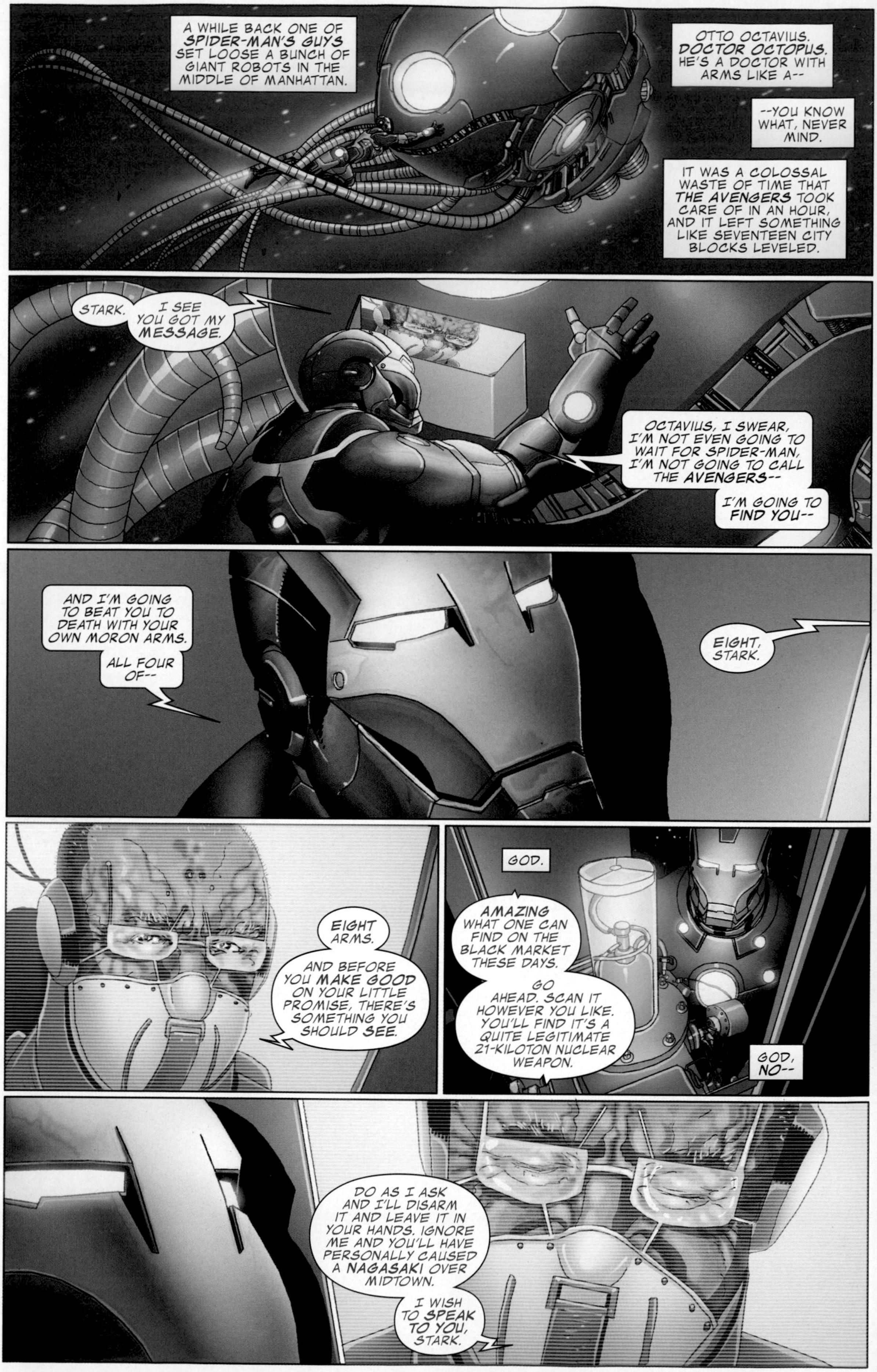
A WHILE BACK ONE OF SPIDER-MAN'S GUYS SET LOOSE A BUNCH OF GIANT ROBOTS IN THE MIDDLE OF MANHATTAN.
OTTO OCTAVIUS. DOCTOR OCTOPUS. HE'S A DOCTOR WITH ARMS LIKE A--
--YOU KNOW WHAT, NEVER MIND.
IT WAS A COLOSSAL WASTE OF TIME THAT THE AVENGERS TOOK CARE OF IN AN HOUR, AND IT LEFT SOMETHING LIKE SEVENTEEN CITY BLOCKS LEVELED.
STARK.
I SEE YOU GOT MY MESSAGE.
OCTAVIUS, I SWEAR, I'M NOT EVEN GOING TO WAIT FOR SPIDER-MAN, I'M NOT GOING TO CALL THE AVENGERS--
I'M GOING TO FIND YOU--
AND I'M GOING TO BEAT YOU TO DEATH WITH YOUR OWN MORON ARMS.
ALL FOUR OF--
EIGHT, STARK.
EIGHT ARMS.
AND BEFORE YOU MAKE GOOD ON YOUR LITTLE PROMISE, THERE'S SOMETHING YOU SHOULD SEE.
GOD.
AMAZING WHAT ONE CAN FIND ON THE BLACK MARKET THESE DAYS.
GO AHEAD. SCAN IT HOWEVER YOU LIKE. YOU'LL FIND IT'S A QUITE LEGITIMATE 21-KILOTON NUCLEAR WEAPON.
GOD, NO--
DO AS I ASK AND I'LL DISARM IT AND LEAVE IT IN YOUR HANDS. IGNORE ME AND YOU'LL HAVE PERSONALLY CAUSED A NAGASAKI OVER MIDTOWN.
I WISH TO SPEAK TO YOU, STARK.

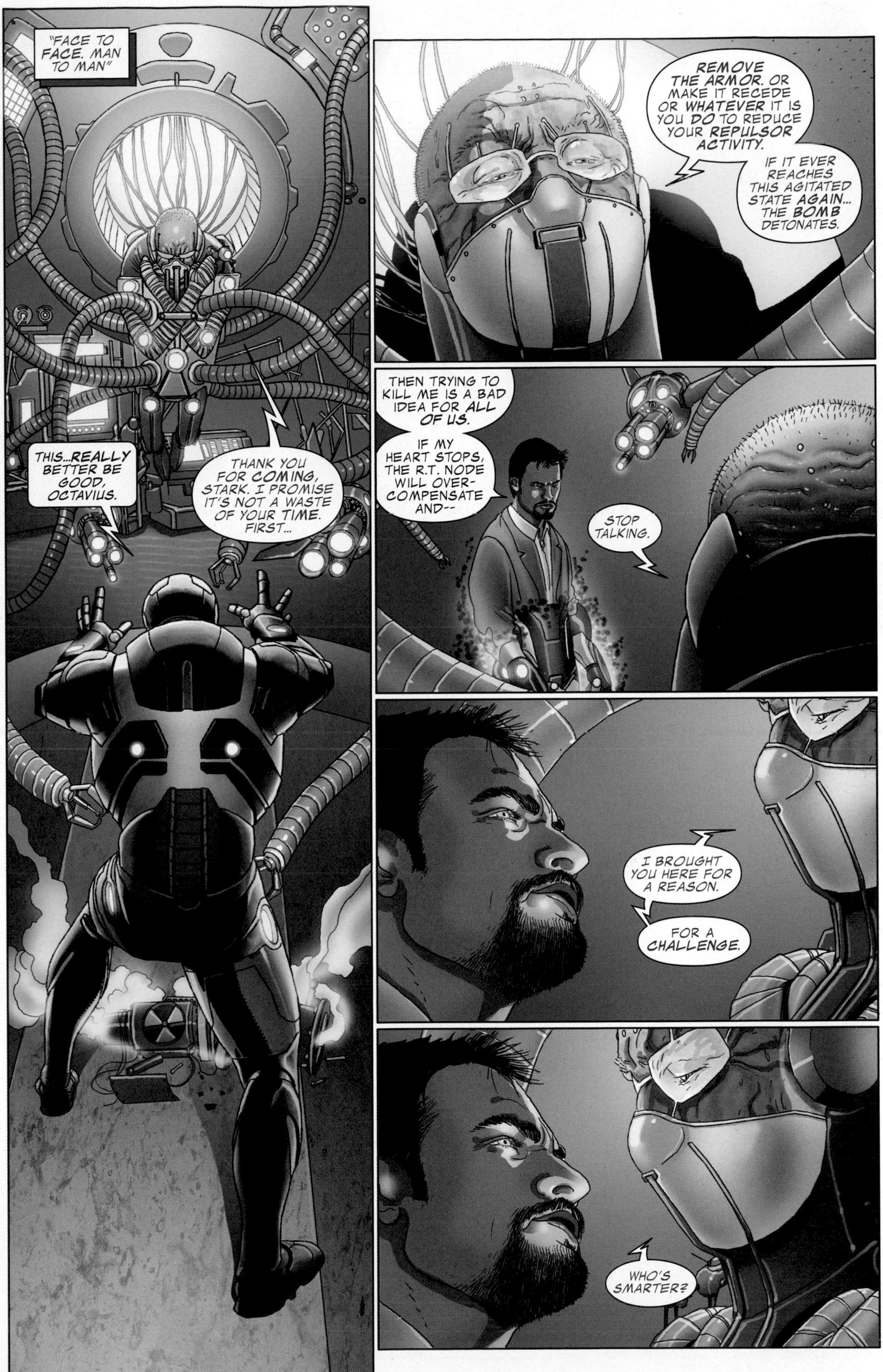
"FACE TO FACE. MAN TO MAN"
THIS...REALLY BETTER BE GOOD, OCTAVIUS.
THANK YOU FOR COMING, STARK. I PROMISE IT'S NOT A WASTE OF YOUR TIME. FIRST...
REMOVE THE ARMOR. OR MAKE IT RECEDE OR WHATEVER IT IS YOU DO TO REDUCE YOUR REPULSOR ACTIVITY.
IF IT EVER REACHES THIS AGITATED STATE AGAIN... THE BOMB DETONATES.
THEN TRYING TO KILL ME IS A BAD IDEA FOR ALL OF US.
IF MY HEART STOPS, THE R.T. NODE WILL OVER-COMPENSATE AND--
STOP TALKING.
I BROUGHT YOU HERE FOR A REASON.
FOR A CHALLENGE.
WHO'S SMARTER?

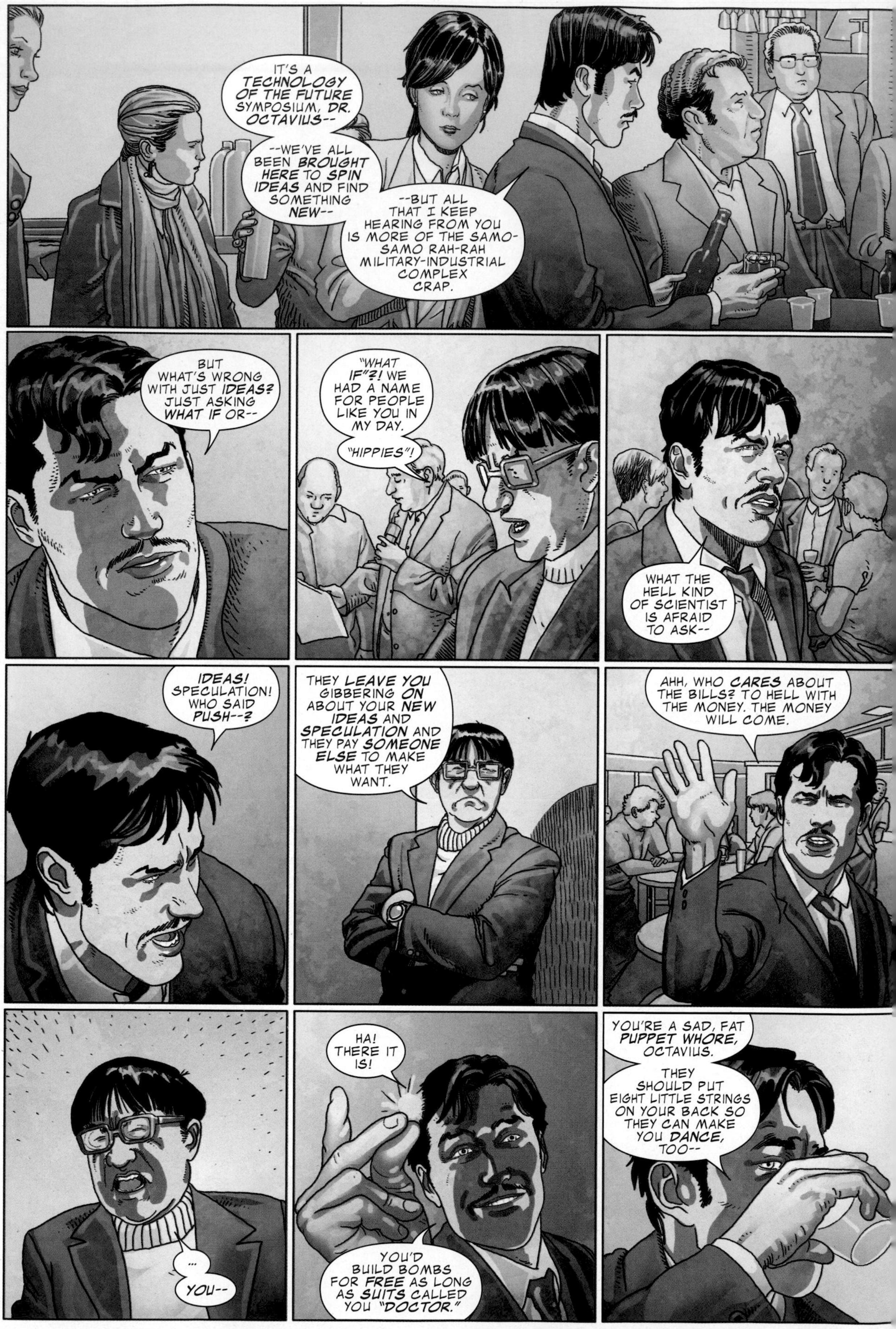
IT'S A TECHNOLOGY OF THE FUTURE SYMPOSIUM, DR. OCTAVIUS--
--WE'VE ALL BEEN BROUGHT HERE TO SPIN IDEAS AND FIND SOMETHING NEW--
--BUT ALL THAT I KEEP HEARING FROM YOU IS MORE OF THE SAMO-SAMO RAH-RAH MILITARY-INDUSTRIAL COMPLEX CRAP.
BUT WHAT'S WRONG WITH JUST IDEAS? JUST ASKING WHAT IF OR--
"WHAT IF"?! WE HAD A NAME FOR PEOPLE LIKE YOU IN MY DAY.
"HIPPIES"!
WHAT THE HELL KIND OF SCIENTIST IS AFRAID TO ASK--
IDEAS! SPECULATION! WHO SAID PUSH--?
THEY LEAVE YOU GIBBERING ON ABOUT YOUR NEW IDEAS AND SPECULATION AND THEY PAY SOMEONE ELSE TO MAKE WHAT THEY WANT.
AHH, WHO CARES ABOUT THE BILLS? TO HELL WITH THE MONEY. THE MONEY WILL COME.
...
YOU--
HA! THERE IT IS!
YOU'D BUILD BOMBS FOR FREE AS LONG AS SUITS CALLED YOU "DOCTOR."
YOU'RE A SAD, FAT PUPPET WHORE, OCTAVIUS.
THEY SHOULD PUT EIGHT LITTLE STRINGS ON YOUR BACK SO THEY CAN MAKE YOU DANCE, TOO--

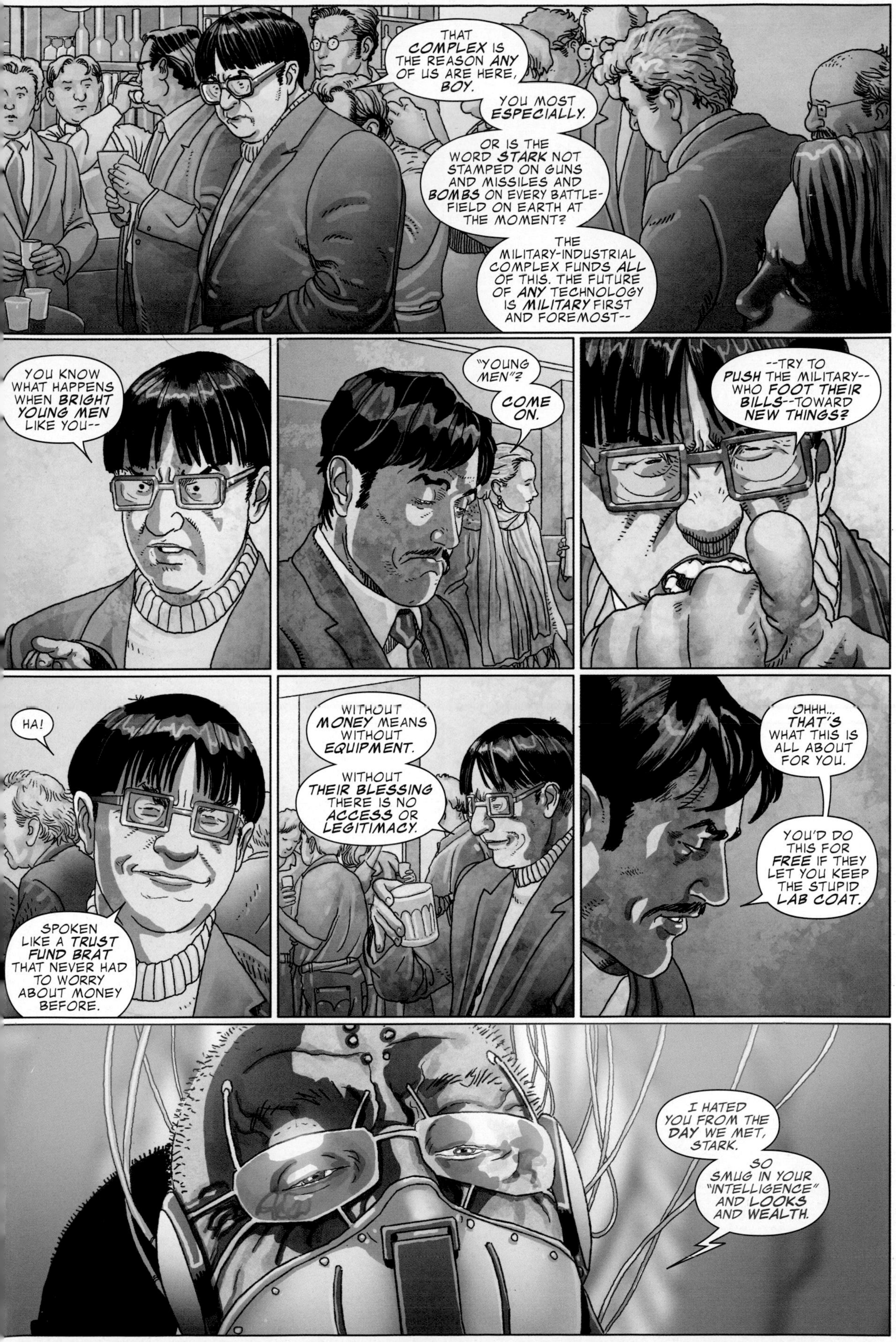
THAT COMPLEX IS THE REASON ANY OF US ARE HERE, BOY.
YOU MOST ESPECIALLY.
OR IS THE WORD STARK NOT STAMPED ON GUNS AND MISSILES AND BOMBS ON EVERY BATTLE-FIELD ON EARTH AT THE MOMENT?
THE MILITARY-INDUSTRIAL COMPLEX FUNDS ALL OF THIS. THE FUTURE OF ANY TECHNOLOGY IS MILITARY FIRST AND FOREMOST--
YOU KNOW WHAT HAPPENS WHEN BRIGHT YOUNG MEN LIKE YOU--
"YOUNG MEN"?
COME ON.
--TRY TO PUSH THE MILITARY-- WHO FOOT THEIR BILLS--TOWARD NEW THINGS?
HA!
SPOKEN LIKE A TRUST FUND BRAT THAT NEVER HAD TO WORRY ABOUT MONEY BEFORE.
WITHOUT MONEY MEANS WITHOUT EQUIPMENT.
WITHOUT THEIR BLESSING THERE IS NO ACCESS OR LEGITIMACY.
OHHH... THAT'S WHAT THIS IS ALL ABOUT FOR YOU.
YOU'D DO THIS FOR FREE IF THEY LET YOU KEEP THE STUPID LAB COAT.
I HATED YOU FROM THE DAY WE MET, STARK.
SO SMUG IN YOUR "INTELLIGENCE" AND LOOKS AND WEALTH.

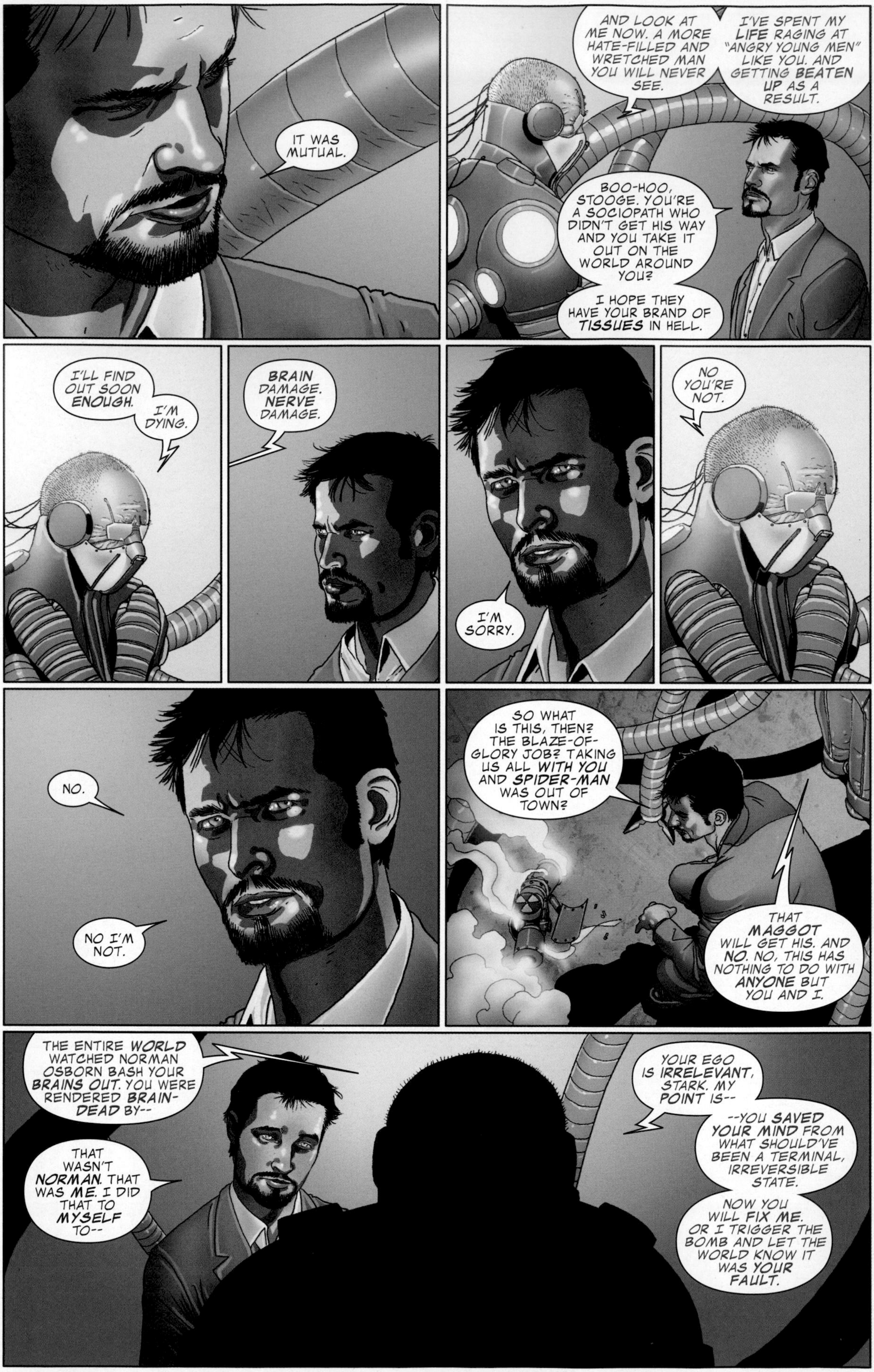
IT WAS MUTUAL.
AND LOOK AT ME NOW. A MORE HATE-FILLED AND WRETCHED MAN YOU WILL NEVER SEE.
I'VE SPENT MY LIFE RAGING AT "ANGRY YOUNG MEN" LIKE YOU. AND GETTING BEATEN UP AS A RESULT.
BOO-HOO, STOOGE. YOU'RE A SOCIOPATH WHO DIDN'T GET HIS WAY AND YOU TAKE IT OUT ON THE WORLD AROUND YOU?
I HOPE THEY HAVE YOUR BRAND OF TISSUES IN HELL.
I'LL FIND OUT SOON ENOUGH.
I'M DYING.
BRAIN DAMAGE. NERVE DAMAGE.
I'M SORRY.
NO YOU'RE NOT.
NO.
NO I'M NOT.
SO WHAT IS THIS, THEN? THE BLAZE-OF-GLORY JOB? TAKING US ALL WITH YOU AND SPIDER-MAN WAS OUT OF TOWN?
THAT MAGGOT WILL GET HIS. AND NO. NO, THIS HAS NOTHING TO DO WITH ANYONE BUT YOU AND I.
THE ENTIRE WORLD WATCHED NORMAN OSBORN BASH YOUR BRAINS OUT. YOU WERE RENDERED BRAIN-DEAD BY--
THAT WASN'T NORMAN. THAT WAS ME. I DID THAT TO MYSELF TO--
YOUR EGO IS IRRELEVANT, STARK. MY POINT IS--
--YOU SAVED YOUR MIND FROM WHAT SHOULD'VE BEEN A TERMINAL, IRREVERSIBLE STATE.
NOW YOU WILL FIX ME. OR I TRIGGER THE BOMB AND LET THE WORLD KNOW IT WAS YOUR FAULT.

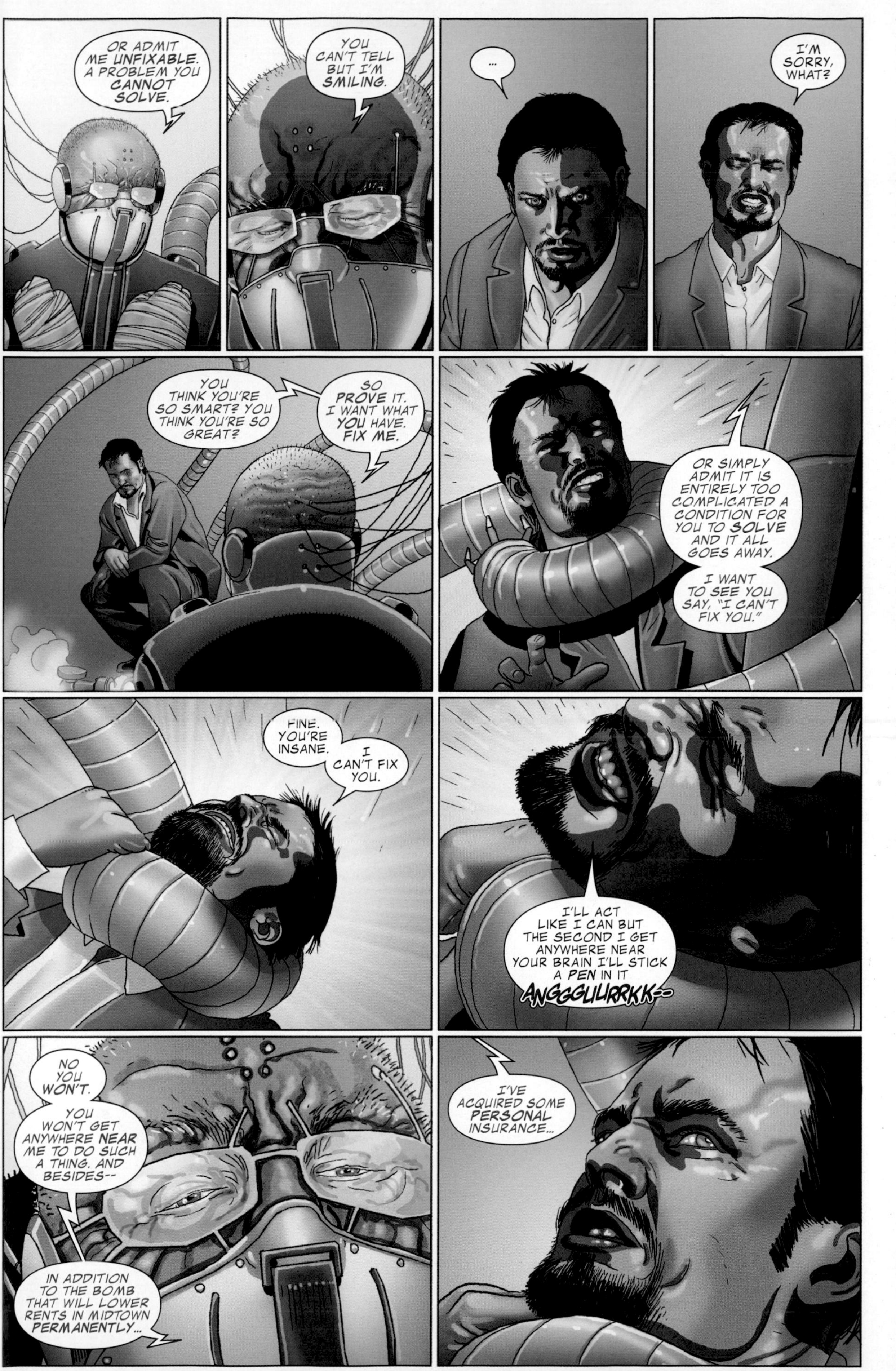
OR ADMIT ME UNFIXABLE. A PROBLEM YOU CANNOT SOLVE.
YOU CAN'T TELL BUT I'M SMILING.
...
I'M SORRY, WHAT?
YOU THINK YOU'RE SO SMART? YOU THINK YOU'RE SO GREAT?
SO PROVE IT. I WANT WHAT YOU HAVE. FIX ME.
OR SIMPLY ADMIT IT IS ENTIRELY TOO COMPLICATED A CONDITION FOR YOU TO SOLVE AND IT ALL GOES AWAY.
I WANT TO SEE YOU SAY, "I CAN'T FIX YOU."
FINE. YOU'RE INSANE.
I CAN'T FIX YOU.
I'LL ACT LIKE I CAN BUT THE SECOND I GET ANYWHERE NEAR YOUR BRAIN I'LL STICK A PEN IN IT
ANGGGUURRKK--
NO YOU WON'T.
YOU WON'T GET ANYWHERE NEAR ME TO DO SUCH A THING. AND BESIDES--
IN ADDITION TO THE BOMB THAT WILL LOWER RENTS IN MIDTOWN PERMANENTLY...
I'VE ACQUIRED SOME PERSONAL INSURANCE...

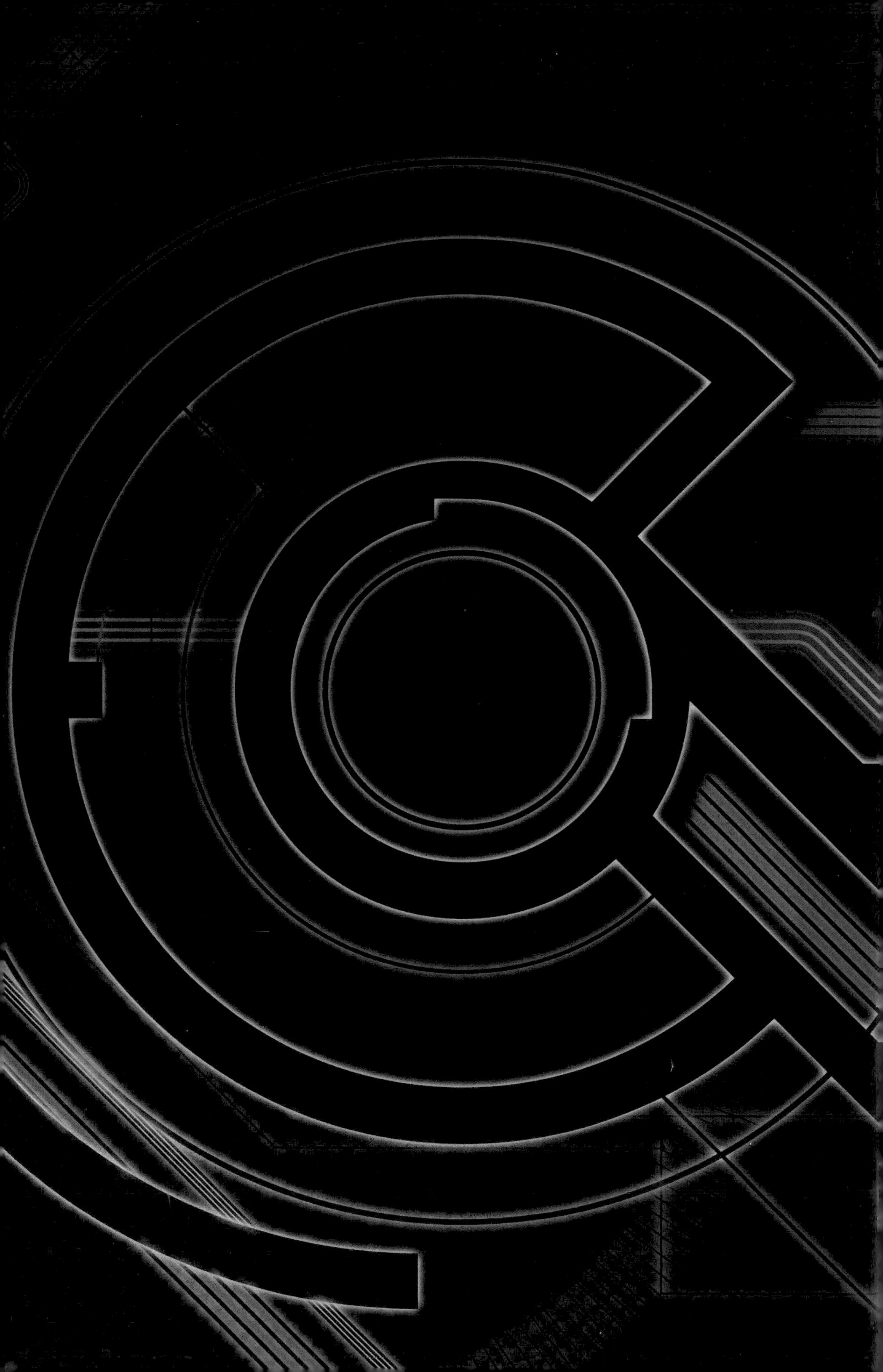

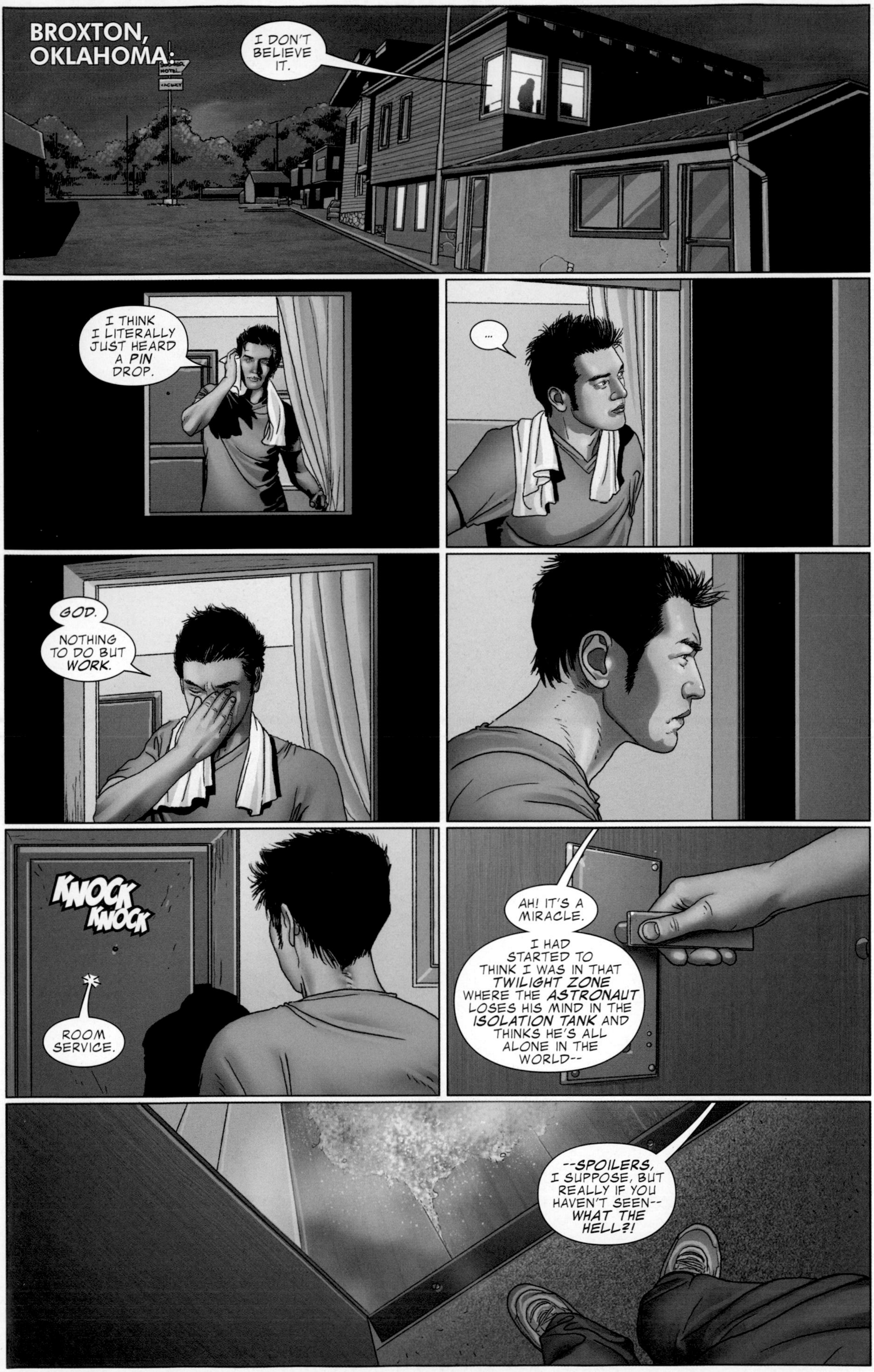
BROXTON, OKLAHOMA:
I DON'T BELIEVE IT.
I THINK I LITERALLY JUST HEARD A PIN DROP.
...
GOD.
NOTHING TO DO BUT WORK.
KNOCK KNOCK
ROOM SERVICE.
AH! IT'S A MIRACLE.
I HAD STARTED TO THINK I WAS IN THAT TWILIGHT ZONE WHERE THE ASTRONAUT LOSES HIS MIND IN THE ISOLATION TANK AND THINKS HE'S ALL ALONE IN THE WORLD--
--SPOILERS, I SUPPOSE, BUT REALLY IF YOU HAVEN'T SEEN-- WHAT THE HELL?!

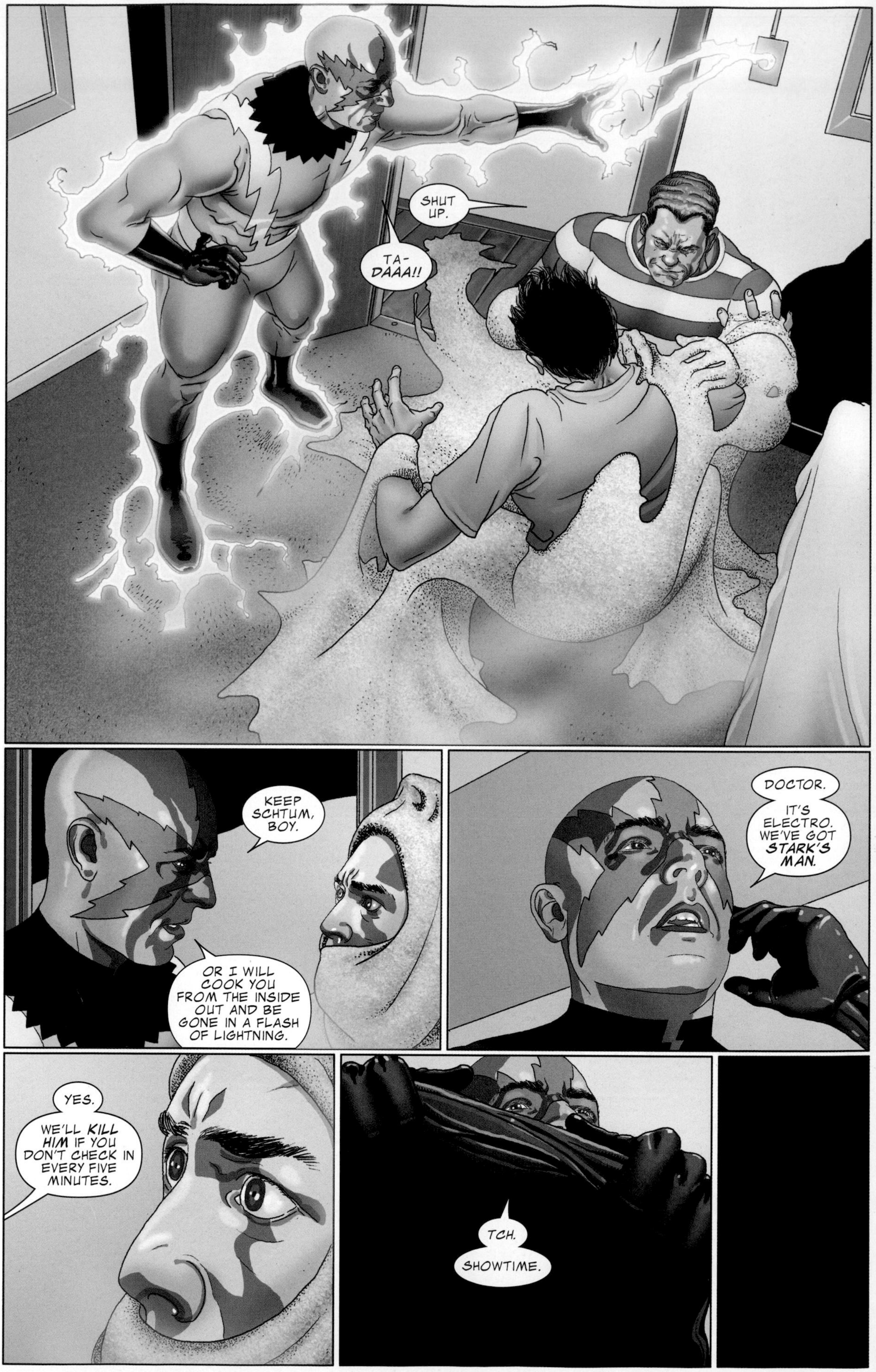
SHUT UP.
TA-DAAA!!
KEEP SCHTUM, BOY.
OR I WILL COOK YOU FROM THE INSIDE OUT AND BE GONE IN A FLASH OF LIGHTNING.
DOCTOR.
IT'S ELECTRO. WE'VE GOT STARK'S MAN.
YES.
WE'LL KILL HIM IF YOU DON'T CHECK IN EVERY FIVE MINUTES.
TCH.
SHOWTIME.

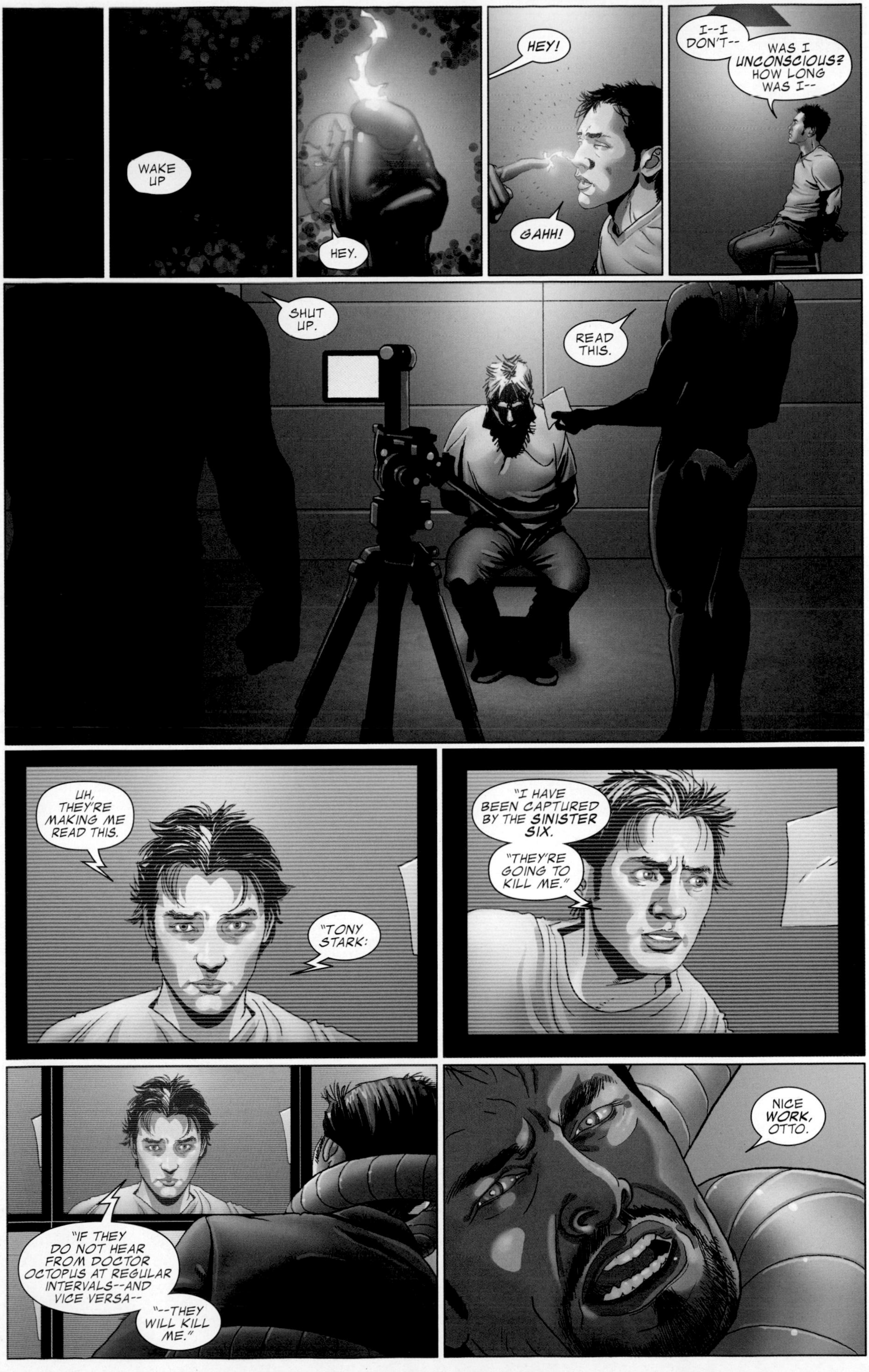
WAKE UP
HEY.
HEY!
GAHH!
I--I DON'T--
WAS I UNCONSCIOUS? HOW LONG WAS I--
SHUT UP.
READ THIS.
UH, THEY'RE MAKING ME READ THIS.
"TONY STARK:
"I HAVE BEEN CAPTURED BY THE SINISTER SIX.
"THEY'RE GOING TO KILL ME."
"IF THEY DO NOT HEAR FROM DOCTOR OCTOPUS AT REGULAR INTERVALS--AND VICE VERSA--
"--THEY WILL KILL ME."
NICE WORK, OTTO.

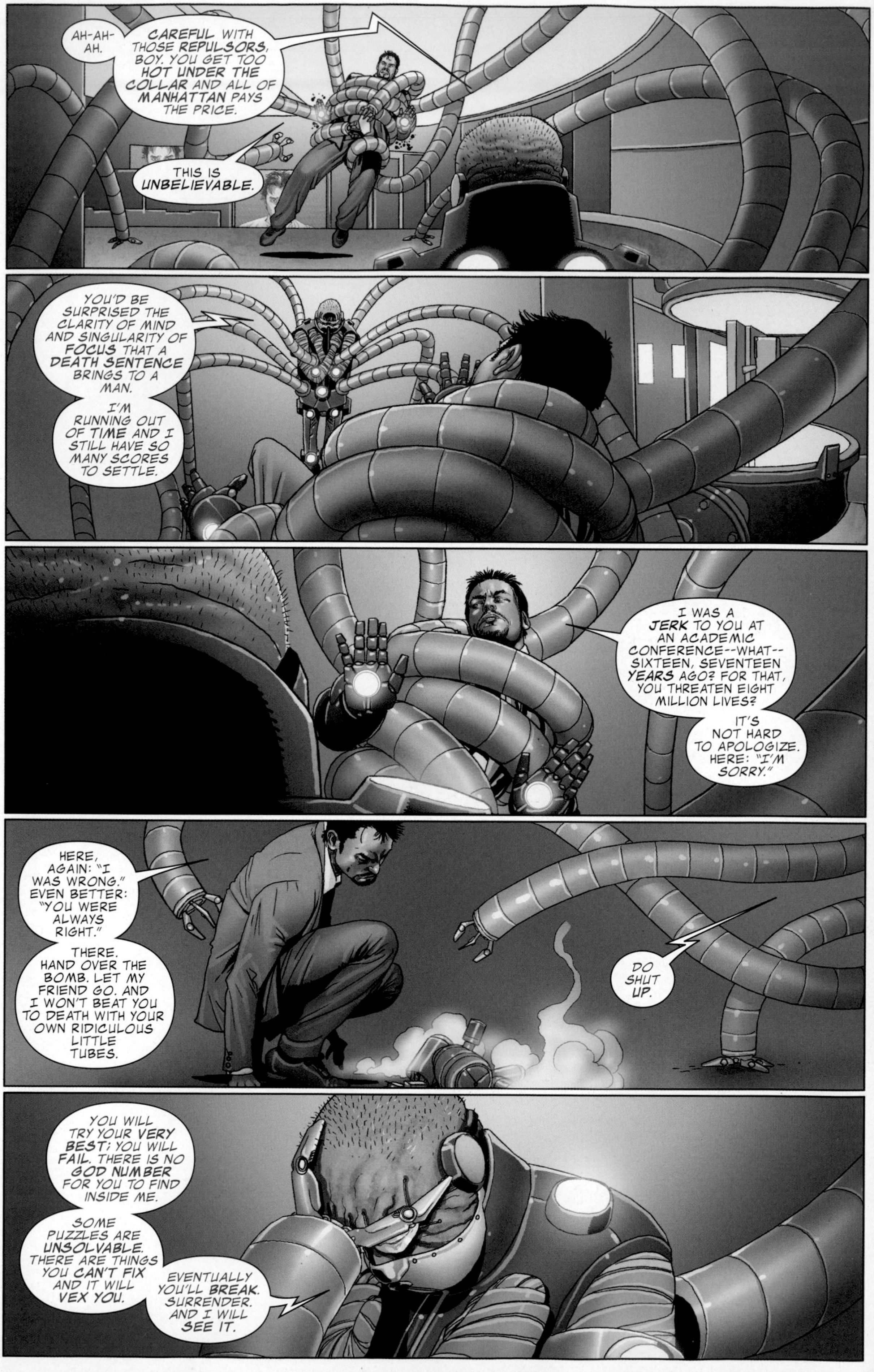
AH-AH-AH.
CAREFUL WITH THOSE REPULSORS, BOY. YOU GET TOO HOT UNDER THE COLLAR AND ALL OF MANHATTAN PAYS THE PRICE.
THIS IS UNBELIEVABLE.
YOU'D BE SURPRISED THE CLARITY OF MIND AND SINGULARITY OF FOCUS THAT A DEATH SENTENCE BRINGS TO A MAN.
I'M RUNNING OUT OF TIME AND I STILL HAVE SO MANY SCORES TO SETTLE.
I WAS A JERK TO YOU AT AN ACADEMIC CONFERENCE--WHAT--SIXTEEN, SEVENTEEN YEARS AGO? FOR THAT, YOU THREATEN EIGHT MILLION LIVES?
IT'S NOT HARD TO APOLOGIZE. HERE: "I'M SORRY."
HERE, AGAIN: "I WAS WRONG." EVEN BETTER: "YOU WERE ALWAYS RIGHT."
THERE. HAND OVER THE BOMB. LET MY FRIEND GO. AND I WON'T BEAT YOU TO DEATH WITH YOUR OWN RIDICULOUS LITTLE TUBES.
DO SHUT UP.
YOU WILL TRY YOUR VERY BEST; YOU WILL FAIL. THERE IS NO GOD NUMBER FOR YOU TO FIND INSIDE ME.
SOME PUZZLES ARE UNSOLVABLE. THERE ARE THINGS YOU CAN'T FIX AND IT WILL VEX YOU.
EVENTUALLY YOU'LL BREAK. SURRENDER. AND I WILL SEE IT.

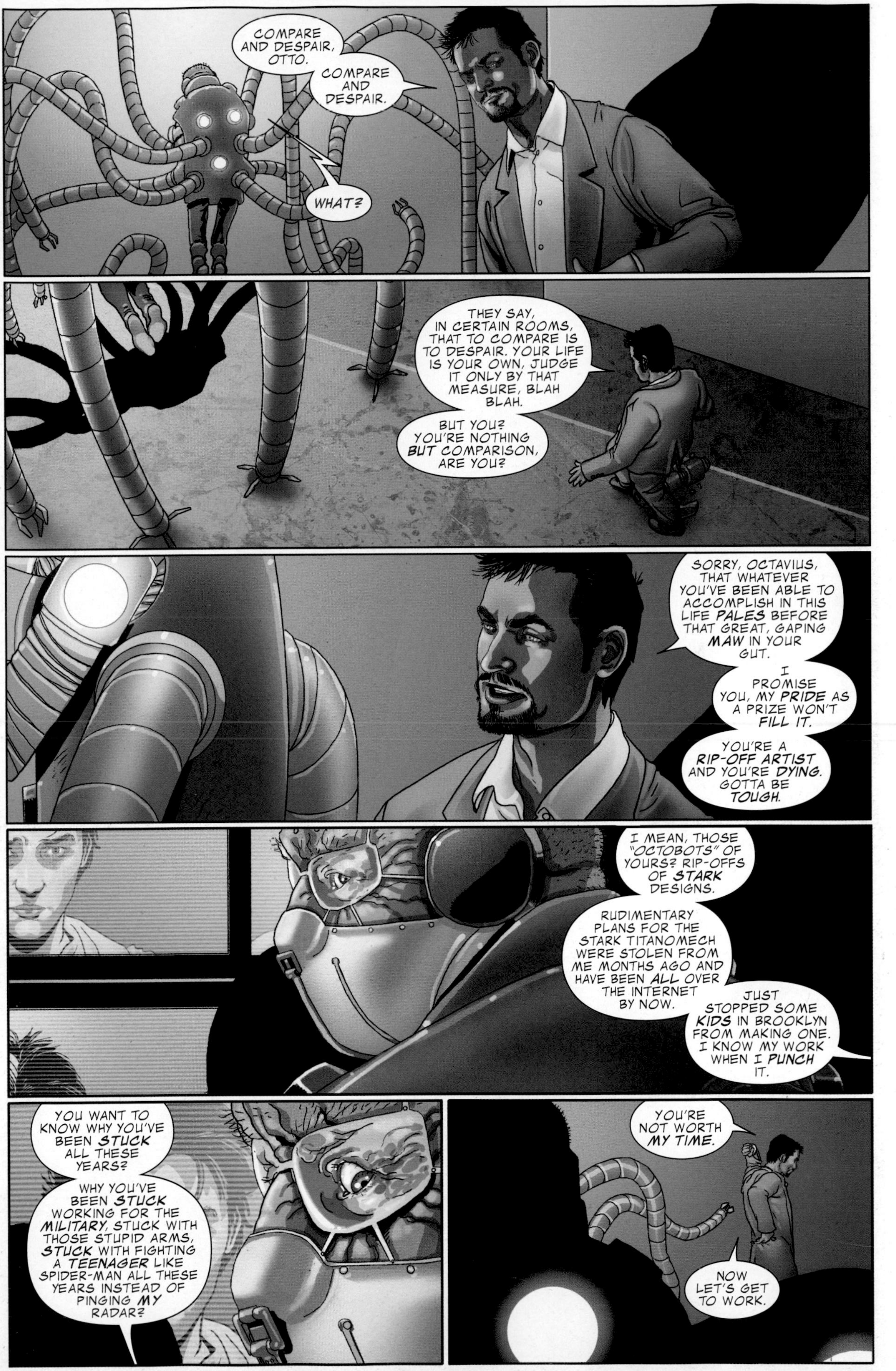
COMPARE AND DESPAIR, OTTO.
COMPARE AND DESPAIR.
WHAT?
THEY SAY, IN CERTAIN ROOMS, THAT TO COMPARE IS TO DESPAIR. YOUR LIFE IS YOUR OWN, JUDGE IT ONLY BY THAT MEASURE, BLAH BLAH.
BUT YOU? YOU'RE NOTHING BUT COMPARISON, ARE YOU?
SORRY, OCTAVIUS, THAT WHATEVER YOU'VE BEEN ABLE TO ACCOMPLISH IN THIS LIFE PALES BEFORE THAT GREAT, GAPING MAW IN YOUR GUT.
I PROMISE YOU, MY PRIDE AS A PRIZE WON'T FILL IT.
YOU'RE A RIP-OFF ARTIST AND YOU'RE DYING. GOTTA BE TOUGH.
I MEAN, THOSE "OCTOBOTS" OF YOURS? RIP-OFFS OF STARK DESIGNS.
RUDIMENTARY PLANS FOR THE STARK TITANOMECH WERE STOLEN FROM ME MONTHS AGO AND HAVE BEEN ALL OVER THE INTERNET BY NOW.
JUST STOPPED SOME KIDS IN BROOKLYN FROM MAKING ONE. I KNOW MY WORK WHEN I PUNCH IT.
YOU WANT TO KNOW WHY YOU'VE BEEN STUCK ALL THESE YEARS?
WHY YOU'VE BEEN STUCK WORKING FOR THE MILITARY, STUCK WITH THOSE STUPID ARMS, STUCK WITH FIGHTING A TEENAGER LIKE SPIDER-MAN ALL THESE YEARS INSTEAD OF PINGING MY RADAR?
YOU'RE NOT WORTH MY TIME.
NOW LET'S GET TO WORK.

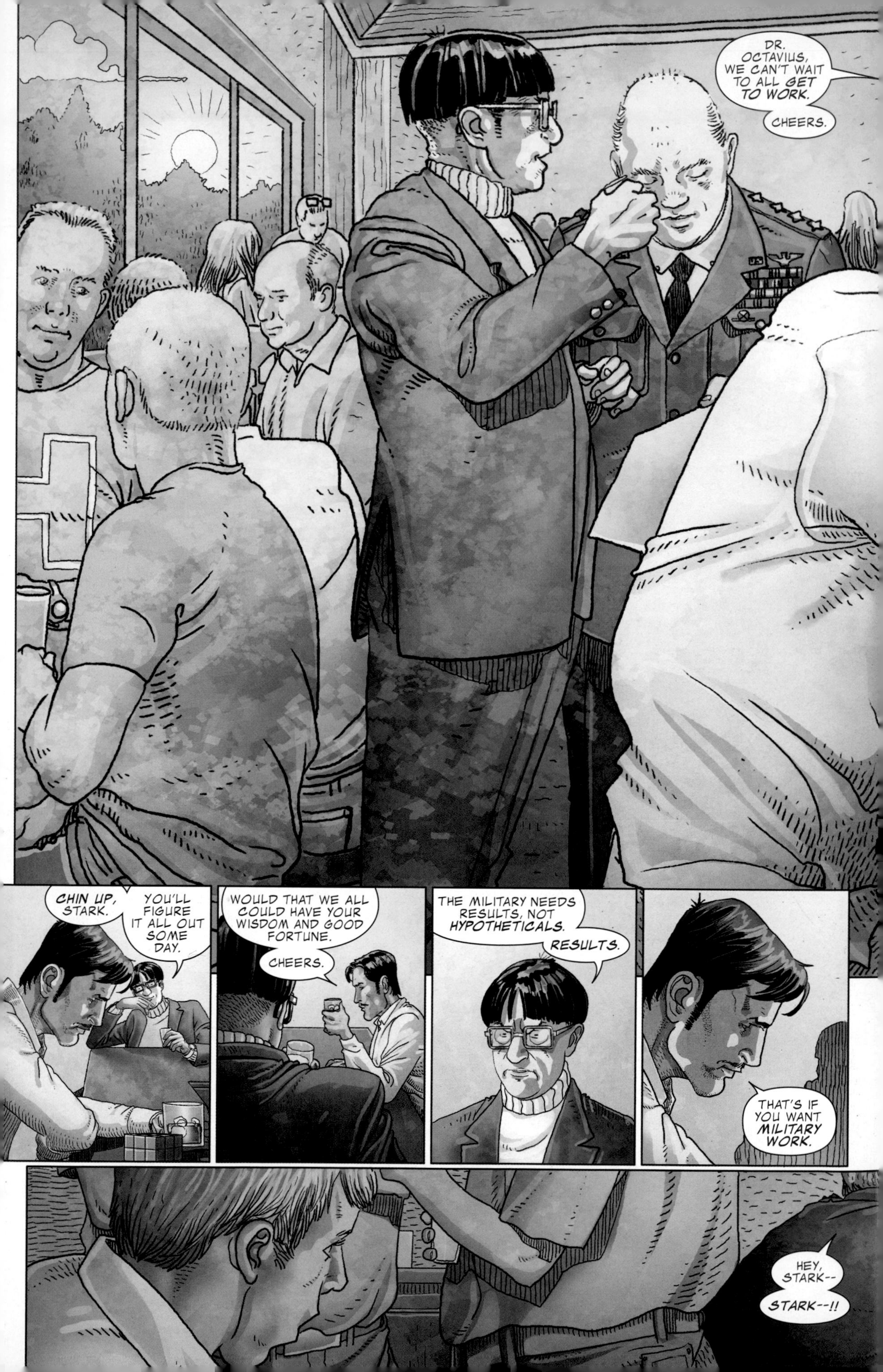
DR. OCTAVIUS, WE CAN'T WAIT TO ALL GET TO WORK.
CHEERS.
CHIN UP, STARK.
YOU'LL FIGURE IT ALL OUT SOME DAY.
WOULD THAT WE ALL COULD HAVE YOUR WISDOM AND GOOD FORTUNE.
CHEERS.
THE MILITARY NEEDS RESULTS, NOT HYPOTHETICALS.
RESULTS.
THAT'S IF YOU WANT MILITARY WORK.
HEY, STARK--
STARK--!!

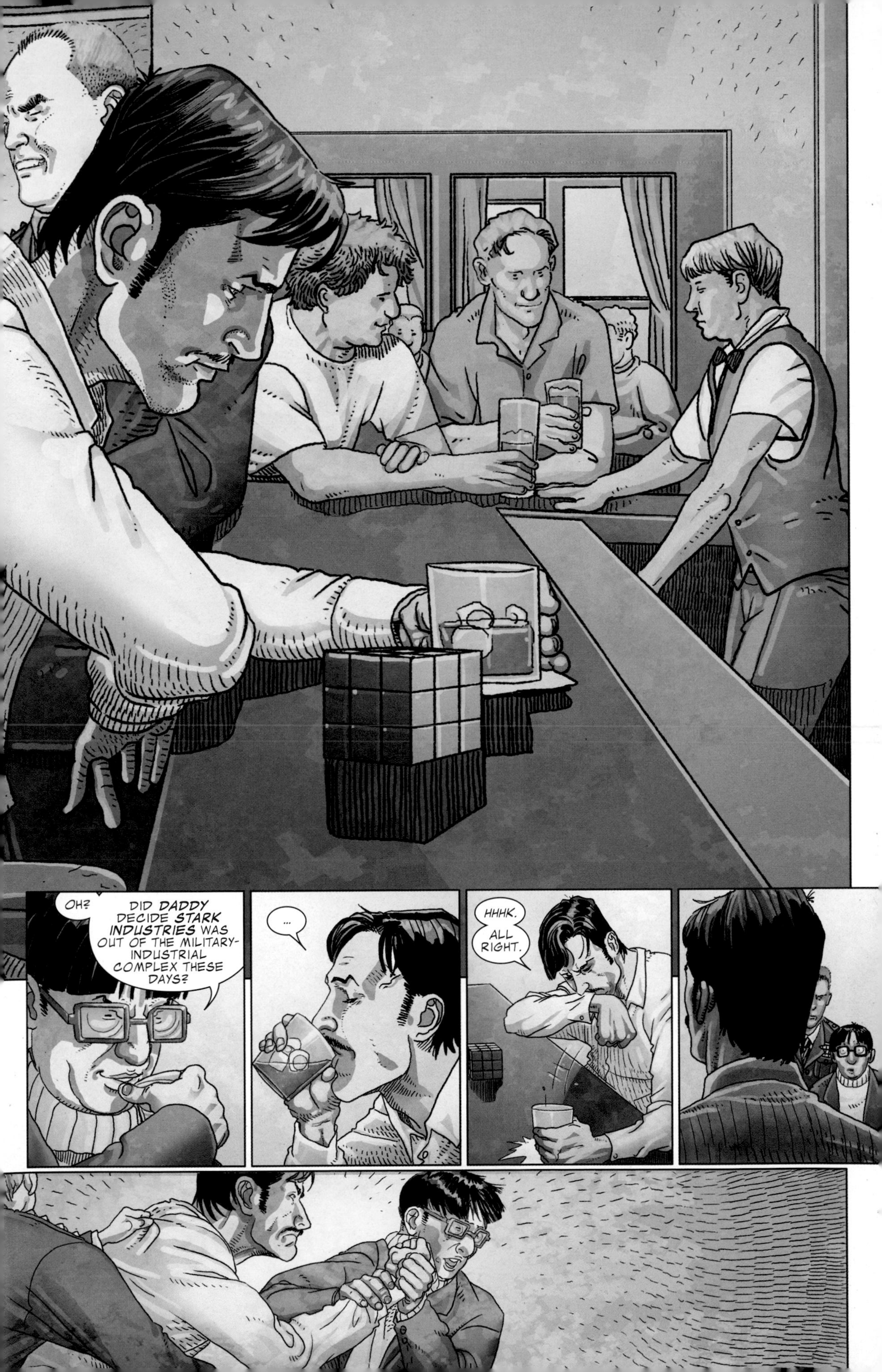

OH?
DID DADDY DECIDE STARK INDUSTRIES WAS OUT OF THE MILITARY-INDUSTRIAL COMPLEX THESE DAYS?
...
HHHK.
ALL RIGHT.

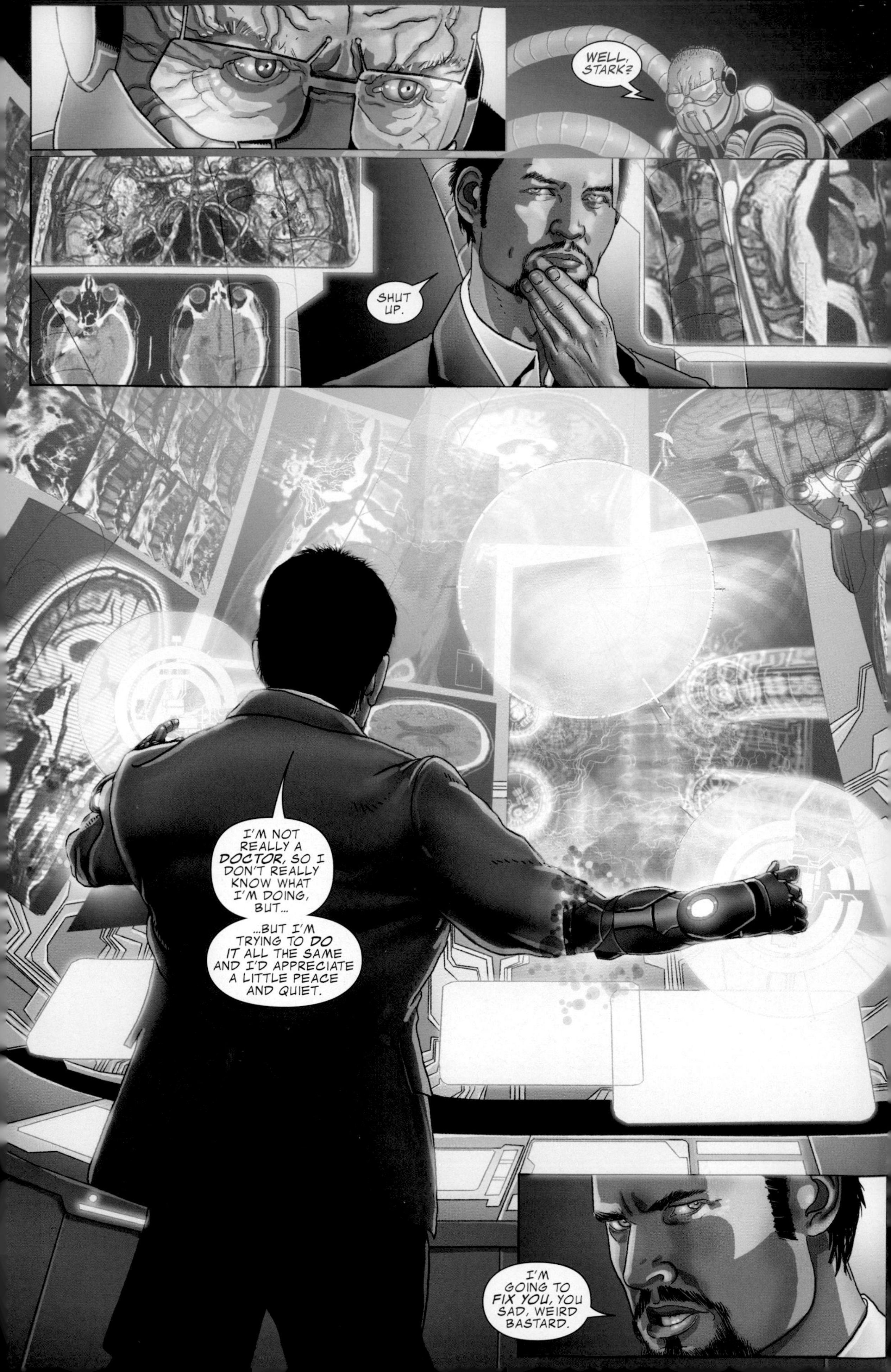
WELL, STARK?
SHUT UP.
I'M NOT REALLY A DOCTOR, SO I DON'T REALLY KNOW WHAT I'M DOING, BUT...
...BUT I'M TRYING TO DO IT ALL THE SAME AND I'D APPRECIATE A LITTLE PEACE AND QUIET.
I'M GOING TO FIX YOU, YOU SAD, WEIRD BASTARD.

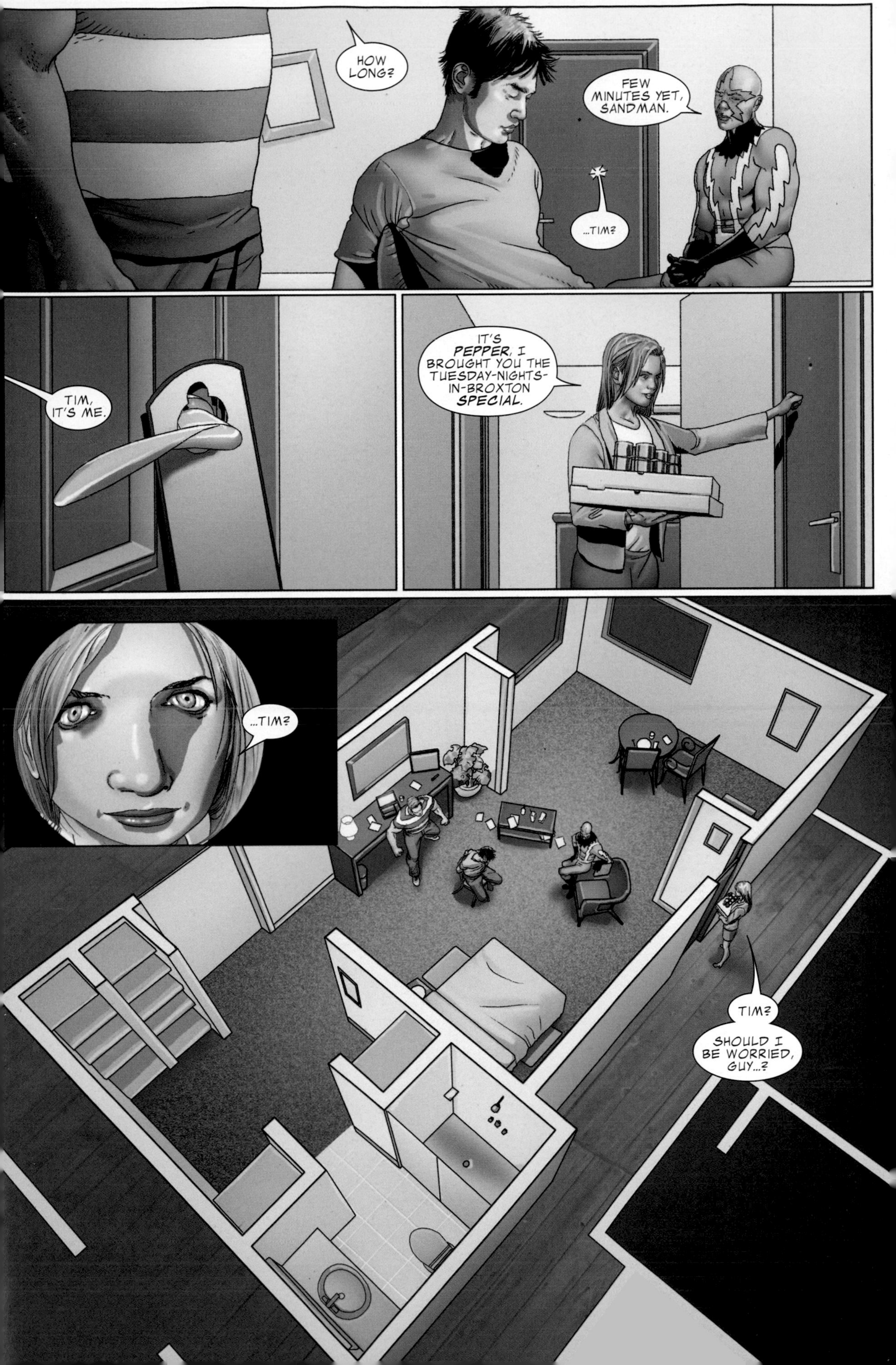
HOW LONG?
FEW MINUTES YET, SANDMAN.
...TIM?
TIM, IT'S ME.
IT'S PEPPER, I BROUGHT YOU THE TUESDAY-NIGHTS-IN-BROXTON SPECIAL.
...TIM?
TIM?
SHOULD I BE WORRIED, GUY...?

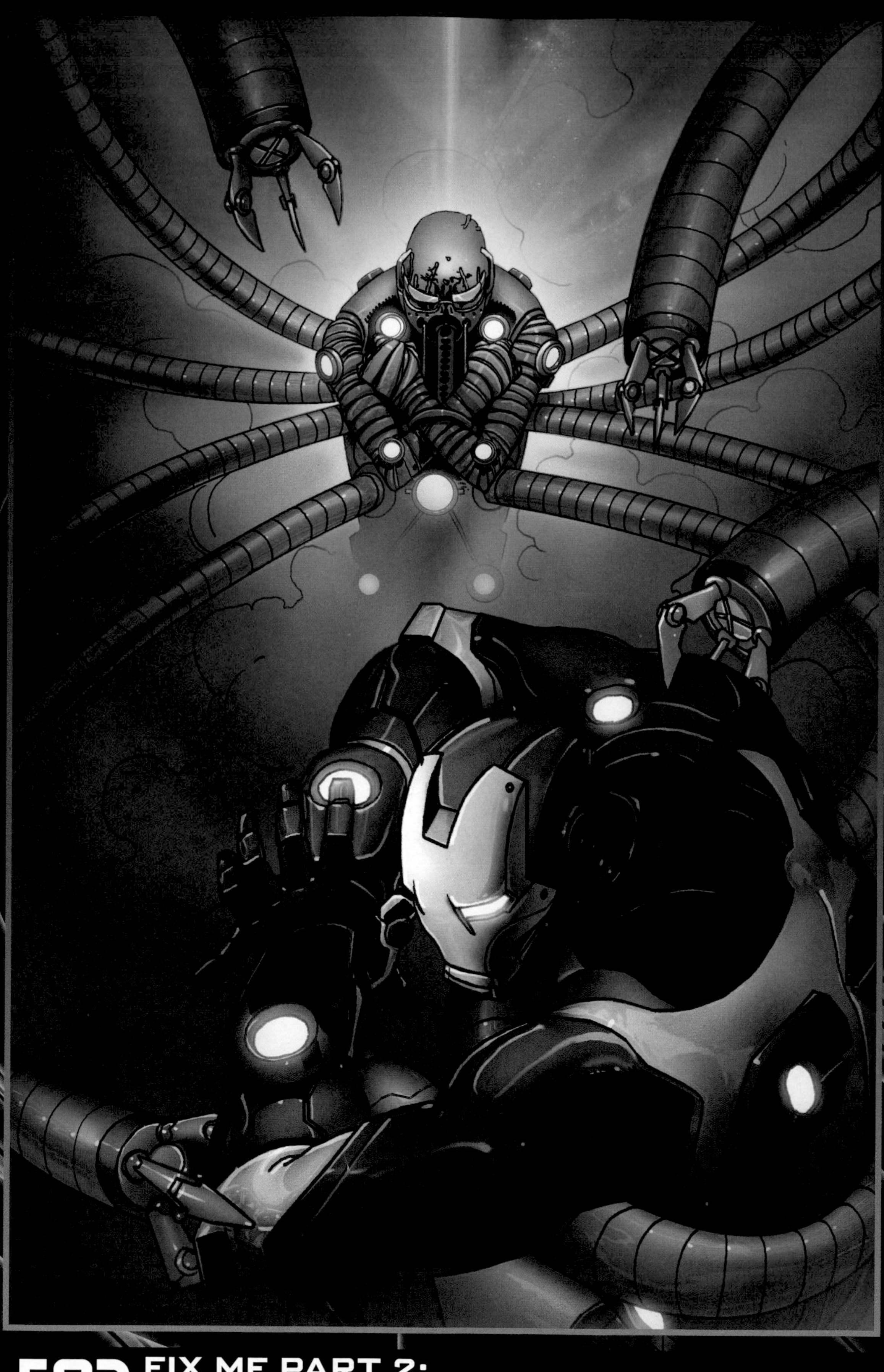

502 FIX ME PART 2: THE GOD NUMBER

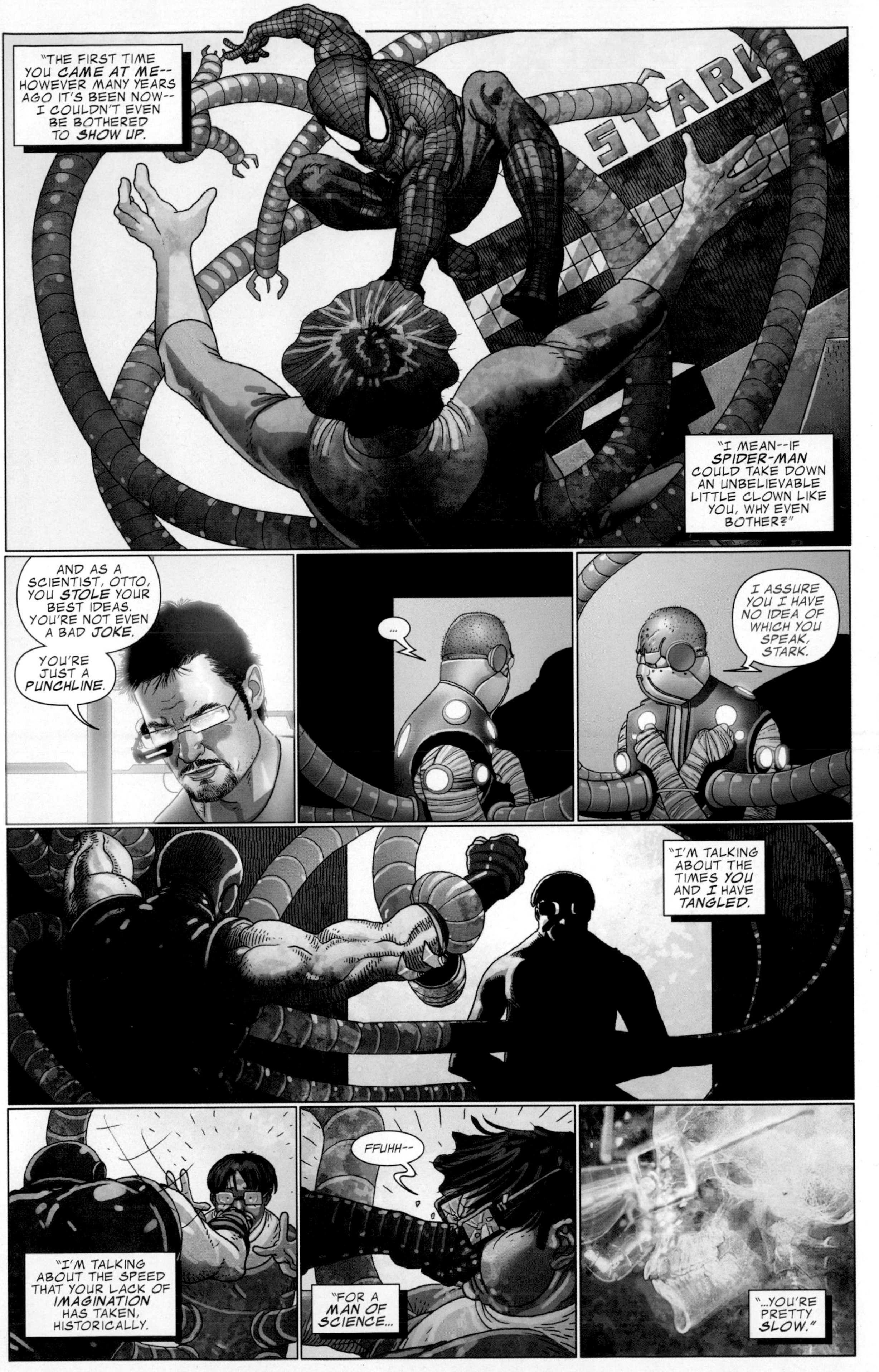
"THE FIRST TIME YOU CAME AT ME-- HOWEVER MANY YEARS AGO IT'S BEEN NOW-- I COULDN'T EVEN BE BOTHERED TO SHOW UP.
STARK
"I MEAN--IF SPIDER-MAN COULD TAKE DOWN AN UNBELIEVABLE LITTLE CLOWN LIKE YOU, WHY EVEN BOTHER?"
AND AS A SCIENTIST, OTTO, YOU STOLE YOUR BEST IDEAS. YOU'RE NOT EVEN A BAD JOKE.
YOU'RE JUST A PUNCHLINE.
...
I ASSURE YOU I HAVE NO IDEA OF WHICH YOU SPEAK, STARK.
"I'M TALKING ABOUT THE TIMES YOU AND I HAVE TANGLED.
"I'M TALKING ABOUT THE SPEED THAT YOUR LACK OF IMAGINATION HAS TAKEN, HISTORICALLY.
FFUHH--
"FOR A MAN OF SCIENCE...
"...YOU'RE PRETTY SLOW."

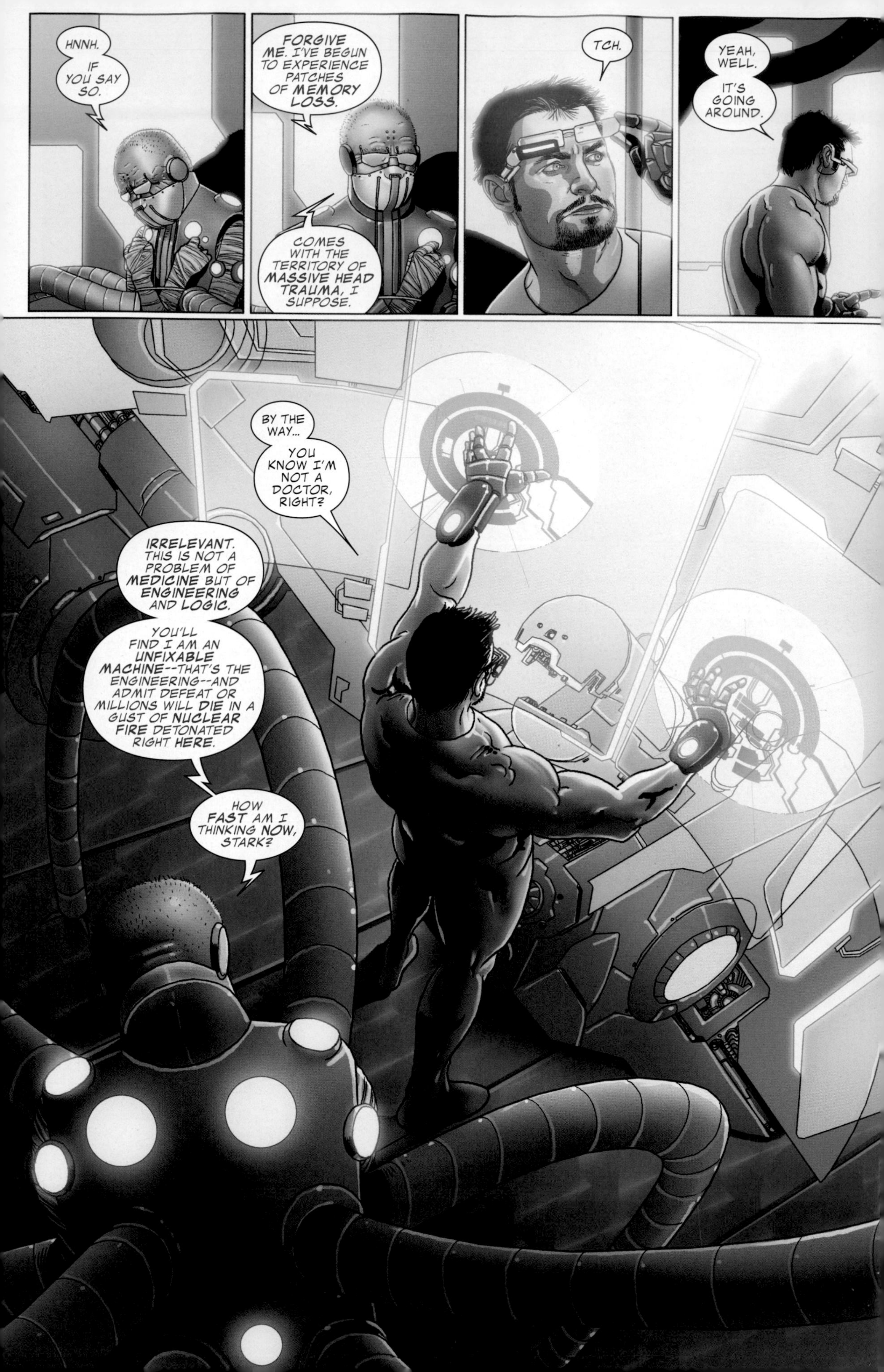
HNNH.
IF YOU SAY SO.
FORGIVE ME. I'VE BEGUN TO EXPERIENCE PATCHES OF MEMORY LOSS.
COMES WITH THE TERRITORY OF MASSIVE HEAD TRAUMA, I SUPPOSE.
TCH.
YEAH, WELL.
IT'S GOING AROUND.
BY THE WAY...
YOU KNOW I'M NOT A DOCTOR, RIGHT?
IRRELEVANT. THIS IS NOT A PROBLEM OF MEDICINE BUT OF ENGINEERING AND LOGIC.
YOU'LL FIND I AM AN UNFIXABLE MACHINE--THAT'S THE ENGINEERING--AND ADMIT DEFEAT OR MILLIONS WILL DIE IN A GUST OF NUCLEAR FIRE DETONATED RIGHT HERE.
HOW FAST AM I THINKING NOW, STARK?

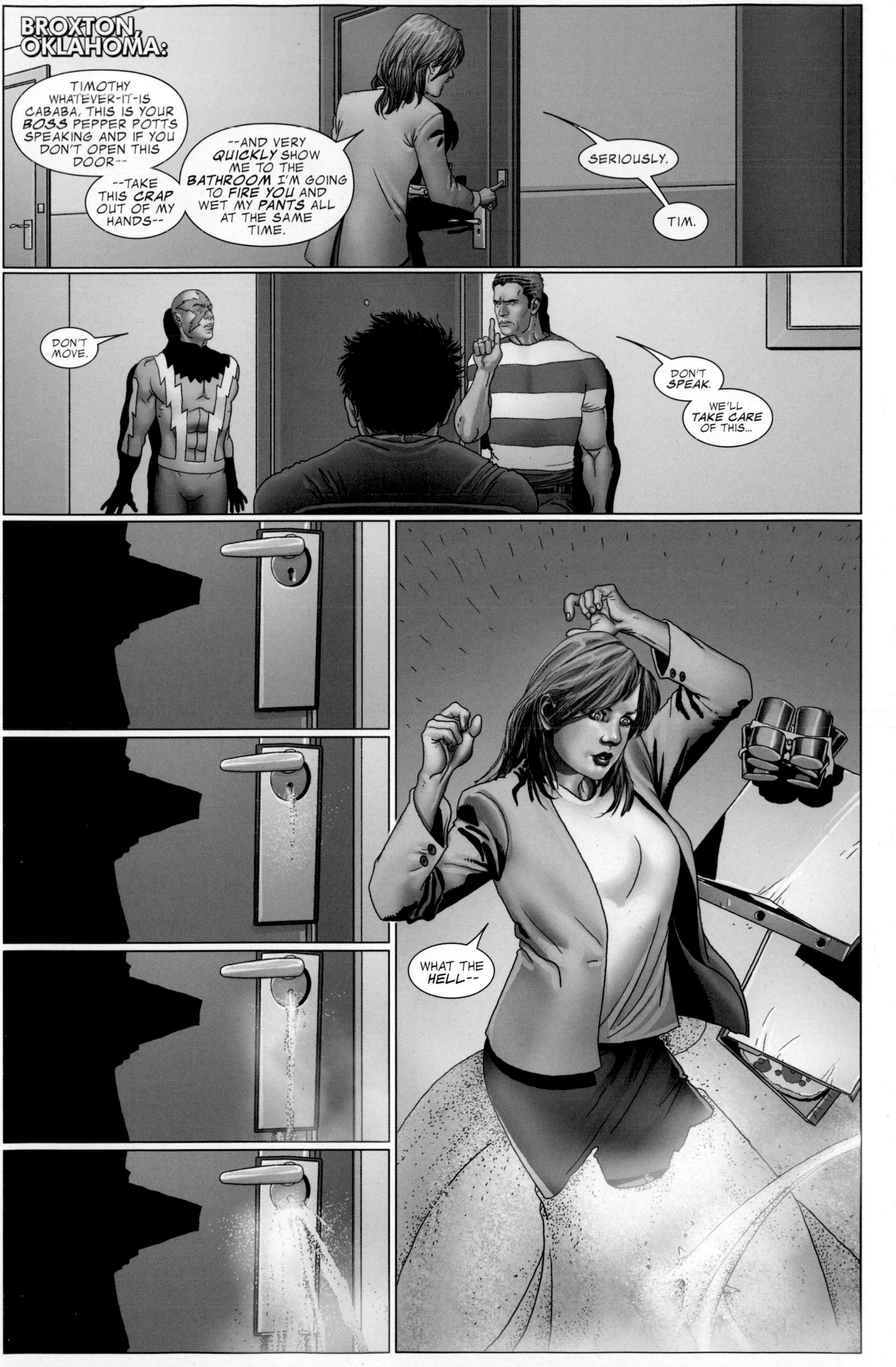
BROXTON, OKLAHOMA:
TIMOTHY WHATEVER-IT-IS CABABA, THIS IS YOUR BOSS PEPPER POTTS SPEAKING AND IF YOU DON'T OPEN THIS DOOR--
--TAKE THIS CRAP OUT OF MY HANDS--
--AND VERY QUICKLY SHOW ME TO THE BATHROOM I'M GOING TO FIRE YOU AND WET MY PANTS ALL AT THE SAME TIME.
SERIOUSLY.
TIM.
DON'T MOVE.
DON'T SPEAK.
WE'LL TAKE CARE OF THIS...
WHAT THE HELL--

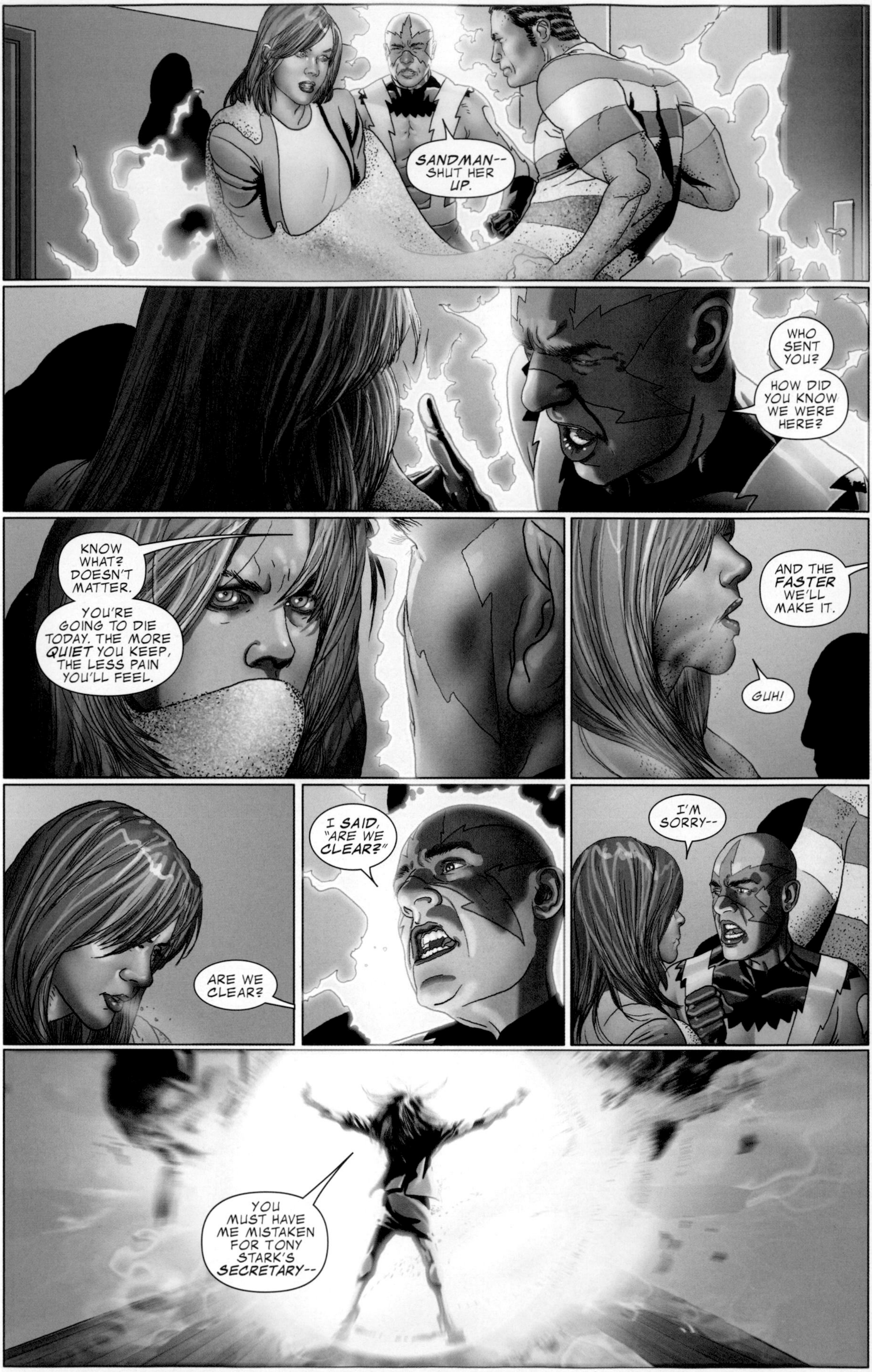
SANDMAN-- SHUT HER UP.
WHO SENT YOU?
HOW DID YOU KNOW WE WERE HERE?
KNOW WHAT? DOESN'T MATTER.
YOU'RE GOING TO DIE TODAY. THE MORE QUIET YOU KEEP, THE LESS PAIN YOU'LL FEEL.
AND THE FASTER WE'LL MAKE IT.
GUH!
ARE WE CLEAR?
I SAID, "ARE WE CLEAR?"
I'M SORRY--
YOU MUST HAVE ME MISTAKEN FOR TONY STARK'S SECRETARY--

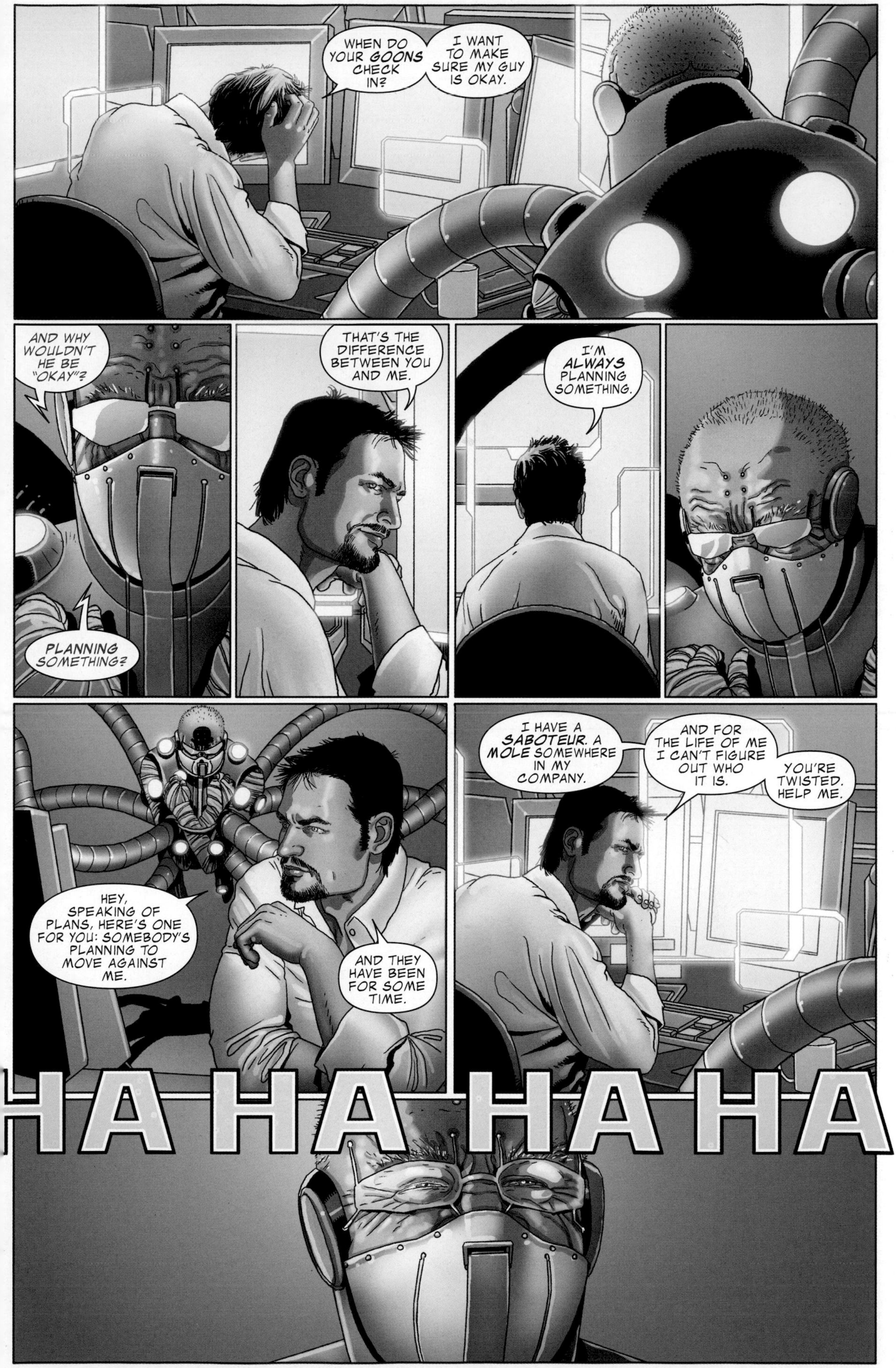
WHEN DO YOUR GOONS CHECK IN?
I WANT TO MAKE SURE MY GUY IS OKAY.
AND WHY WOULDN'T HE BE "OKAY"?
PLANNING SOMETHING?
THAT'S THE DIFFERENCE BETWEEN YOU AND ME.
I'M ALWAYS PLANNING SOMETHING.
HEY, SPEAKING OF PLANS, HERE'S ONE FOR YOU: SOMEBODY'S PLANNING TO MOVE AGAINST ME.
AND THEY HAVE BEEN FOR SOME TIME.
I HAVE A SABOTEUR. A MOLE SOMEWHERE IN MY COMPANY.
AND FOR THE LIFE OF ME I CAN'T FIGURE OUT WHO IT IS.
YOU'RE TWISTED. HELP ME.
HA HA HA HA HA HA

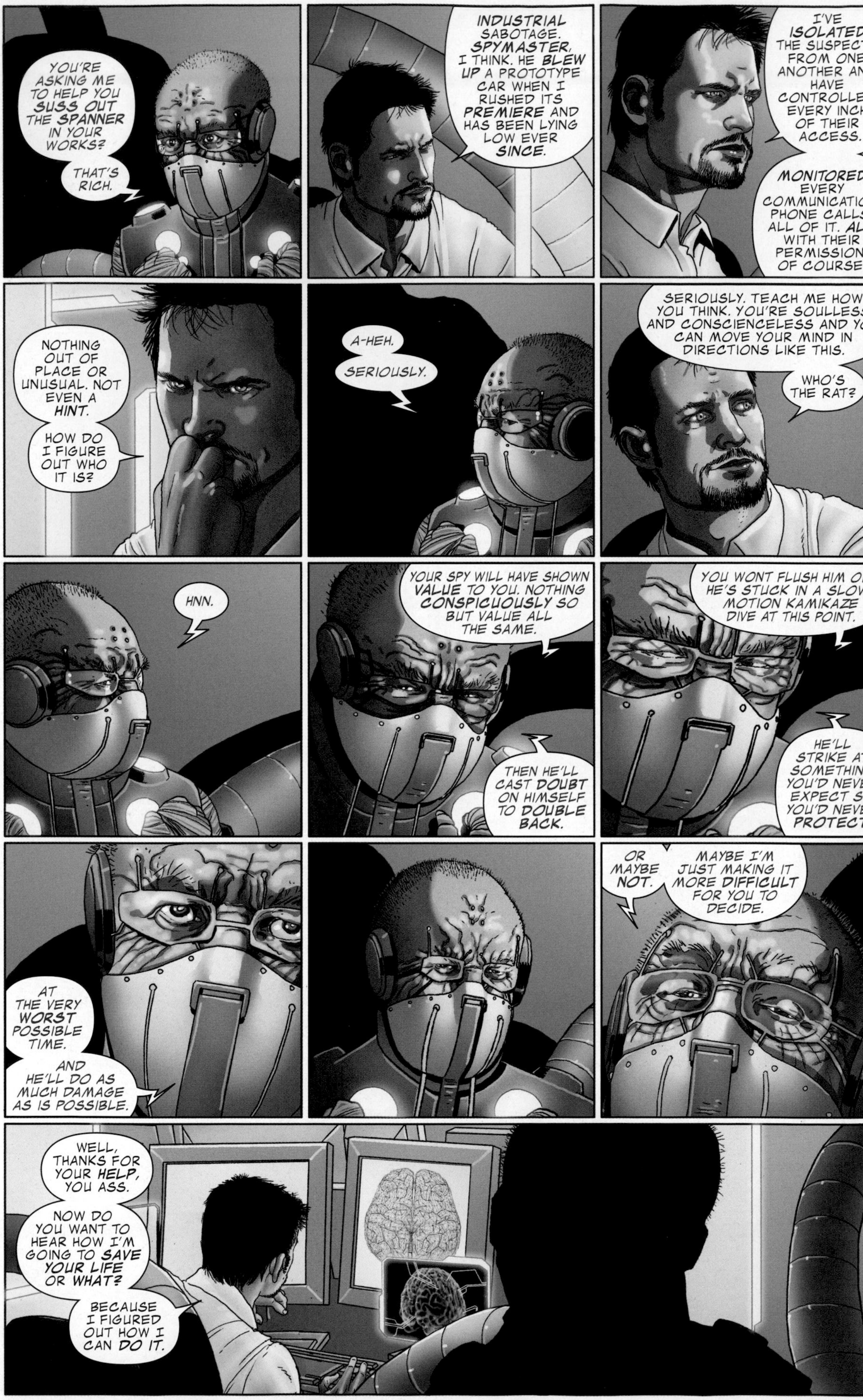
YOU'RE ASKING ME TO HELP YOU SUSS OUT THE SPANNER IN YOUR WORKS?
THAT'S RICH.
INDUSTRIAL SABOTAGE. SPYMASTER, I THINK. HE BLEW UP A PROTOTYPE CAR WHEN I RUSHED ITS PREMIERE AND HAS BEEN LYING LOW EVER SINCE.
I'VE ISOLATED THE SUSPECTS FROM ONE ANOTHER AND HAVE CONTROLLED EVERY INCH OF THEIR ACCESS.
MONITORED EVERY COMMUNICATION, PHONE CALLS, ALL OF IT. ALL WITH THEIR PERMISSION, OF COURSE.
NOTHING OUT OF PLACE OR UNUSUAL. NOT EVEN A HINT.
HOW DO I FIGURE OUT WHO IT IS?
A-HEH.
SERIOUSLY.
SERIOUSLY. TEACH ME HOW YOU THINK. YOU'RE SOULLESS AND CONSCIENCELESS AND YOU CAN MOVE YOUR MIND IN DIRECTIONS LIKE THIS.
WHO'S THE RAT?
HNN.
YOUR SPY WILL HAVE SHOWN VALUE TO YOU. NOTHING CONSPICUOUSLY SO BUT VALUE ALL THE SAME.
THEN HE'LL CAST DOUBT ON HIMSELF TO DOUBLE BACK.
YOU WONT FLUSH HIM OUT. HE'S STUCK IN A SLOW-MOTION KAMIKAZE DIVE AT THIS POINT.
HE'LL STRIKE AT SOMETHING YOU'D NEVER EXPECT SO YOU'D NEVER PROTECT.
AT THE VERY WORST POSSIBLE TIME.
AND HE'LL DO AS MUCH DAMAGE AS IS POSSIBLE.
OR MAYBE NOT.
MAYBE I'M JUST MAKING IT MORE DIFFICULT FOR YOU TO DECIDE.
WELL, THANKS FOR YOUR HELP, YOU ASS.
NOW DO YOU WANT TO HEAR HOW I'M GOING TO SAVE YOUR LIFE OR WHAT?
BECAUSE I FIGURED OUT HOW I CAN DO IT.

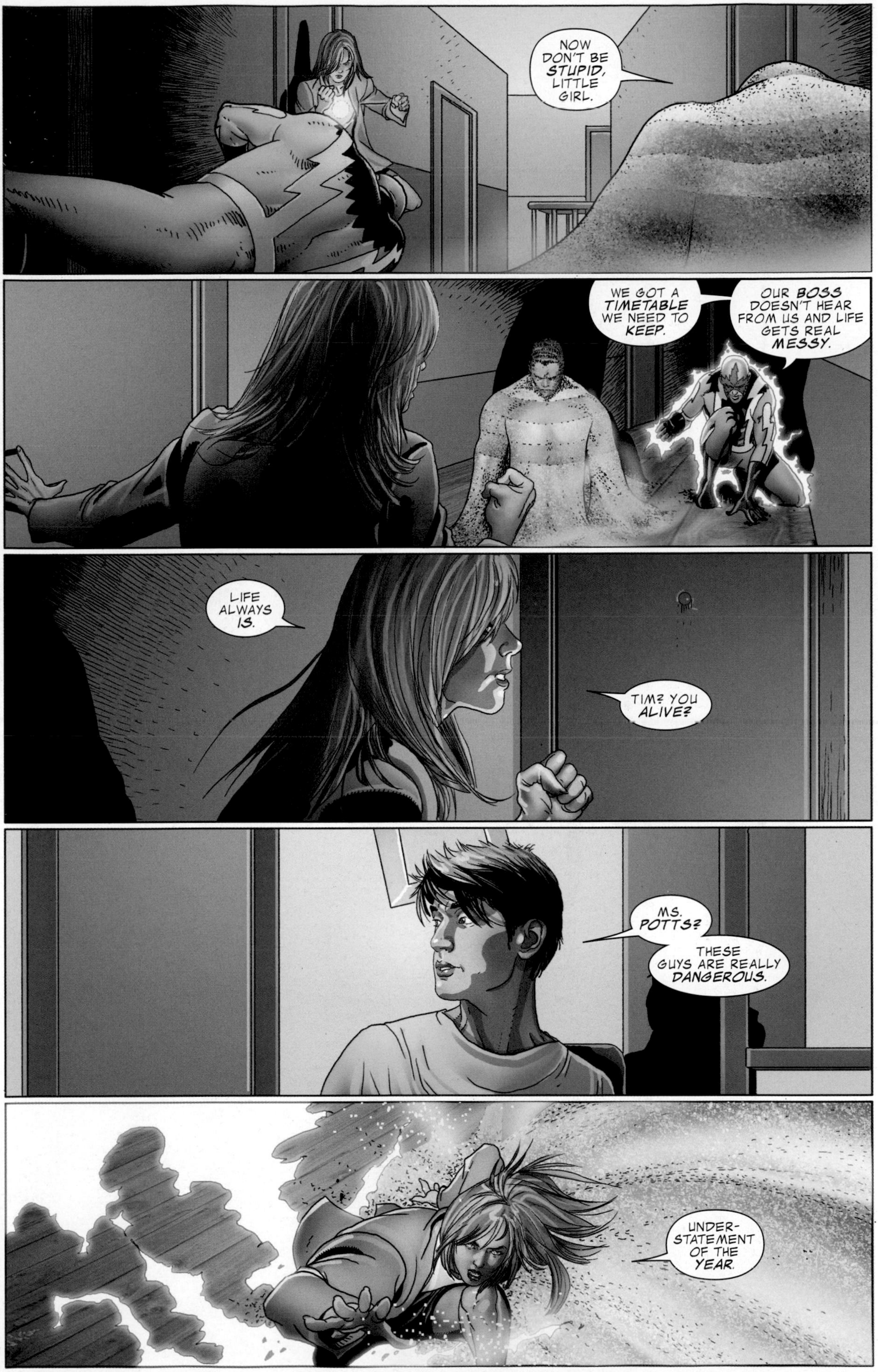
NOW DON'T BE STUPID, LITTLE GIRL.
WE GOT A TIMETABLE WE NEED TO KEEP.
OUR BOSS DOESN'T HEAR FROM US AND LIFE GETS REAL MESSY.
LIFE ALWAYS IS.
TIM? YOU ALIVE?
MS. POTTS?
THESE GUYS ARE REALLY DANGEROUS.
UNDER-STATEMENT OF THE YEAR.

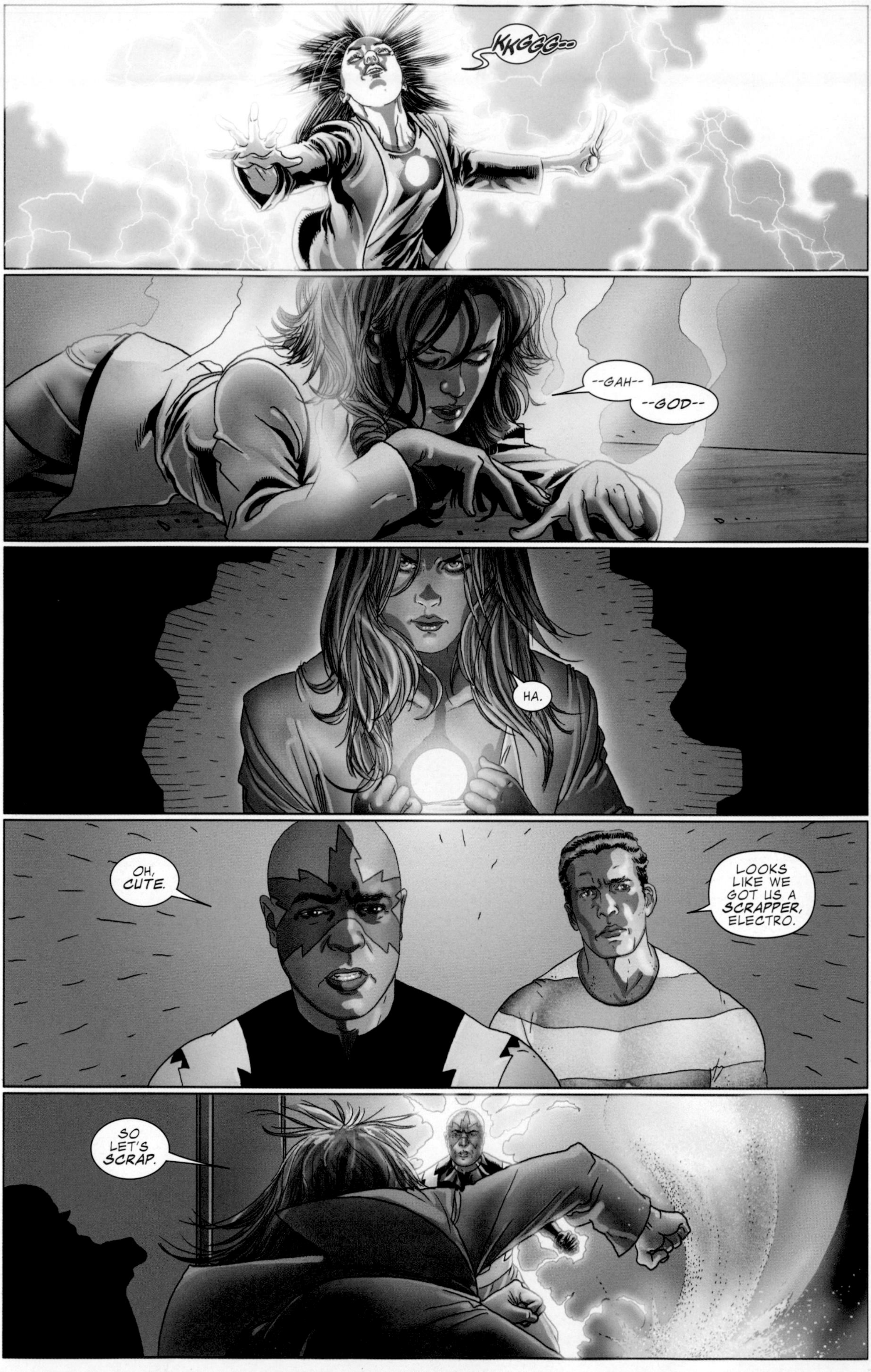
KKGGG--
--GAH--
--GOD--
HA.
OH, CUTE.
LOOKS LIKE WE GOT US A SCRAPPER, ELECTRO.
SO LET'S SCRAP.

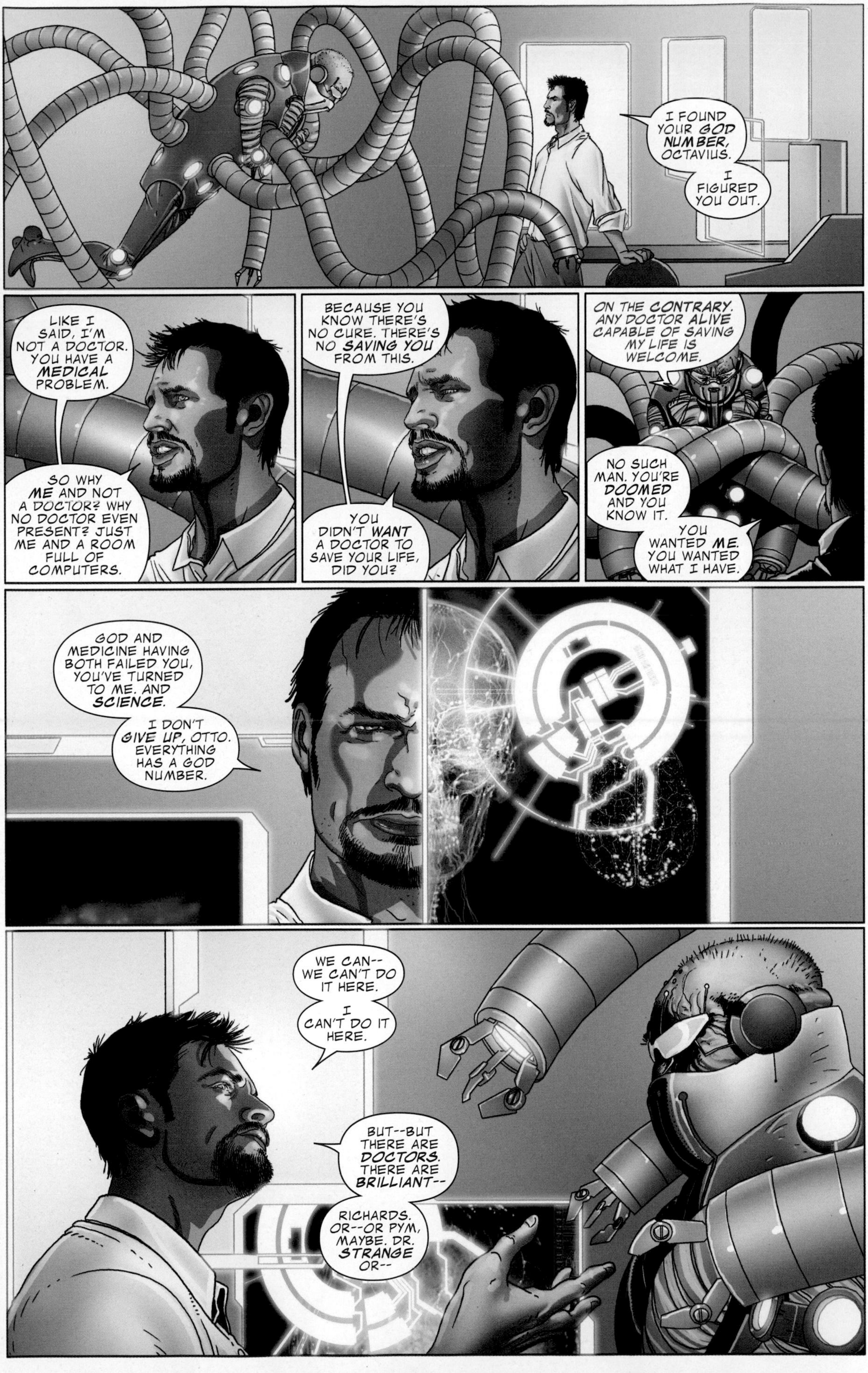
I FOUND YOUR GOD NUMBER, OCTAVIUS.
I FIGURED YOU OUT.
LIKE I SAID, I'M NOT A DOCTOR. YOU HAVE A MEDICAL PROBLEM.
SO WHY ME AND NOT A DOCTOR? WHY NO DOCTOR EVEN PRESENT? JUST ME AND A ROOM FULL OF COMPUTERS.
BECAUSE YOU KNOW THERE'S NO CURE. THERE'S NO SAVING YOU FROM THIS.
YOU DIDN'T WANT A DOCTOR TO SAVE YOUR LIFE, DID YOU?
ON THE CONTRARY. ANY DOCTOR ALIVE CAPABLE OF SAVING MY LIFE IS WELCOME.
NO SUCH MAN. YOU'RE DOOMED AND YOU KNOW IT.
YOU WANTED ME. YOU WANTED WHAT I HAVE.
GOD AND MEDICINE HAVING BOTH FAILED YOU, YOU'VE TURNED TO ME. AND SCIENCE.
I DON'T GIVE UP, OTTO. EVERYTHING HAS A GOD NUMBER.
WE CAN-- WE CAN'T DO IT HERE.
I CAN'T DO IT HERE.
BUT--BUT THERE ARE DOCTORS. THERE ARE BRILLIANT--
RICHARDS. OR--OR PYM, MAYBE. DR. STRANGE OR--

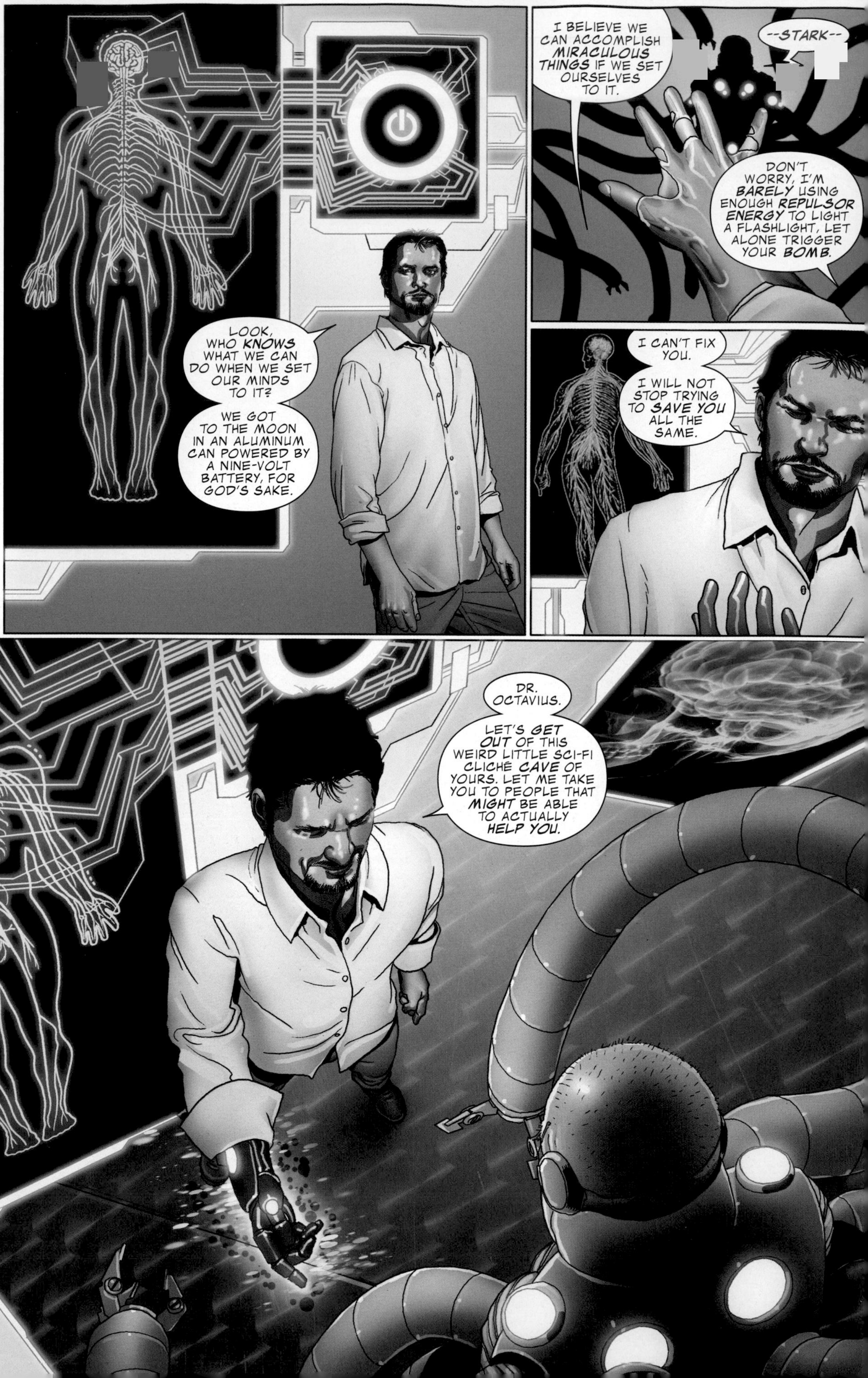
LOOK, WHO KNOWS WHAT WE CAN DO WHEN WE SET OUR MINDS TO IT?
WE GOT TO THE MOON IN AN ALUMINUM CAN POWERED BY A NINE-VOLT BATTERY, FOR GOD'S SAKE.
I BELIEVE WE CAN ACCOMPLISH MIRACULOUS THINGS IF WE SET OURSELVES TO IT.
--STARK--
DON'T WORRY, I'M BARELY USING ENOUGH REPULSOR ENERGY TO LIGHT A FLASHLIGHT, LET ALONE TRIGGER YOUR BOMB.
I CAN'T FIX YOU.
I WILL NOT STOP TRYING TO SAVE YOU ALL THE SAME.
DR. OCTAVIUS.
LET'S GET OUT OF THIS WEIRD LITTLE SCI-FI CLICHÉ CAVE OF YOURS. LET ME TAKE YOU TO PEOPLE THAT MIGHT BE ABLE TO ACTUALLY HELP YOU.

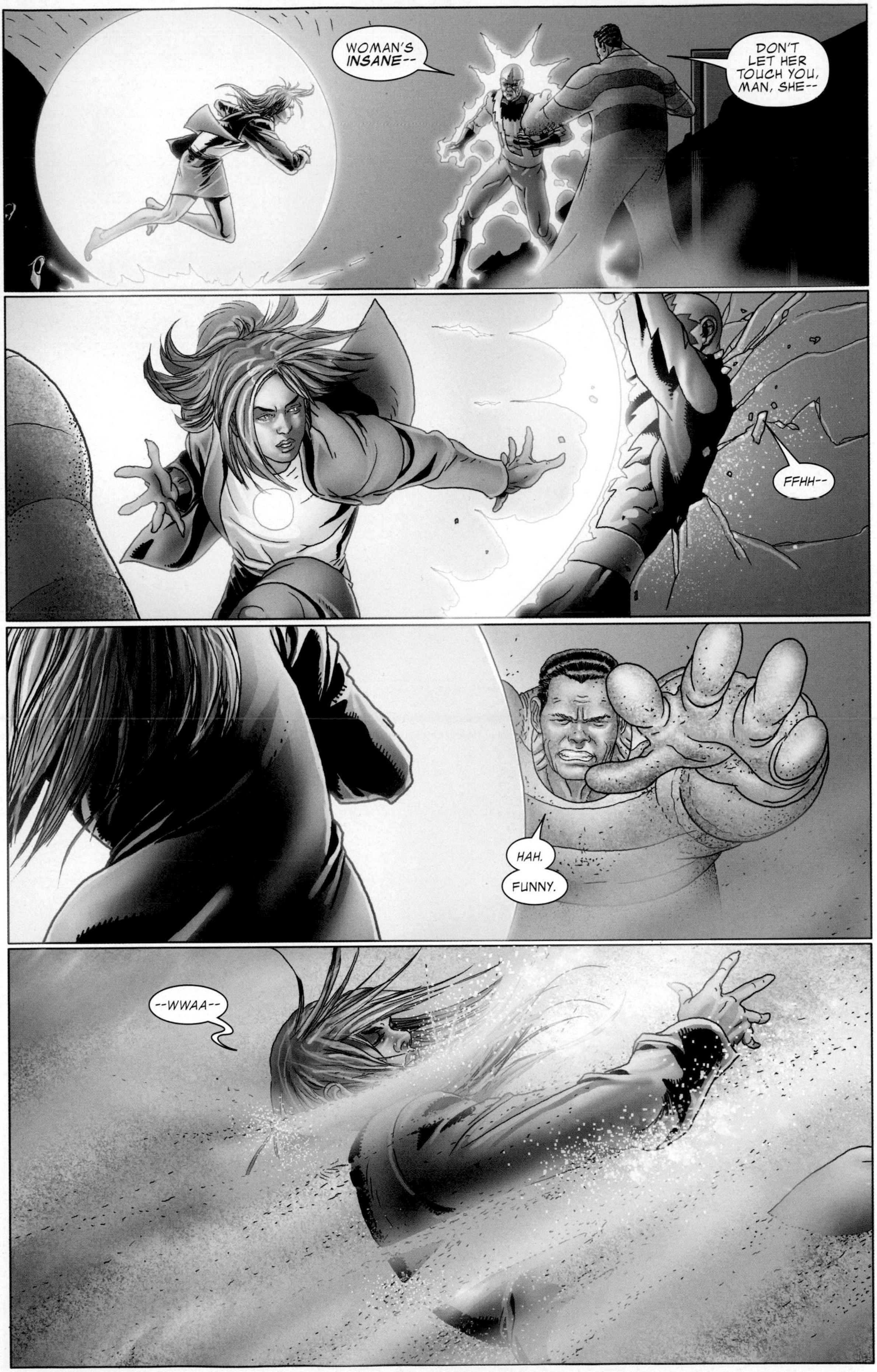
WOMAN'S INSANE--
DON'T LET HER TOUCH YOU, MAN, SHE--
FFHH--
HAH.
FUNNY.
--WWAA--

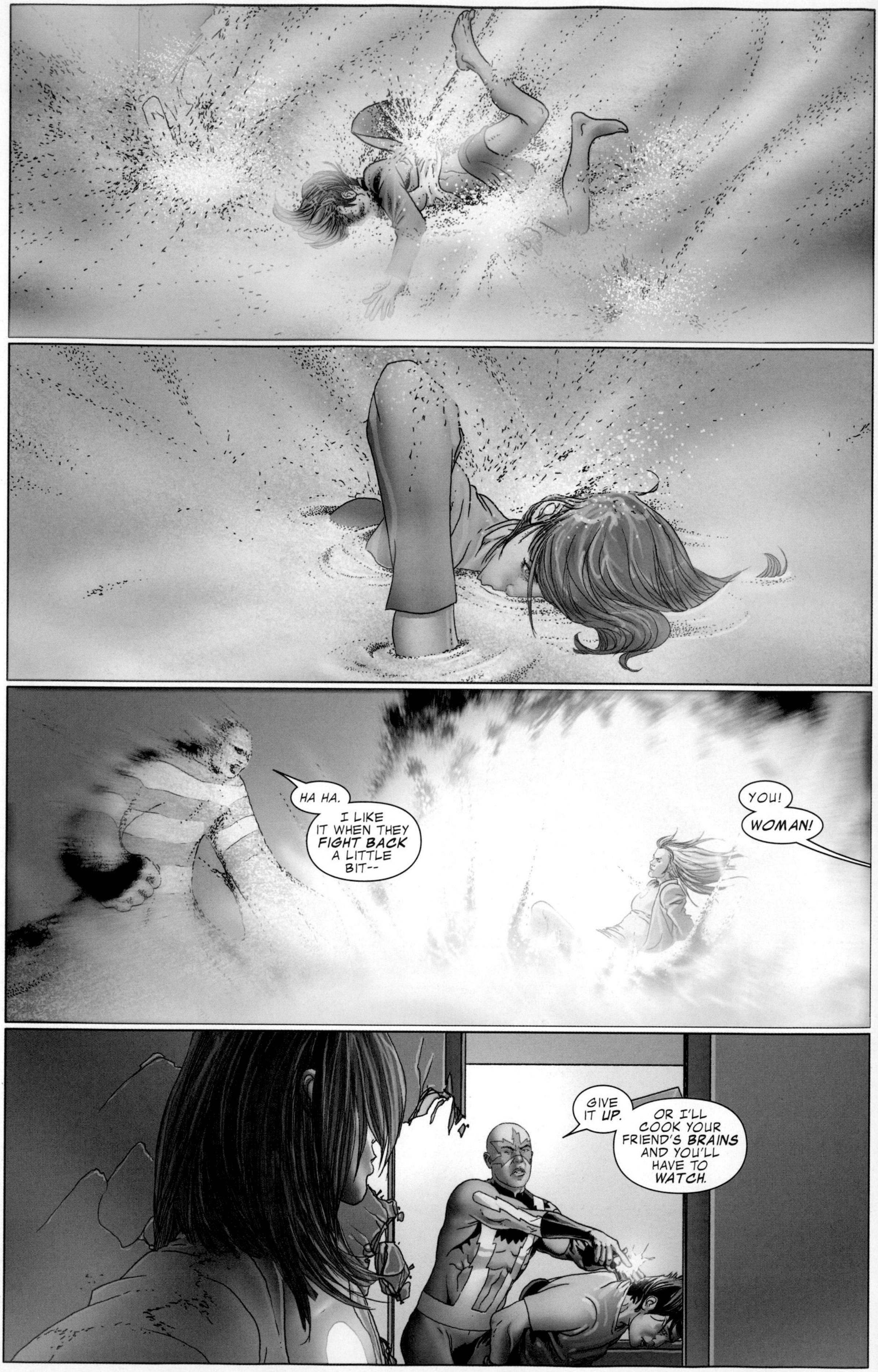
HA HA.
I LIKE IT WHEN THEY FIGHT BACK A LITTLE BIT--
YOU!
WOMAN!
GIVE IT UP.
OR I'LL COOK YOUR FRIEND'S BRAINS AND YOU'LL HAVE TO WATCH.

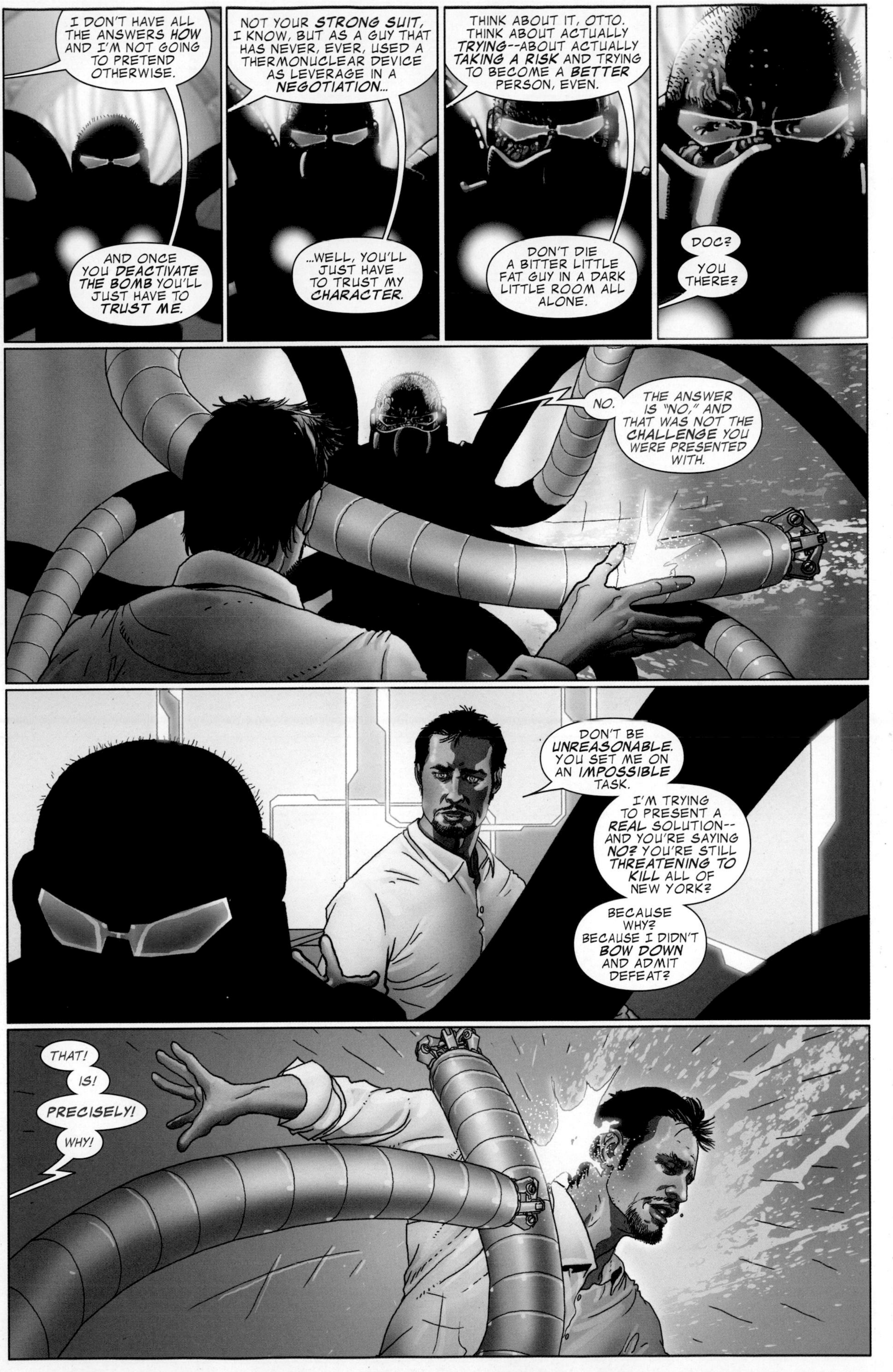
I DON'T HAVE ALL THE ANSWERS HOW AND I'M NOT GOING TO PRETEND OTHERWISE.
AND ONCE YOU DEACTIVATE THE BOMB YOU'LL JUST HAVE TO TRUST ME.
NOT YOUR STRONG SUIT, I KNOW, BUT AS A GUY THAT HAS NEVER, EVER, USED A THERMONUCLEAR DEVICE AS LEVERAGE IN A NEGOTIATION...
...WELL, YOU'LL JUST HAVE TO TRUST MY CHARACTER.
THINK ABOUT IT, OTTO. THINK ABOUT ACTUALLY TRYING--ABOUT ACTUALLY TAKING A RISK AND TRYING TO BECOME A BETTER PERSON, EVEN.
DON'T DIE A BITTER LITTLE FAT GUY IN A DARK LITTLE ROOM ALL ALONE.
DOC?
YOU THERE?
NO.
THE ANSWER IS "NO," AND THAT WAS NOT THE CHALLENGE YOU WERE PRESENTED WITH.
DON'T BE UNREASONABLE. YOU SET ME ON AN IMPOSSIBLE TASK.
I'M TRYING TO PRESENT A REAL SOLUTION--AND YOU'RE SAYING NO? YOU'RE STILL THREATENING TO KILL ALL OF NEW YORK?
BECAUSE WHY? BECAUSE I DIDN'T BOW DOWN AND ADMIT DEFEAT?
THAT!
IS!
PRECISELY!
WHY!

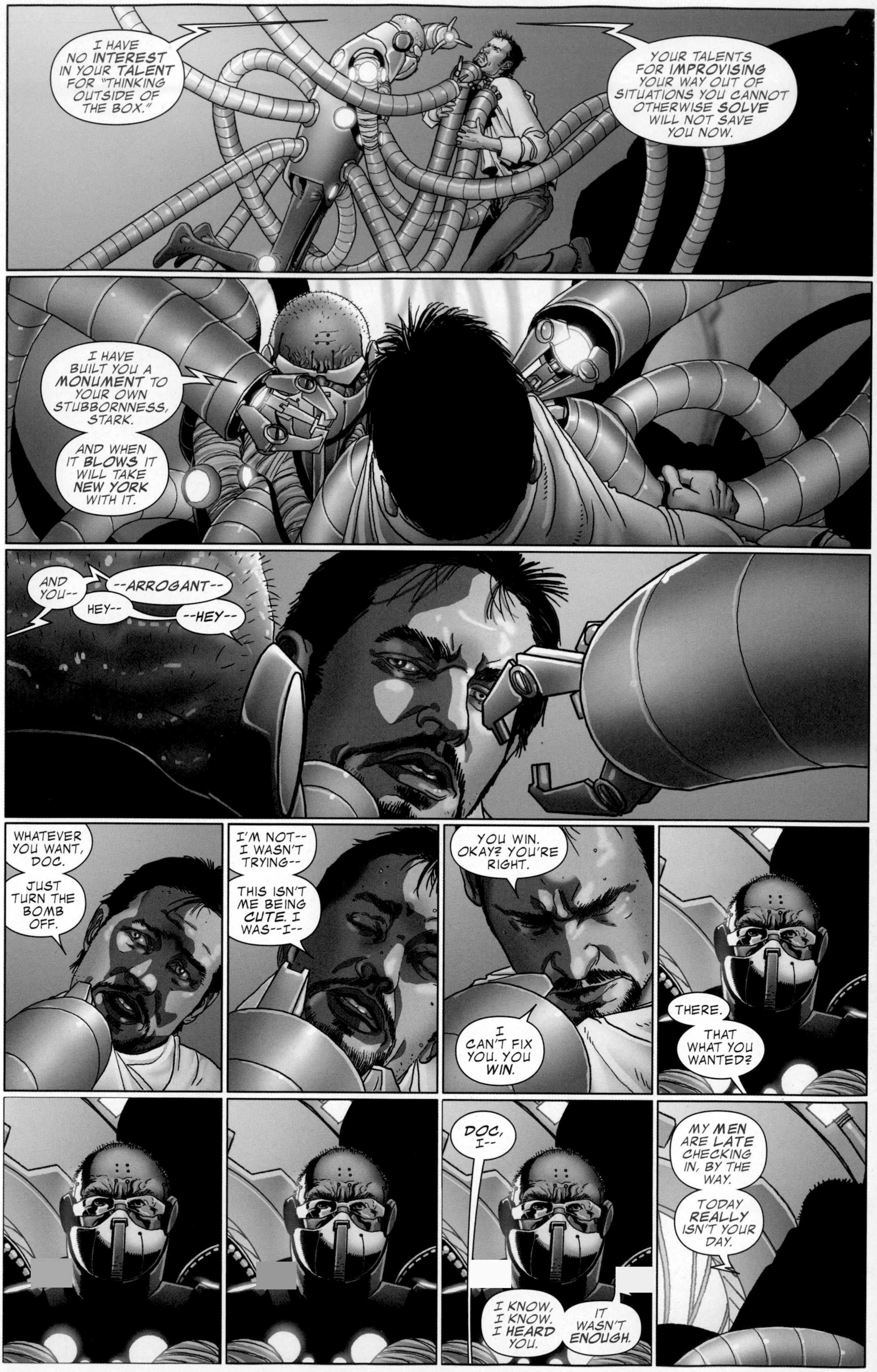

I HAVE NO INTEREST IN YOUR TALENT FOR "THINKING OUTSIDE OF THE BOX."
YOUR TALENTS FOR IMPROVISING YOUR WAY OUT OF SITUATIONS YOU CANNOT OTHERWISE SOLVE WILL NOT SAVE YOU NOW.
I HAVE BUILT YOU A MONUMENT TO YOUR OWN STUBBORNNESS, STARK.
AND WHEN IT BLOWS IT WILL TAKE NEW YORK WITH IT.
AND YOU--
--ARROGANT--
HEY--
--HEY--
WHATEVER YOU WANT, DOC.
JUST TURN THE BOMB OFF.
I'M NOT-- I WASN'T TRYING--
THIS ISN'T ME BEING CUTE. I WAS--I--
YOU WIN. OKAY? YOU'RE RIGHT.
I CAN'T FIX YOU. YOU WIN.
THERE.
THAT WHAT YOU WANTED?
DOC, I--
I KNOW, I KNOW. I HEARD YOU.
IT WASN'T ENOUGH.
MY MEN ARE LATE CHECKING IN, BY THE WAY.
TODAY REALLY ISN'T YOUR DAY.

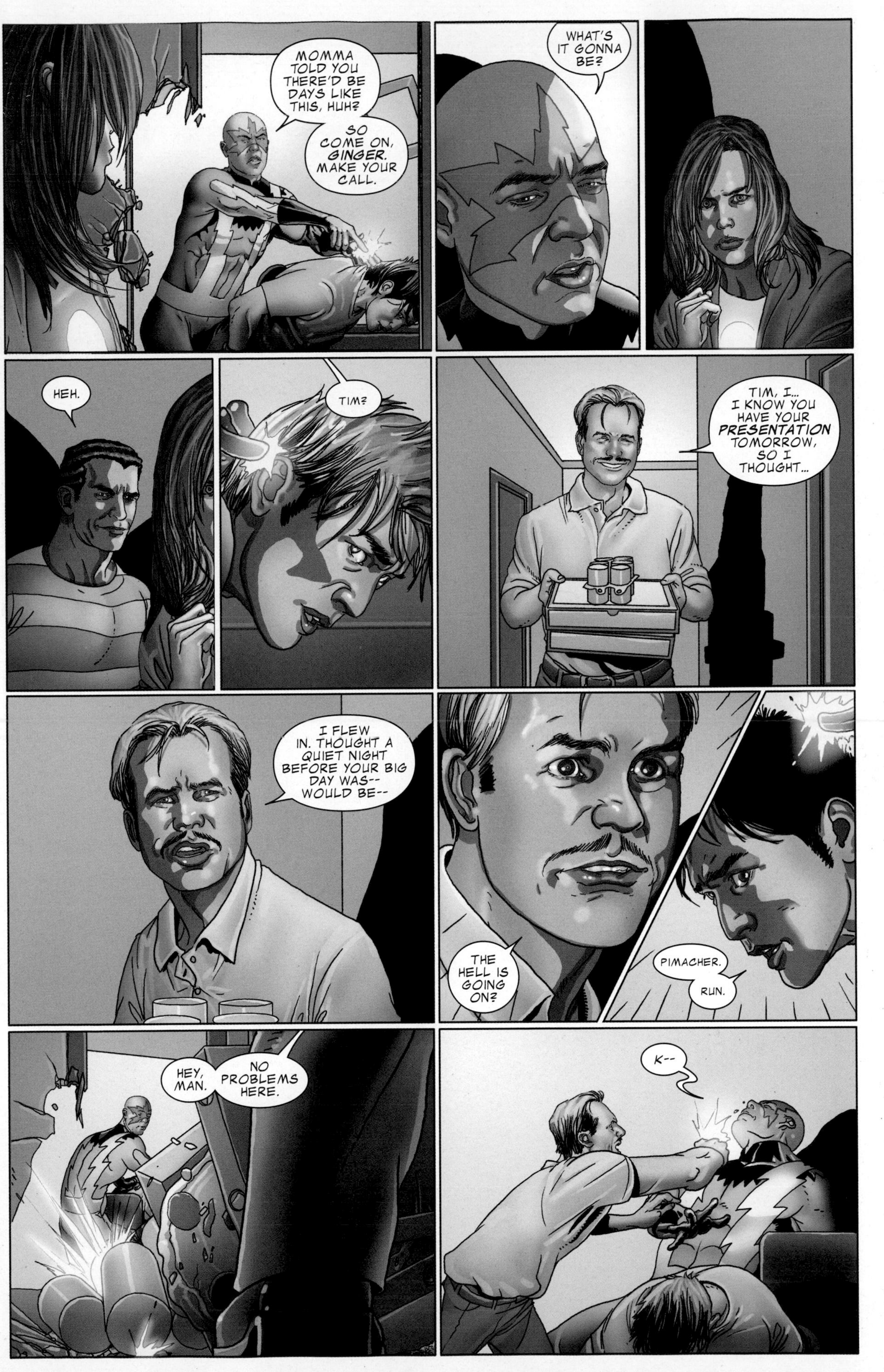
MOMMA TOLD YOU THERE'D BE DAYS LIKE THIS, HUH?
SO COME ON, GINGER. MAKE YOUR CALL.
WHAT'S IT GONNA BE?
HEH.
TIM?
TIM, I... I KNOW YOU HAVE YOUR PRESENTATION TOMORROW, SO I THOUGHT...
I FLEW IN. THOUGHT A QUIET NIGHT BEFORE YOUR BIG DAY WAS-- WOULD BE--
THE HELL IS GOING ON?
PIMACHER.
RUN.
HEY, MAN.
NO PROBLEMS HERE.
K--

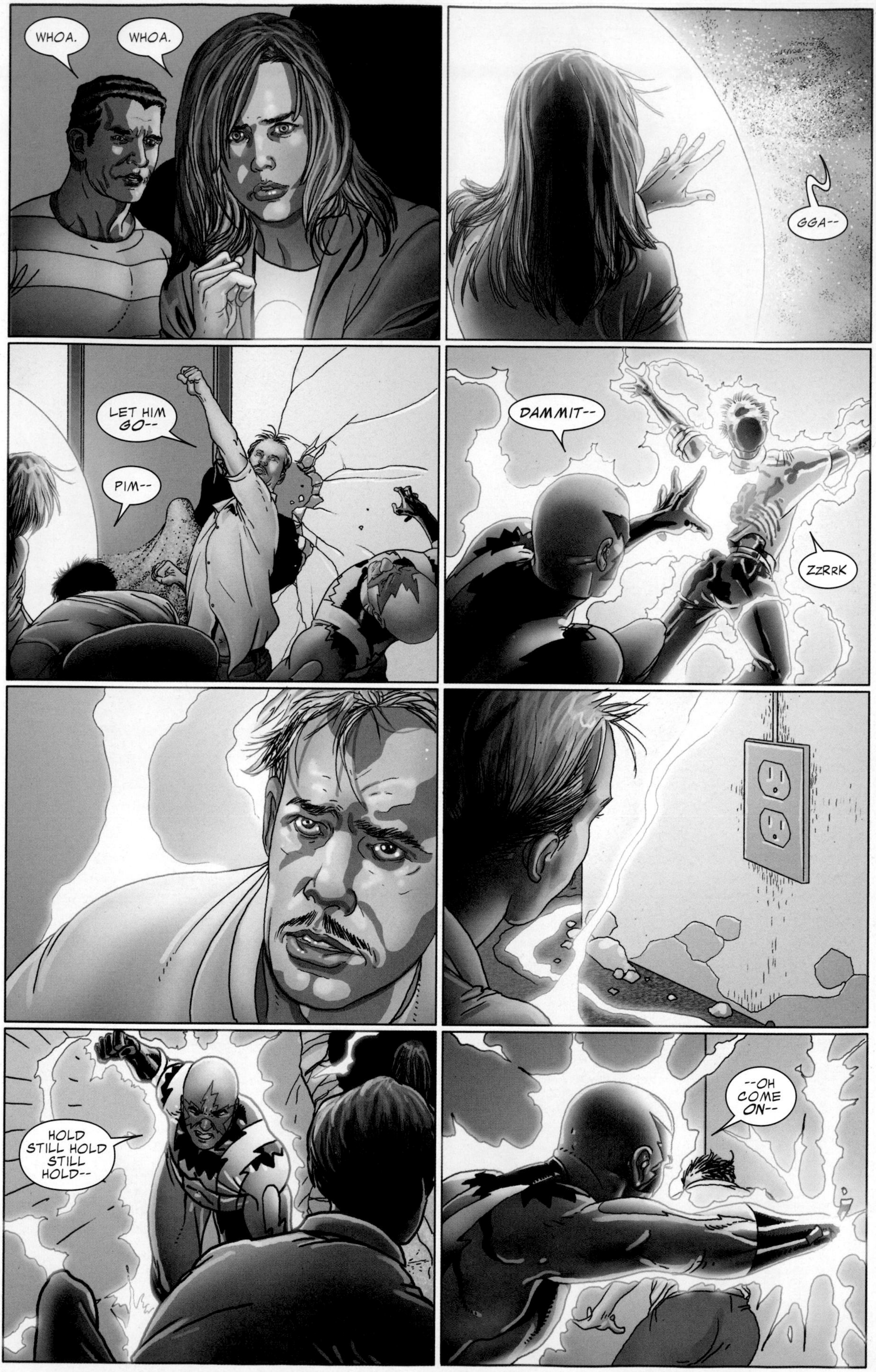
WHOA.
WHOA.
GGA--
LET HIM GO--
PIM--
DAMMIT--
ZZRRK
HOLD STILL HOLD STILL HOLD--
--OH COME ON--

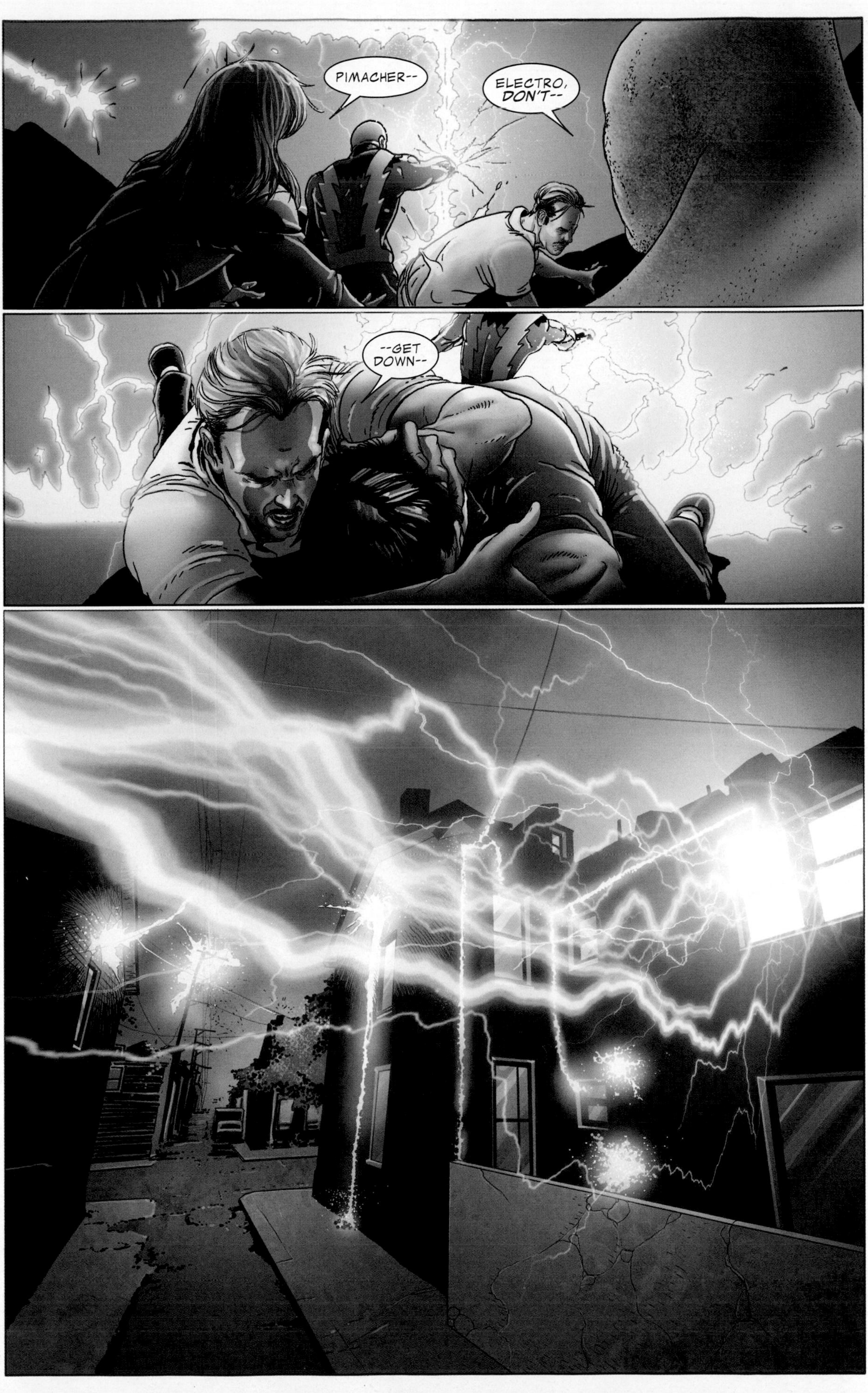
PIMACHER--
ELECTRO, DON'T--
--GET DOWN--

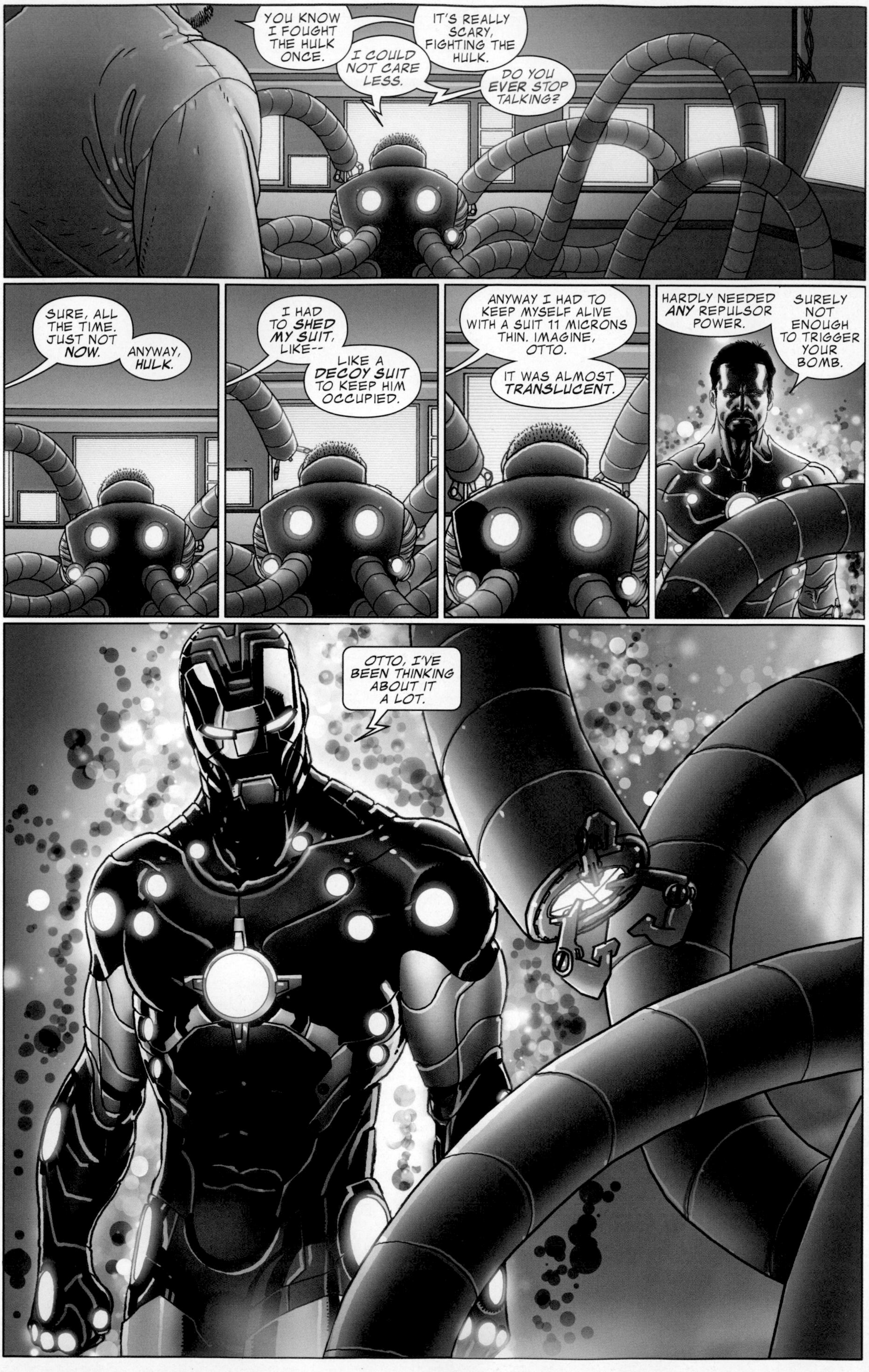
YOU KNOW I FOUGHT THE HULK ONCE.
IT'S REALLY SCARY, FIGHTING THE HULK.
I COULD NOT CARE LESS.
DO YOU EVER STOP TALKING?
SURE, ALL THE TIME. JUST NOT NOW.
ANYWAY, HULK.
I HAD TO SHED MY SUIT, LIKE--
LIKE A DECOY SUIT TO KEEP HIM OCCUPIED.
ANYWAY I HAD TO KEEP MYSELF ALIVE WITH A SUIT 11 MICRONS THIN. IMAGINE, OTTO.
IT WAS ALMOST TRANSLUCENT.
HARDLY NEEDED ANY REPULSOR POWER.
SURELY NOT ENOUGH TO TRIGGER YOUR BOMB.
OTTO, I'VE BEEN THINKING ABOUT IT A LOT.

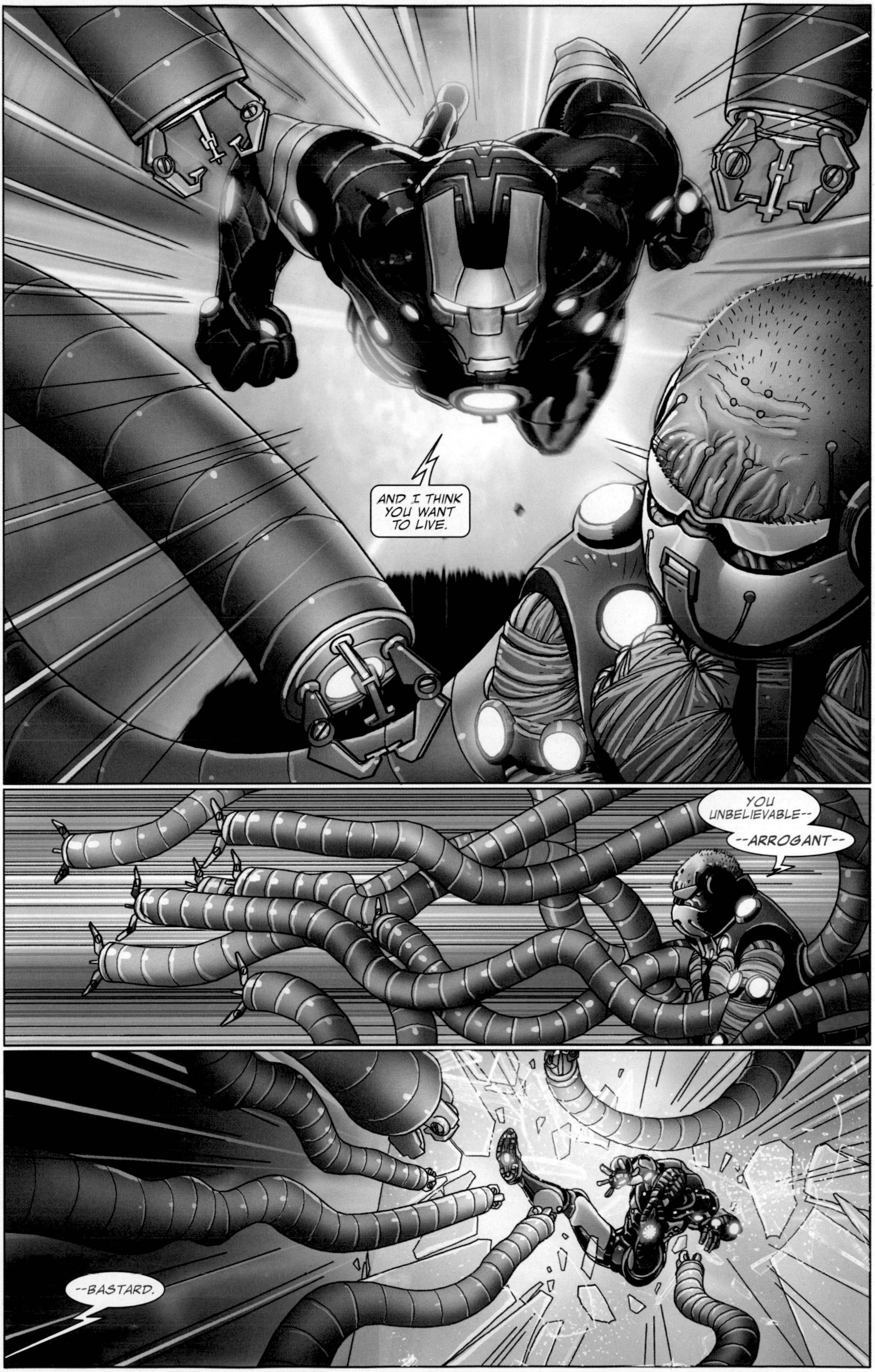
AND I THINK YOU WANT TO LIVE.
YOU UNBELIEVABLE--
--ARROGANT--
--BASTARD.

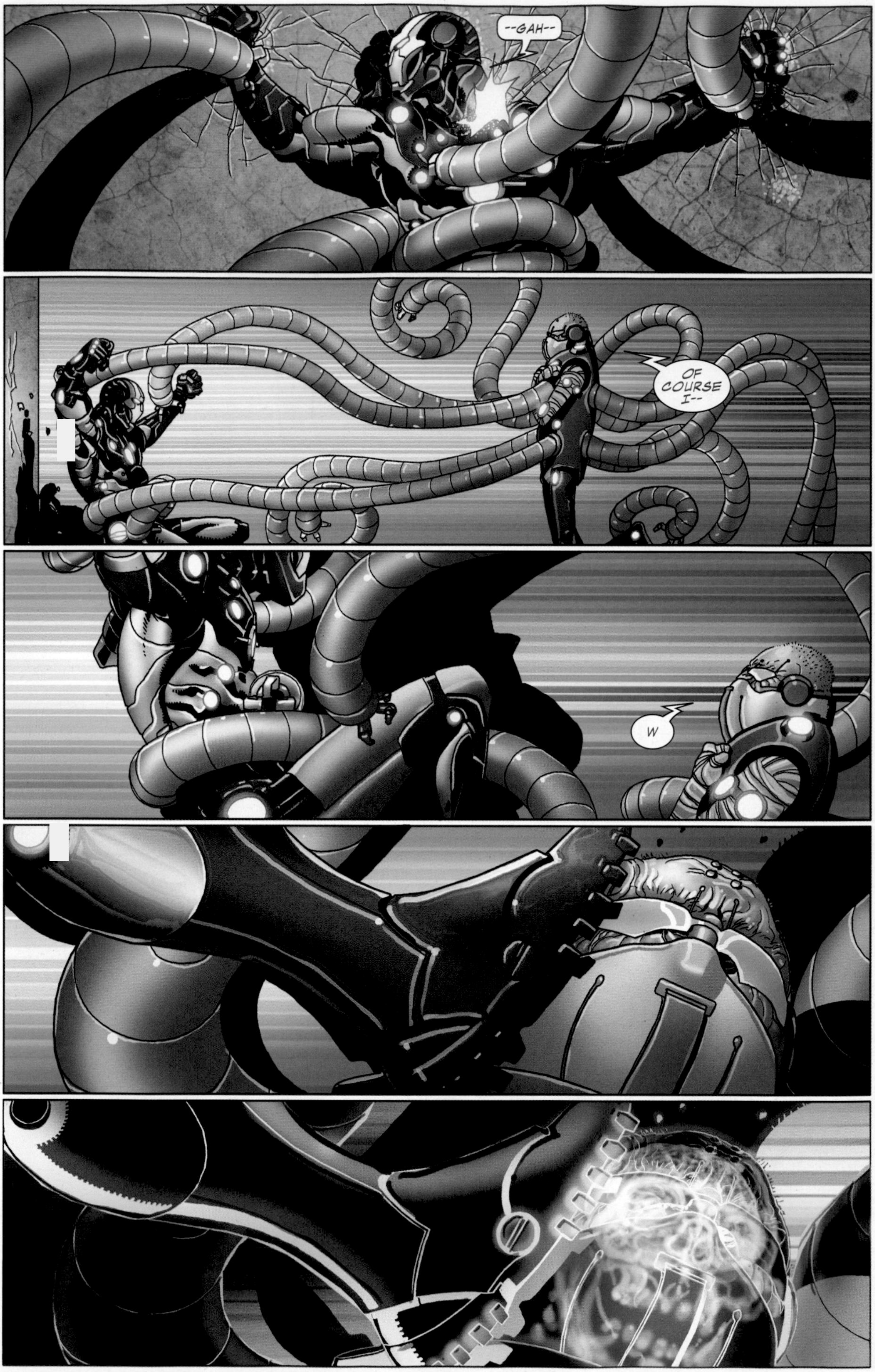
--GAH--
OF COURSE I--
W

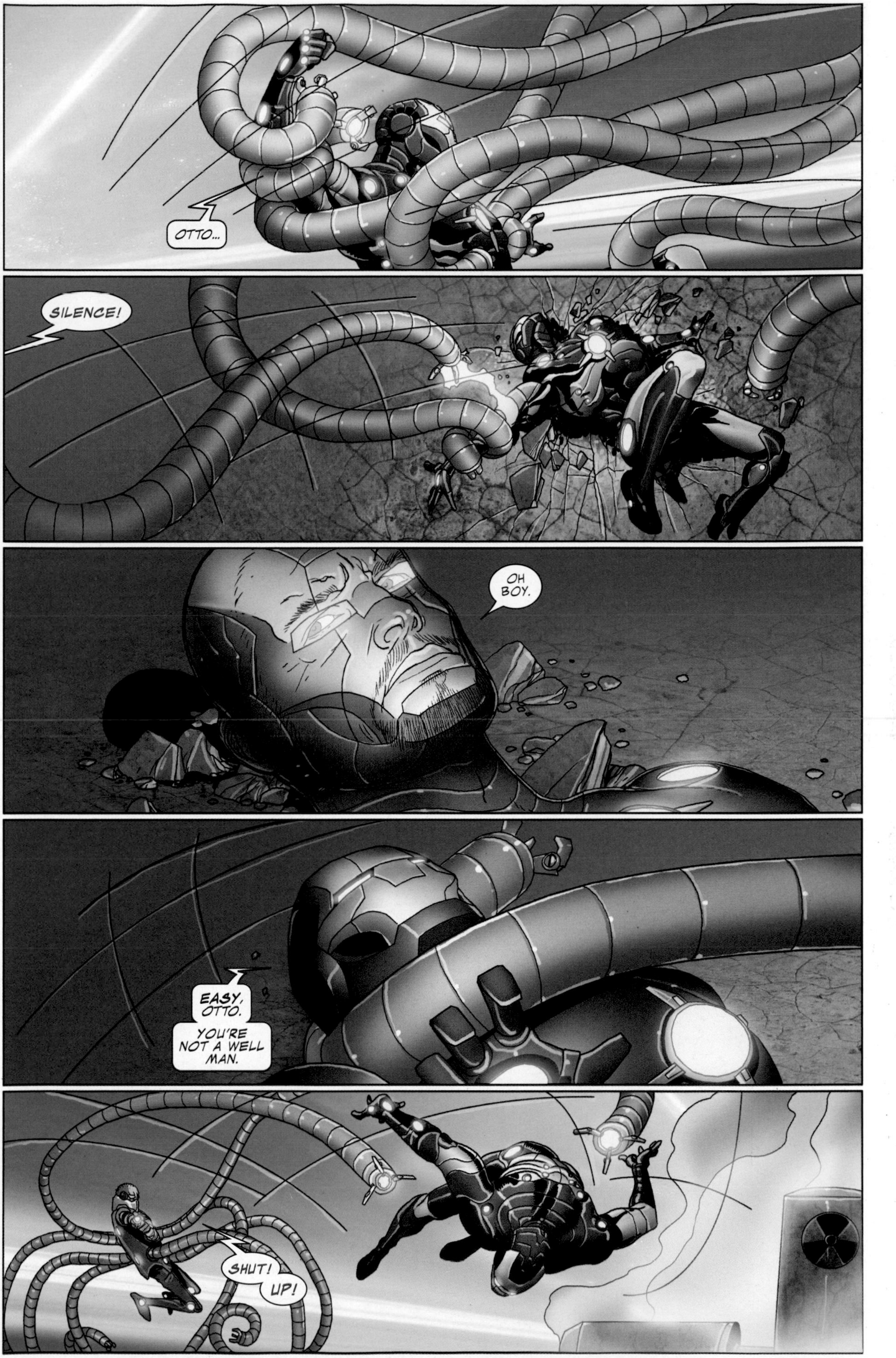
OTTO...
SILENCE!
OH BOY.
EASY, OTTO.
YOU'RE NOT A WELL MAN.
SHUT!
UP!

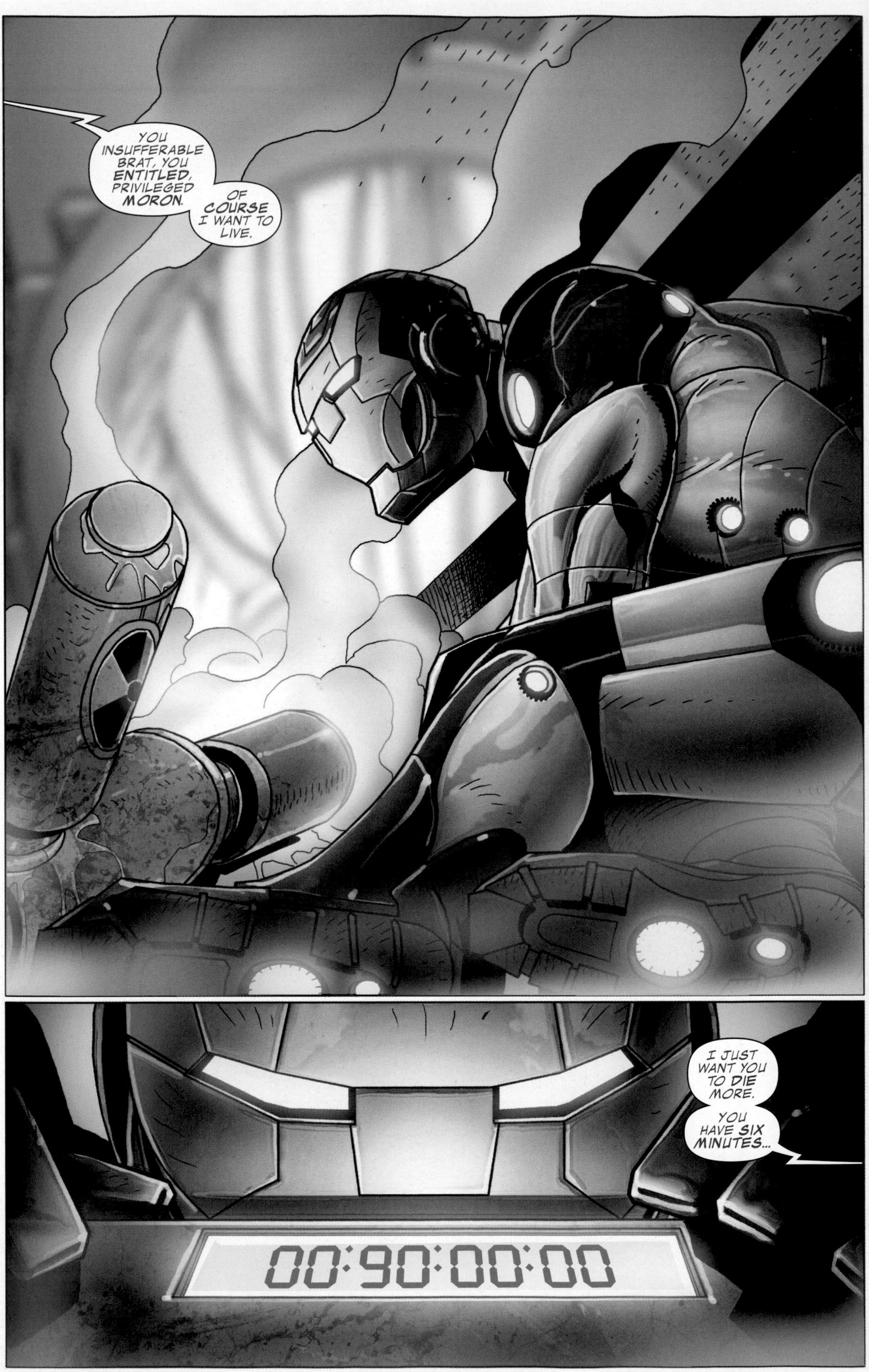
YOU INSUFFERABLE BRAT, YOU ENTITLED, PRIVILEGED MORON.
OF COURSE I WANT TO LIVE.
I JUST WANT YOU TO DIE MORE.
YOU HAVE SIX MINUTES...
00:90:00:00

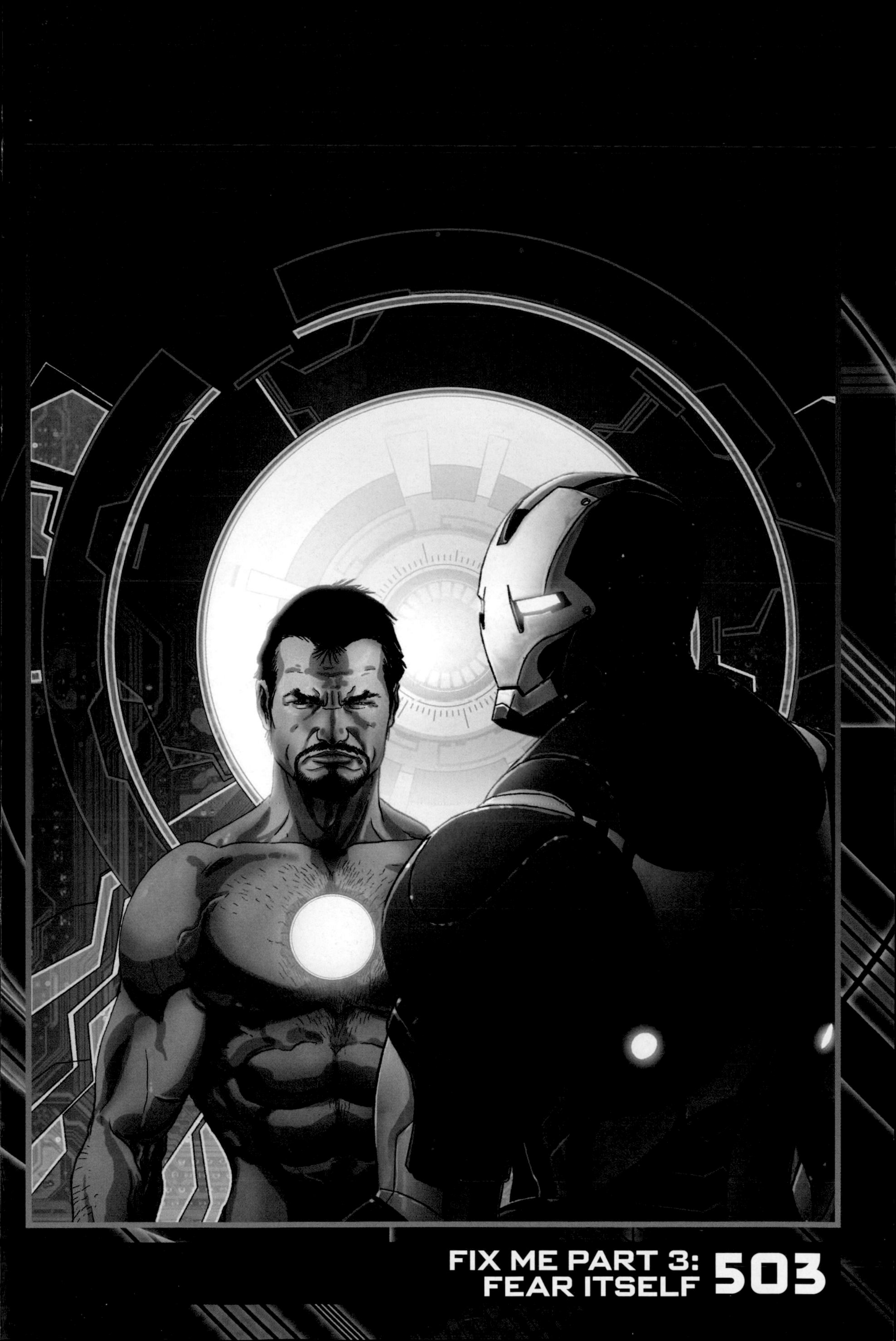

FIX ME PART 3:
FEAR ITSELF 503

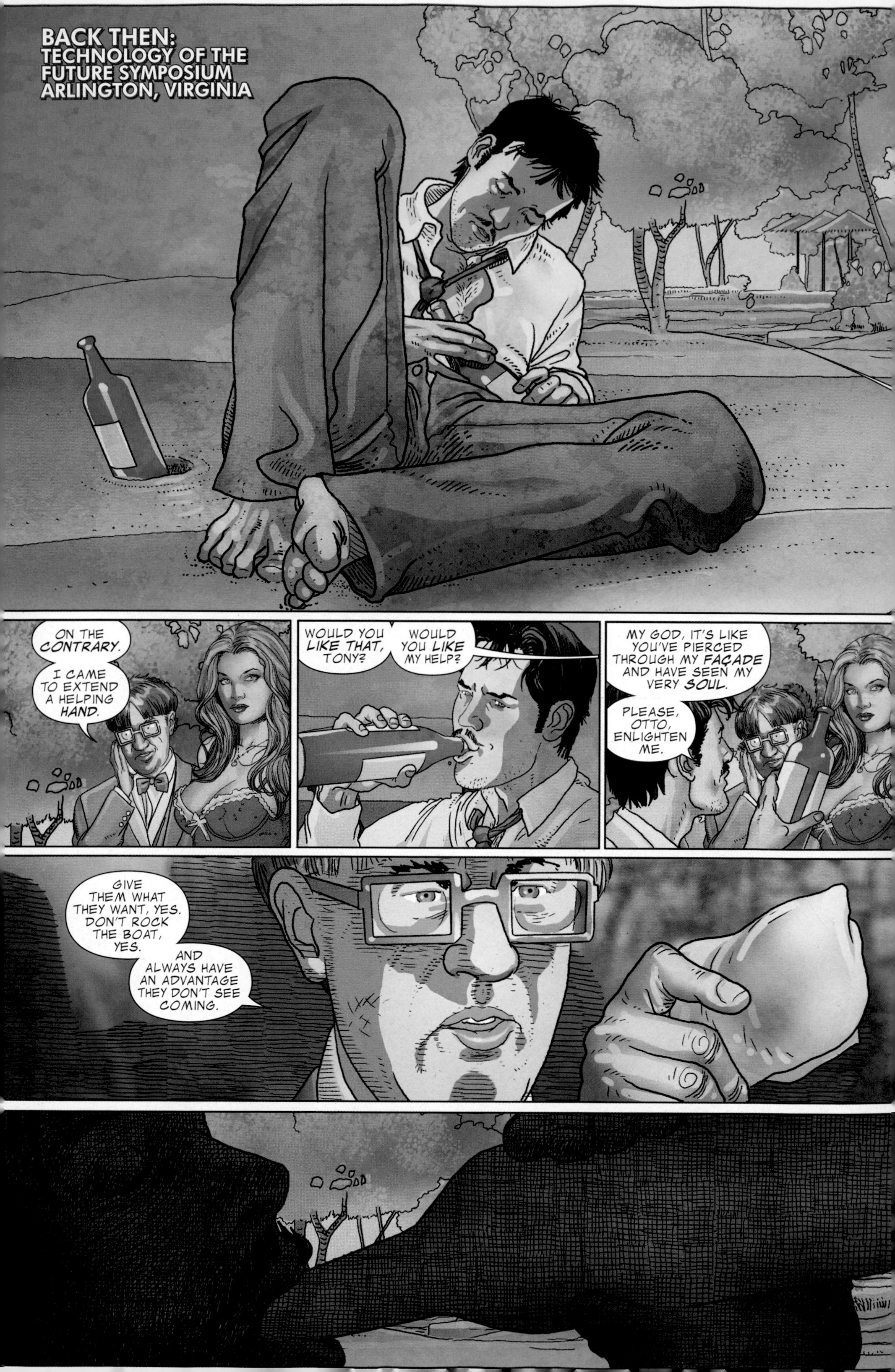
BACK THEN: TECHNOLOGY OF THE FUTURE SYMPOSIUM ARLINGTON, VIRGINIA
ON THE CONTRARY.
I CAME TO EXTEND A HELPING HAND.
WOULD YOU LIKE THAT, TONY?
WOULD YOU LIKE MY HELP?
MY GOD, IT'S LIKE YOU'VE PIERCED THROUGH MY FAÇADE AND HAVE SEEN MY VERY SOUL.
PLEASE, OTTO, ENLIGHTEN ME.
GIVE THEM WHAT THEY WANT, YES. DON'T ROCK THE BOAT, YES.
AND ALWAYS HAVE AN ADVANTAGE THEY DON'T SEE COMING.

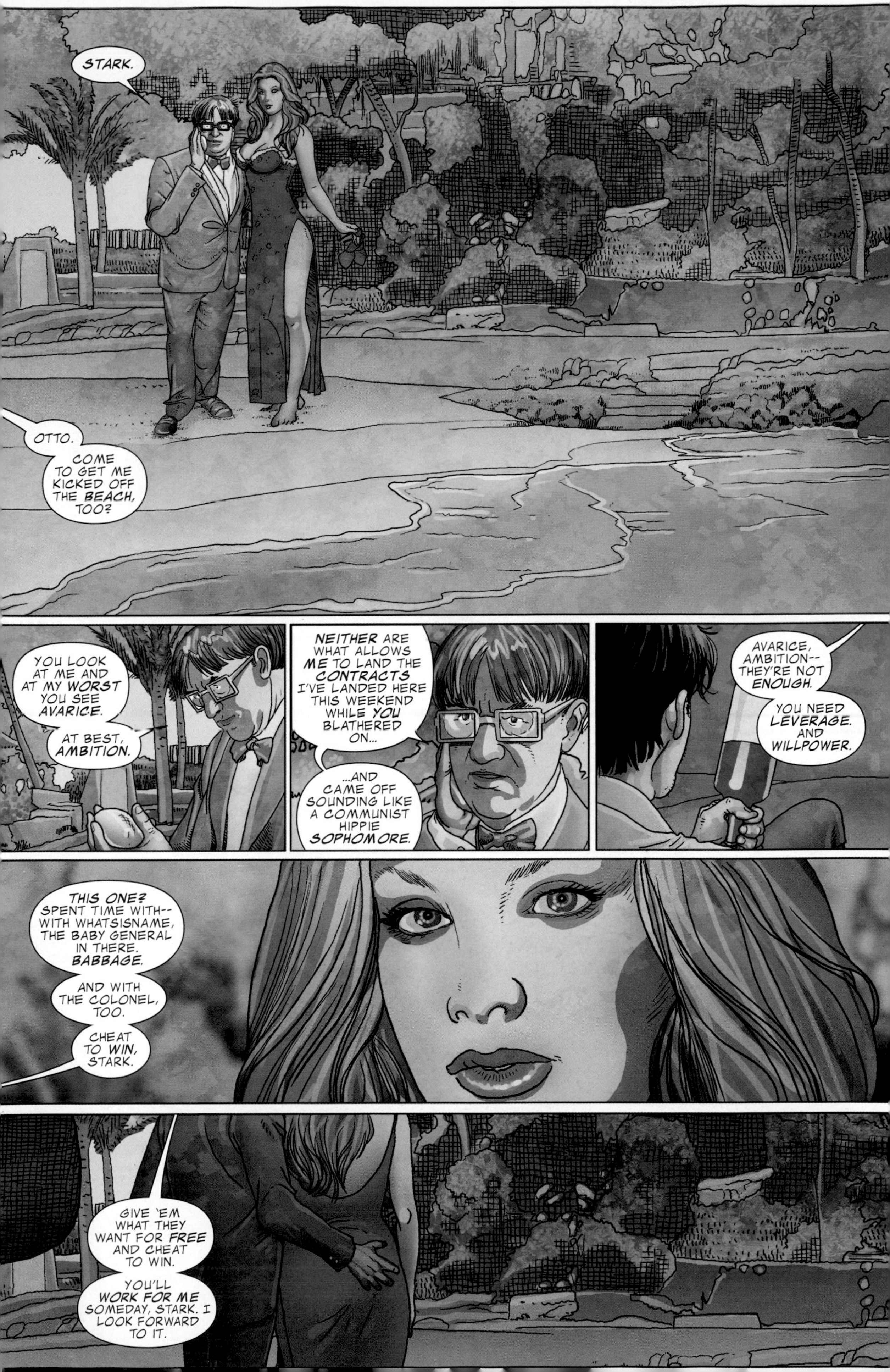
STARK.
OTTO.
COME TO GET ME KICKED OFF THE BEACH, TOO?
YOU LOOK AT ME AND AT MY WORST YOU SEE AVARICE.
AT BEST, AMBITION.
NEITHER ARE WHAT ALLOWS ME TO LAND THE CONTRACTS I'VE LANDED HERE THIS WEEKEND WHILE YOU BLATHERED ON...
...AND CAME OFF SOUNDING LIKE A COMMUNIST HIPPIE SOPHOMORE.
AVARICE, AMBITION-- THEY'RE NOT ENOUGH.
YOU NEED LEVERAGE. AND WILLPOWER.
THIS ONE? SPENT TIME WITH-- WITH WHATSISNAME, THE BABY GENERAL IN THERE. BABBAGE.
AND WITH THE COLONEL, TOO.
CHEAT TO WIN, STARK.
GIVE 'EM WHAT THEY WANT FOR FREE AND CHEAT TO WIN.
YOU'LL WORK FOR ME SOMEDAY, STARK. I LOOK FORWARD TO IT.

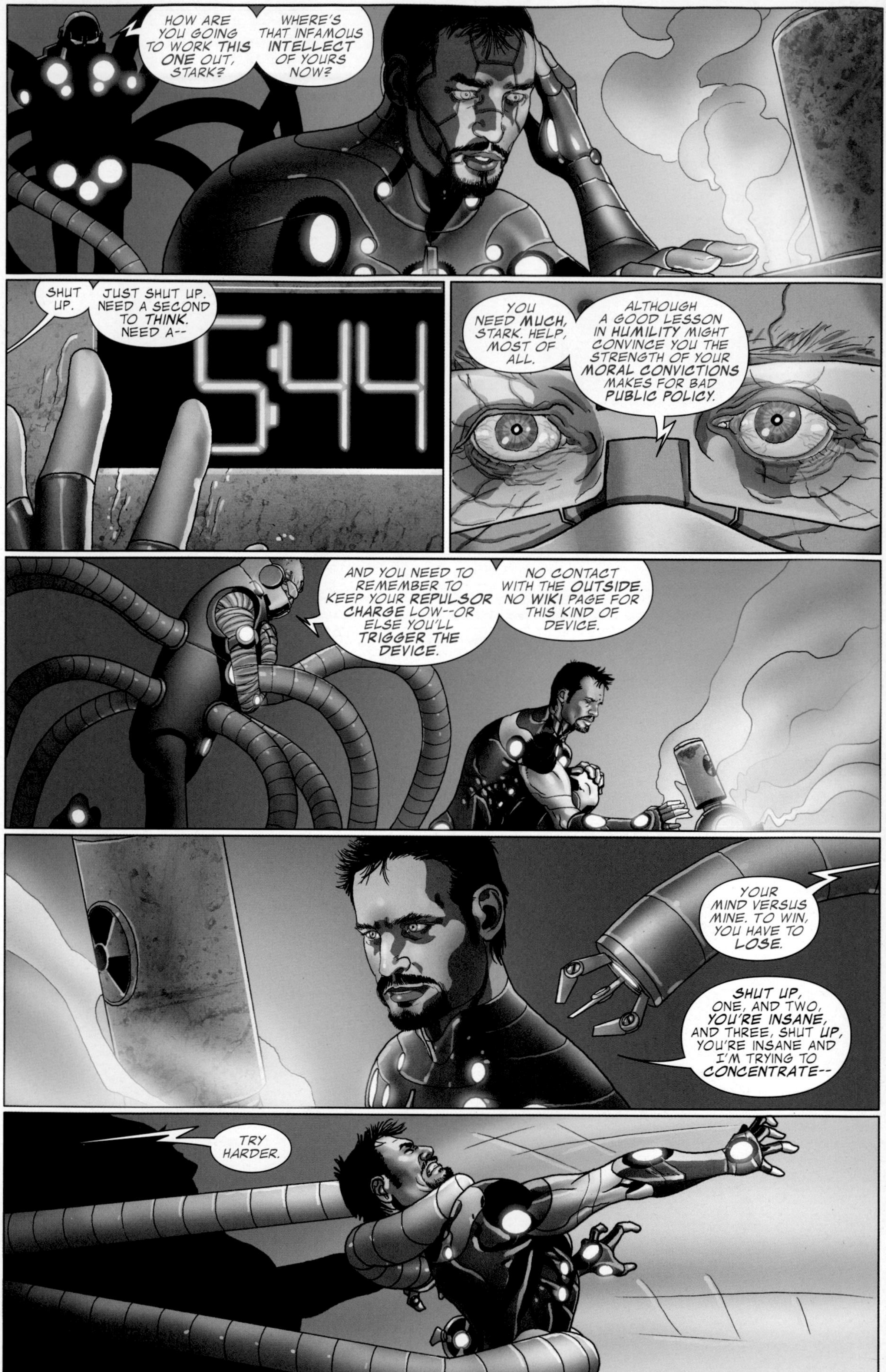
HOW ARE YOU GOING TO WORK THIS ONE OUT, STARK?
WHERE'S THAT INFAMOUS INTELLECT OF YOURS NOW?
SHUT UP.
JUST SHUT UP. NEED A SECOND TO THINK. NEED A--
5:44
YOU NEED MUCH, STARK. HELP, MOST OF ALL.
ALTHOUGH A GOOD LESSON IN HUMILITY MIGHT CONVINCE YOU THE STRENGTH OF YOUR MORAL CONVICTIONS MAKES FOR BAD PUBLIC POLICY.
AND YOU NEED TO REMEMBER TO KEEP YOUR REPULSOR CHARGE LOW--OR ELSE YOU'LL TRIGGER THE DEVICE.
NO CONTACT WITH THE OUTSIDE. NO WIKI PAGE FOR THIS KIND OF DEVICE.
YOUR MIND VERSUS MINE. TO WIN, YOU HAVE TO LOSE.
SHUT UP, ONE, AND TWO, YOU'RE INSANE, AND THREE, SHUT UP, YOU'RE INSANE AND I'M TRYING TO CONCENTRATE--
TRY HARDER.

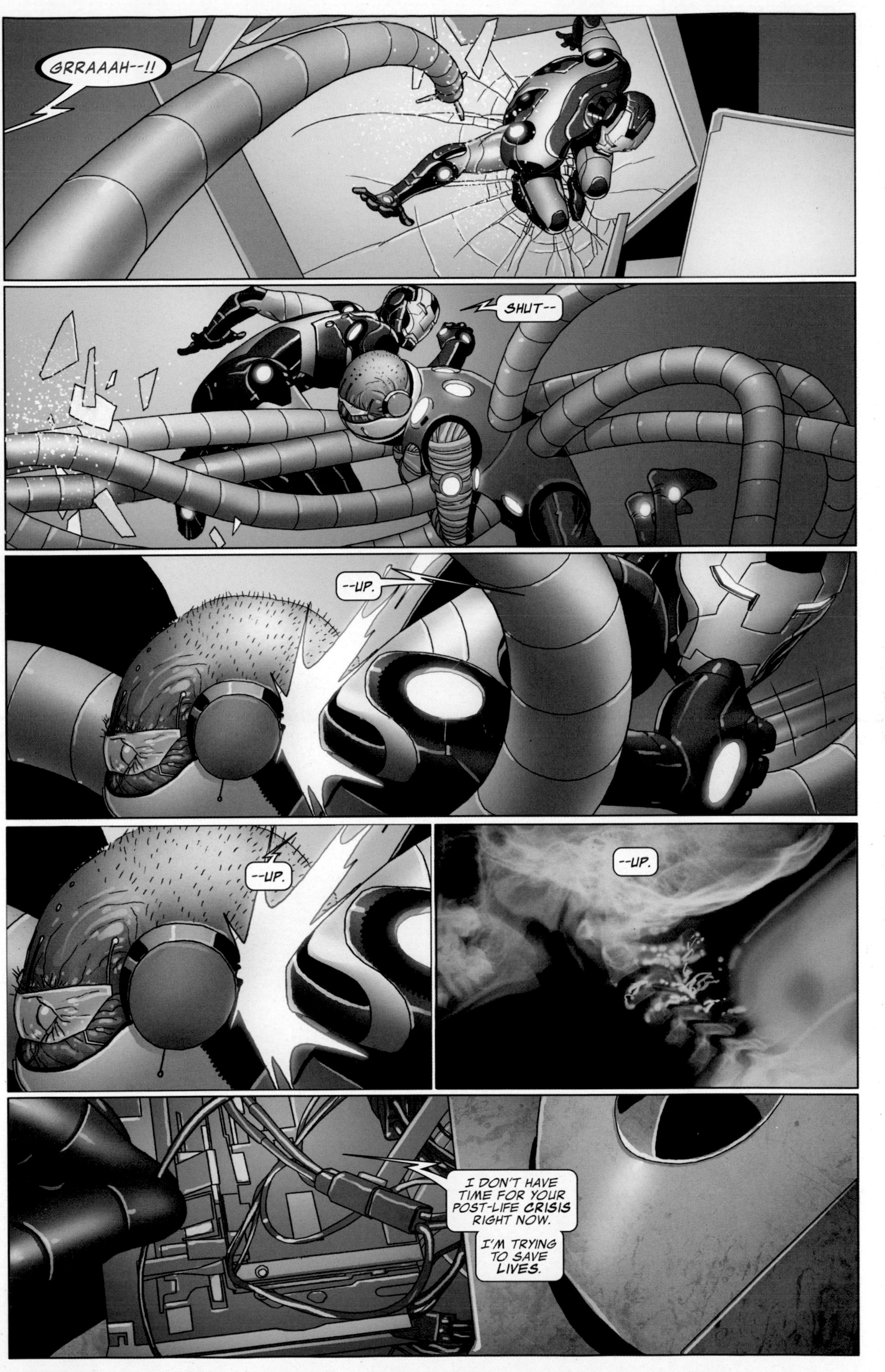
GRRAAAH--!!
SHUT--
--UP.
--UP.
--UP.
I DON'T HAVE TIME FOR YOUR POST-LIFE CRISIS RIGHT NOW.
I'M TRYING TO SAVE LIVES.

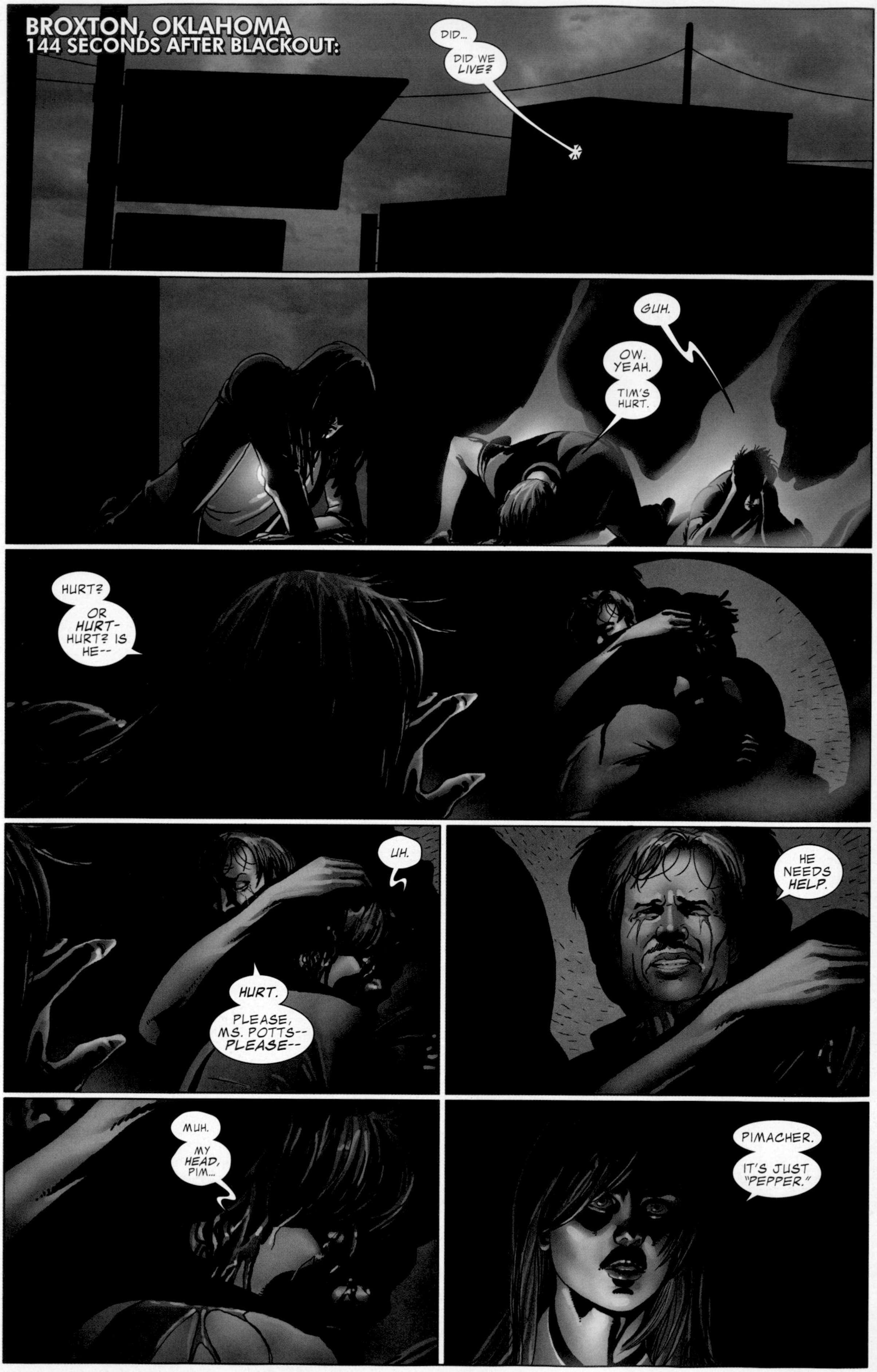
BROXTON, OKLAHOMA
144 SECONDS AFTER BLACKOUT:
DID...
DID WE LIVE?
GUH.
OW. YEAH.
TIM'S HURT.
HURT?
OR HURT-HURT? IS HE--
UH.
HURT.
PLEASE, MS. POTTS-- PLEASE--
HE NEEDS HELP.
MUH.
MY HEAD, PIM...
PIMACHER.
IT'S JUST "PEPPER."

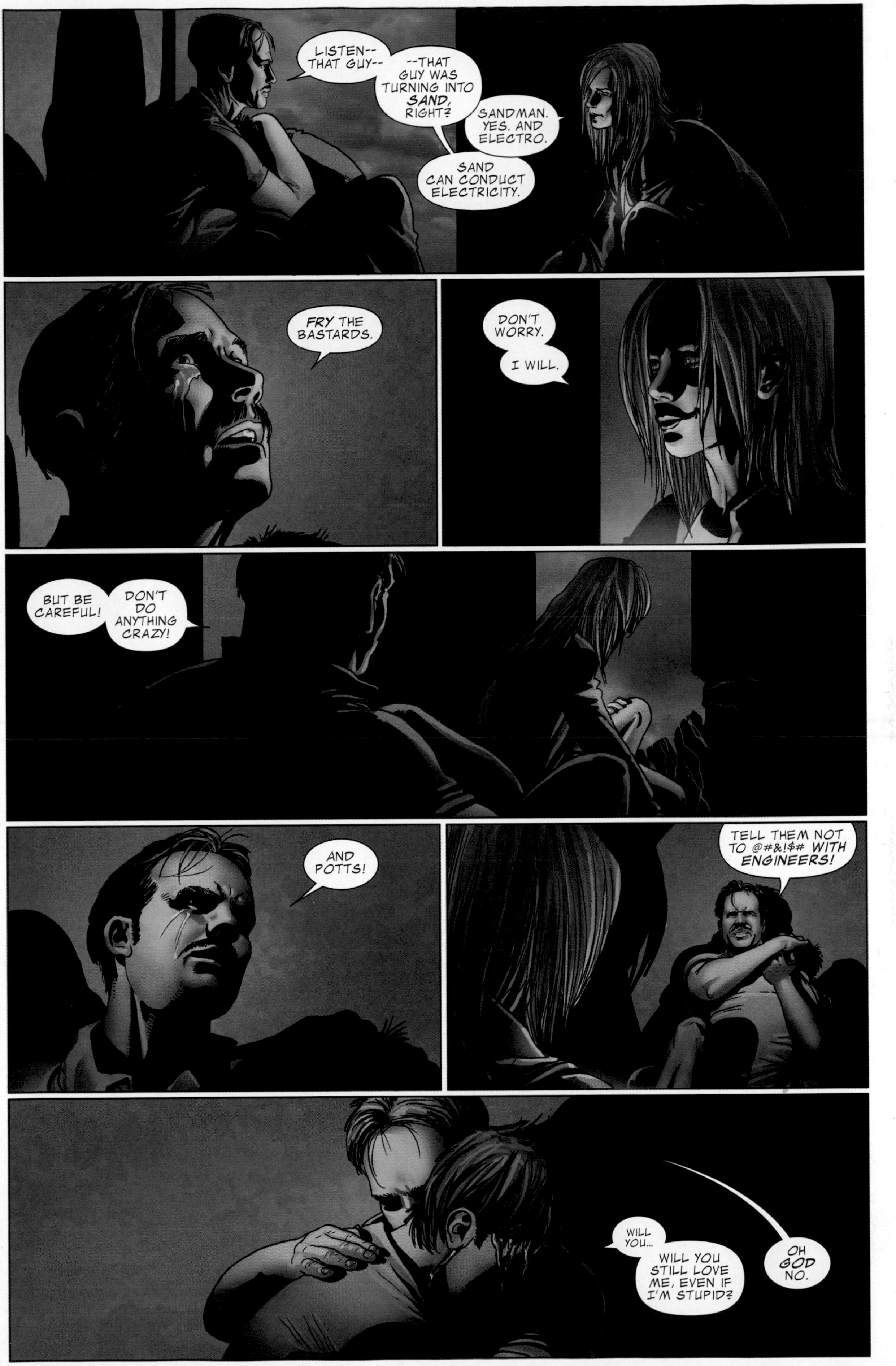
LISTEN-- THAT GUY--
--THAT GUY WAS TURNING INTO SAND, RIGHT?
SANDMAN. YES. AND ELECTRO.
SAND CAN CONDUCT ELECTRICITY.
FRY THE BASTARDS.
DON'T WORRY.
I WILL.
BUT BE CAREFUL!
DON'T DO ANYTHING CRAZY!
AND POTTS!
TELL THEM NOT TO @#&!$# WITH ENGINEERS!
WILL YOU...
WILL YOU STILL LOVE ME, EVEN IF I'M STUPID?
OH GOD NO.

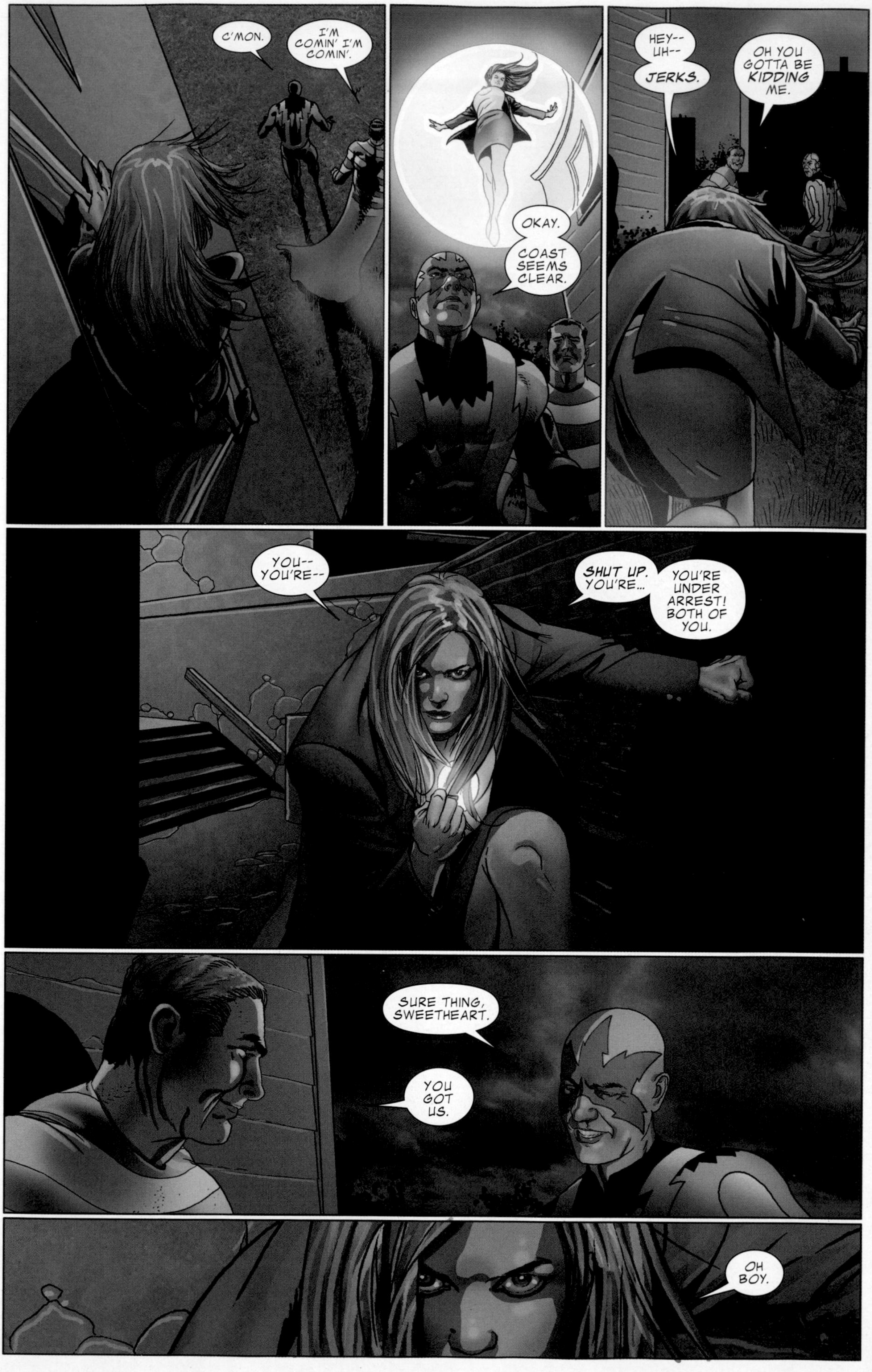
C'MON.
I'M COMIN' I'M COMIN'.
OKAY.
COAST SEEMS CLEAR.
HEY-- UH--
JERKS.
OH YOU GOTTA BE KIDDING ME.
YOU-- YOU'RE--
SHUT UP. YOU'RE...
YOU'RE UNDER ARREST! BOTH OF YOU.
SURE THING, SWEETHEART.
YOU GOT US.
OH BOY.

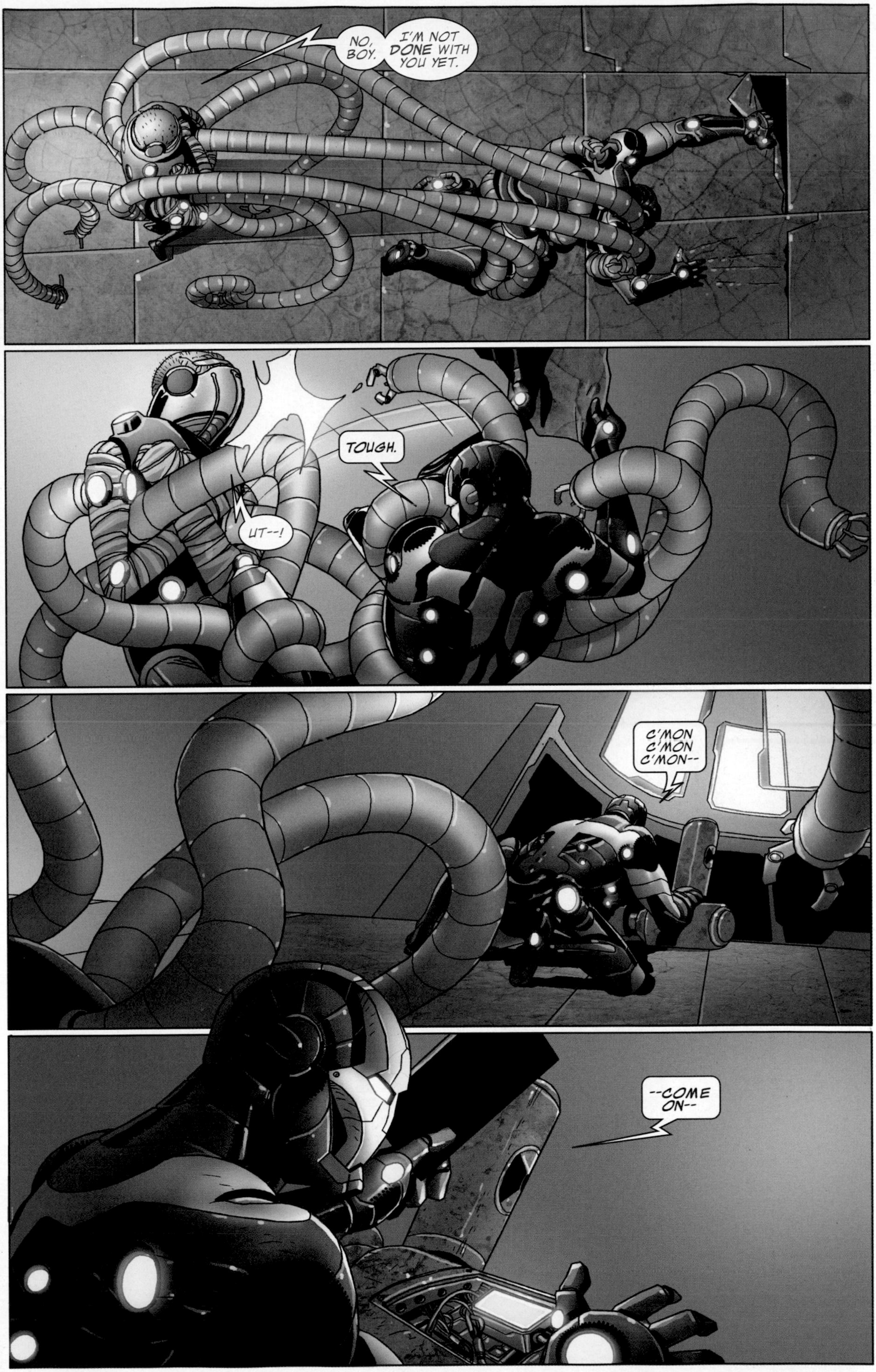
NO, BOY.
I'M NOT DONE WITH YOU YET.
TOUGH.
UT--!
C'MON C'MON C'MON--
--COME ON--

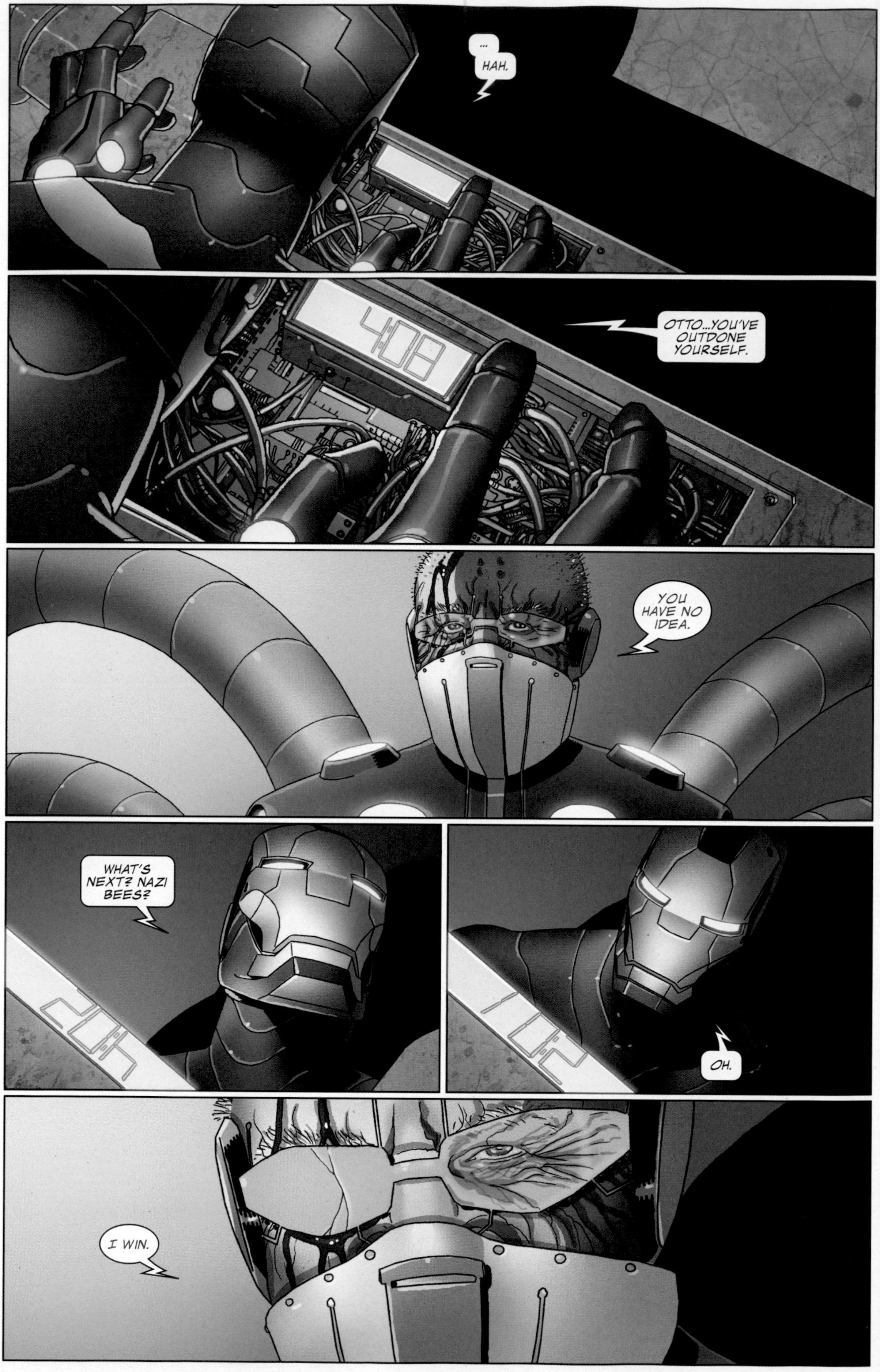
...HAH.
OTTO...YOU'VE OUTDONE YOURSELF.
4:08
YOU HAVE NO IDEA.
WHAT'S NEXT? NAZI BEES?
OH.
I WIN.

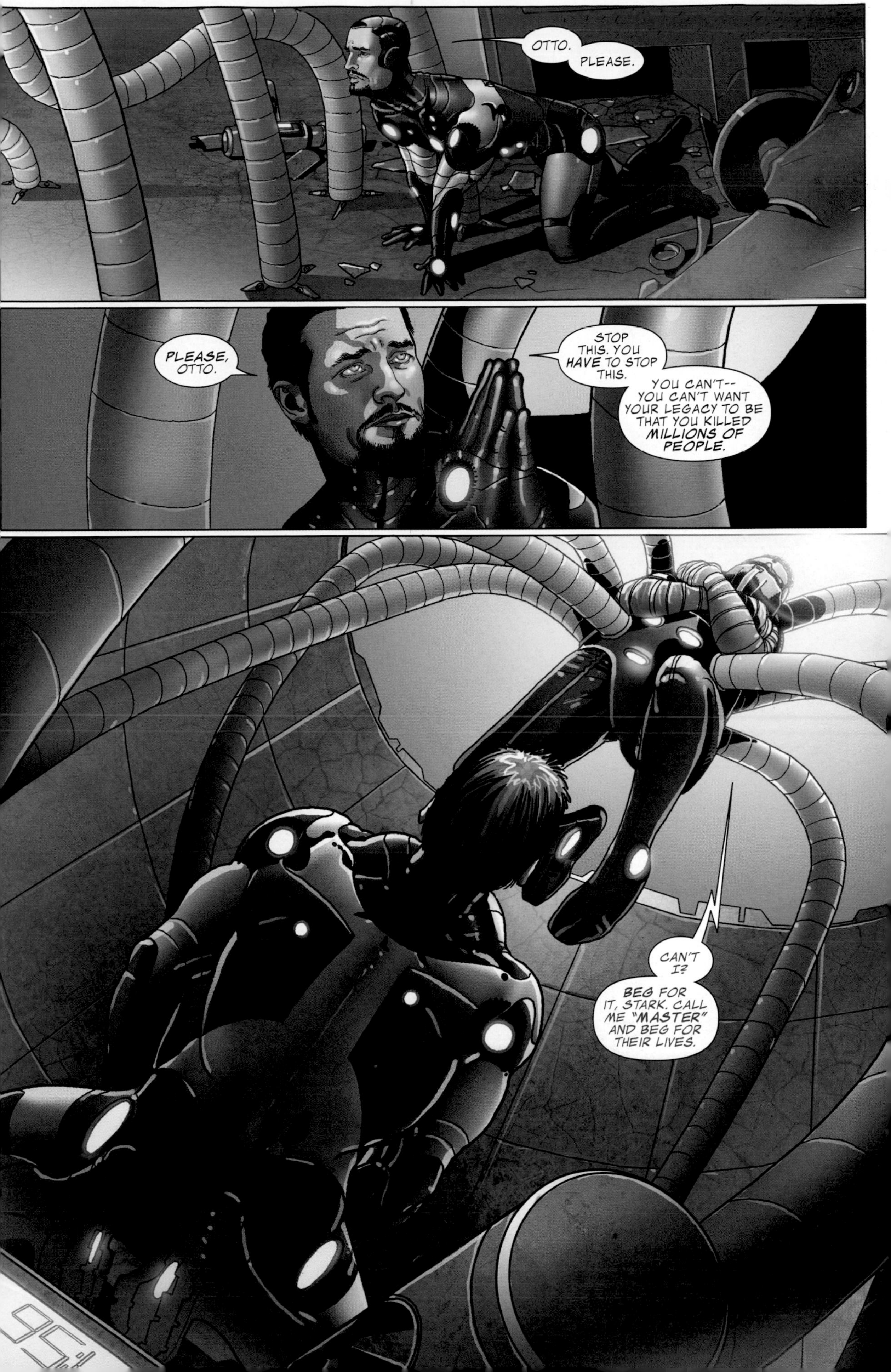
OTTO.
PLEASE.
PLEASE, OTTO.
STOP THIS. YOU HAVE TO STOP THIS.
YOU CAN'T-- YOU CAN'T WANT YOUR LEGACY TO BE THAT YOU KILLED MILLIONS OF PEOPLE.
CAN'T I?
BEG FOR IT, STARK. CALL ME "MASTER" AND BEG FOR THEIR LIVES.

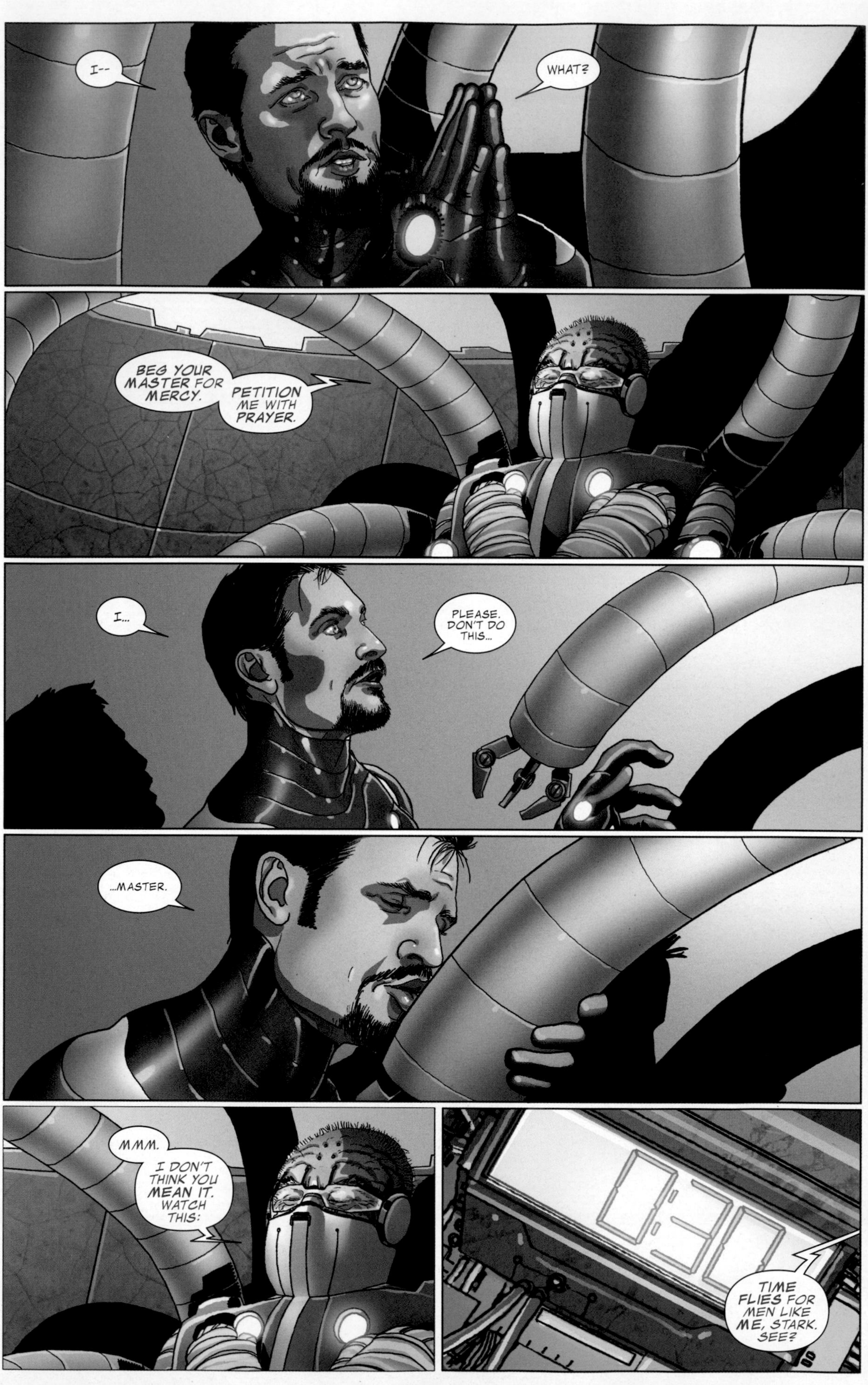
I--
WHAT?
BEG YOUR MASTER FOR MERCY.
PETITION ME WITH PRAYER.
I...
PLEASE. DON'T DO THIS...
...MASTER.
MMM.
I DON'T THINK YOU MEAN IT. WATCH THIS:
0:30
TIME FLIES FOR MEN LIKE ME, STARK. SEE?

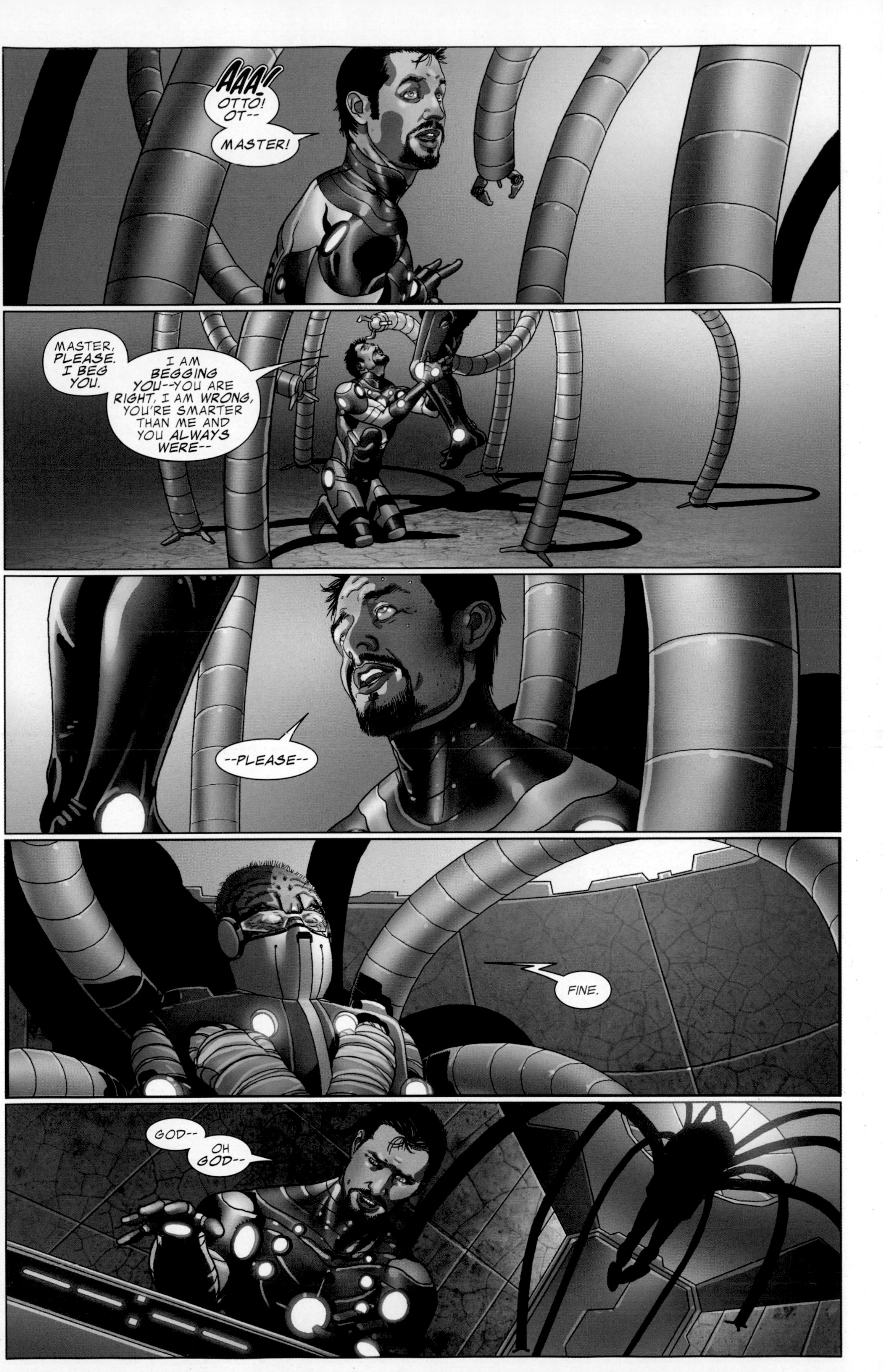
AAA!!
OTTO! OT--
MASTER!
MASTER, PLEASE. I BEG YOU.
I AM BEGGING YOU--YOU ARE RIGHT, I AM WRONG, YOU'RE SMARTER THAN ME AND YOU ALWAYS WERE--
--PLEASE--
FINE.
GOD--
OH GOD--

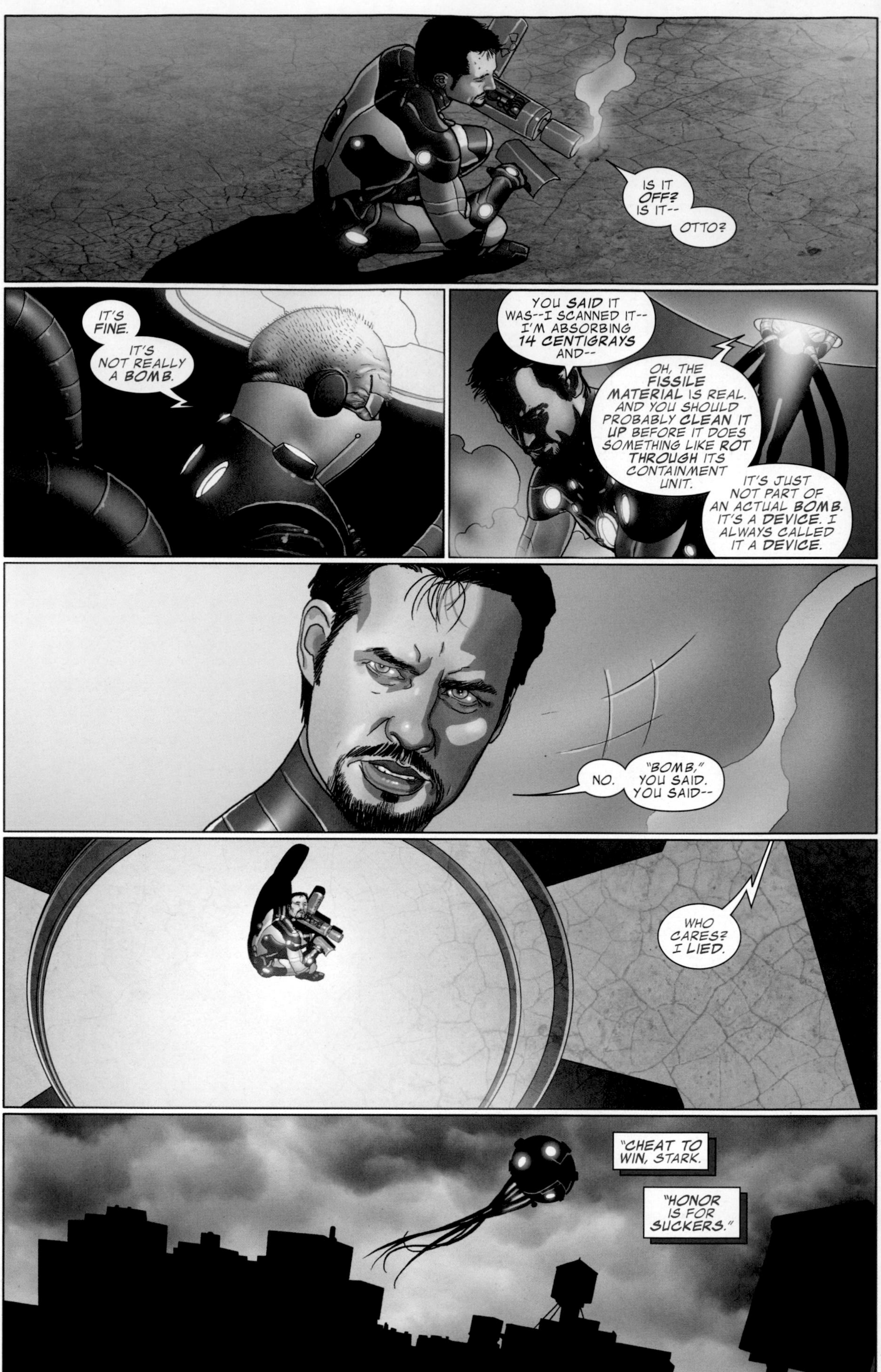
IS IT OFF? IS IT--
OTTO?
IT'S FINE.
IT'S NOT REALLY A BOMB.
YOU SAID IT WAS--I SCANNED IT-- I'M ABSORBING 14 CENTIGRAYS AND--
OH, THE FISSILE MATERIAL IS REAL. AND YOU SHOULD PROBABLY CLEAN IT UP BEFORE IT DOES SOMETHING LIKE ROT THROUGH ITS CONTAINMENT UNIT.
IT'S JUST NOT PART OF AN ACTUAL BOMB. IT'S A DEVICE. I ALWAYS CALLED IT A DEVICE.
NO.
"BOMB," YOU SAID. YOU SAID--
WHO CARES? I LIED.
"CHEAT TO WIN, STARK.
"HONOR IS FOR SUCKERS."

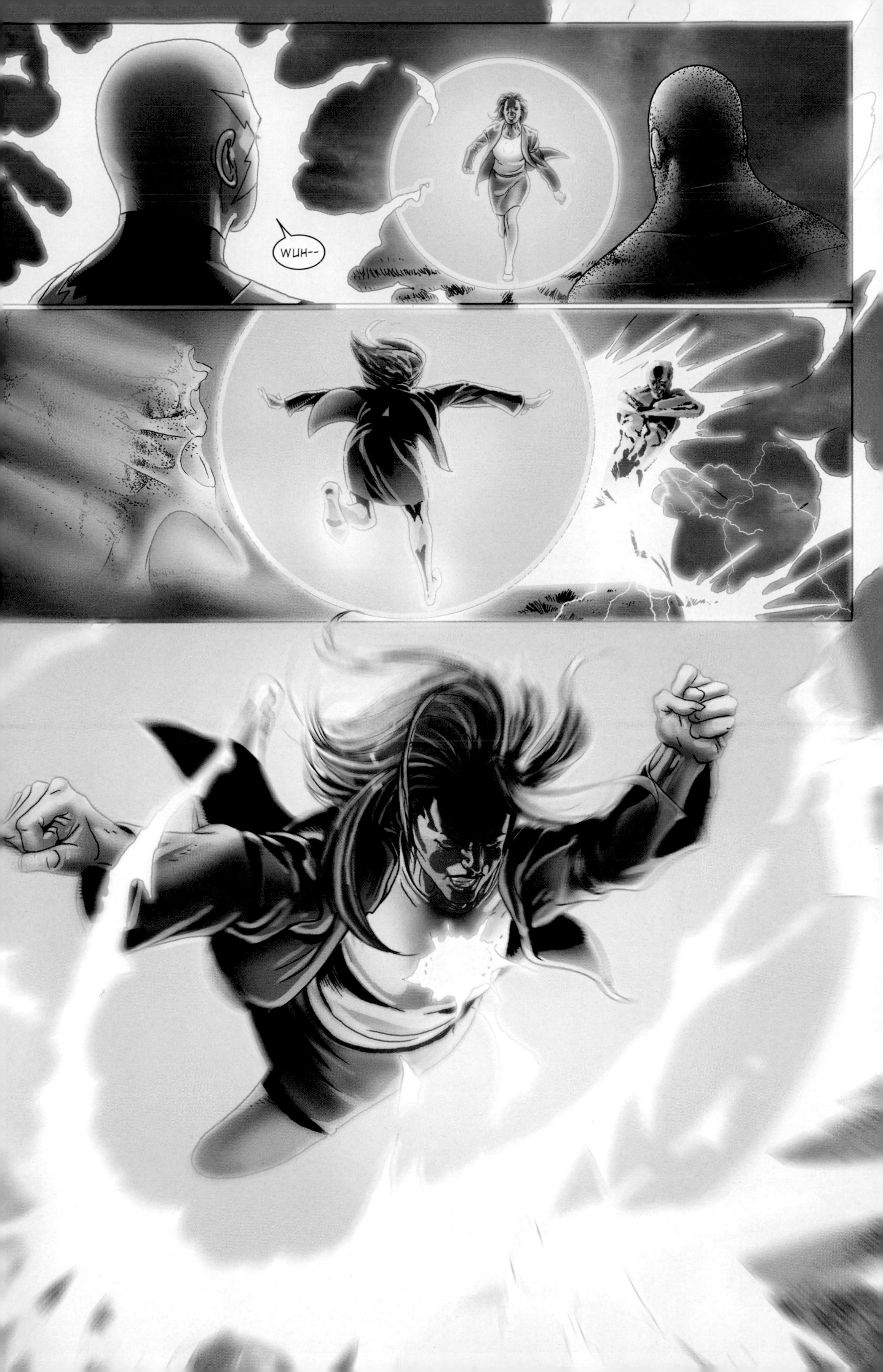
WUH--

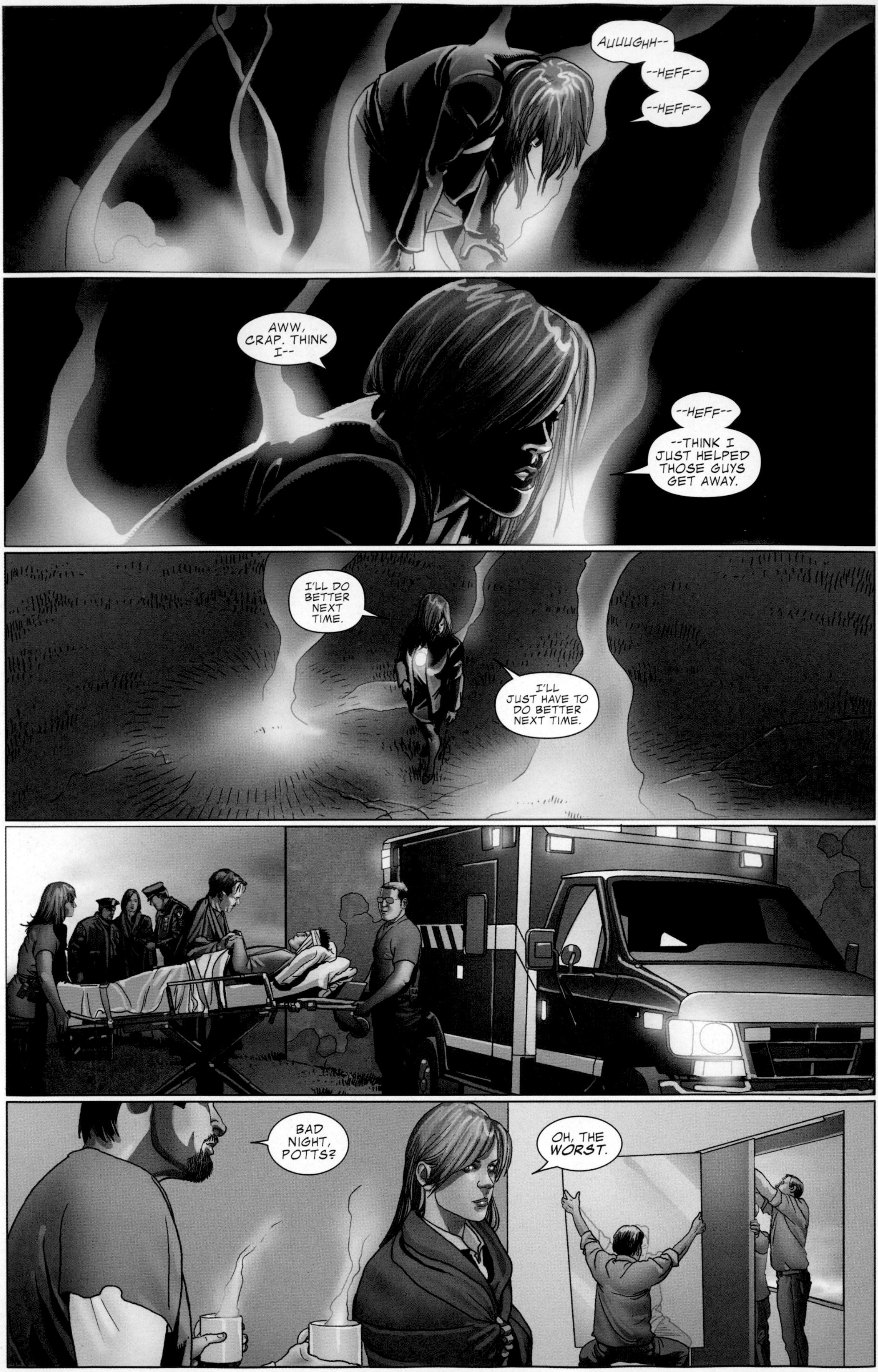
AUUUGHH--
--HEFF--
--HEFF--
AWW, CRAP. THINK I--
--HEFF--
--THINK I JUST HELPED THOSE GUYS GET AWAY.
I'LL DO BETTER NEXT TIME.
I'LL JUST HAVE TO DO BETTER NEXT TIME.
BAD NIGHT, POTTS?
OH, THE *WORST*.

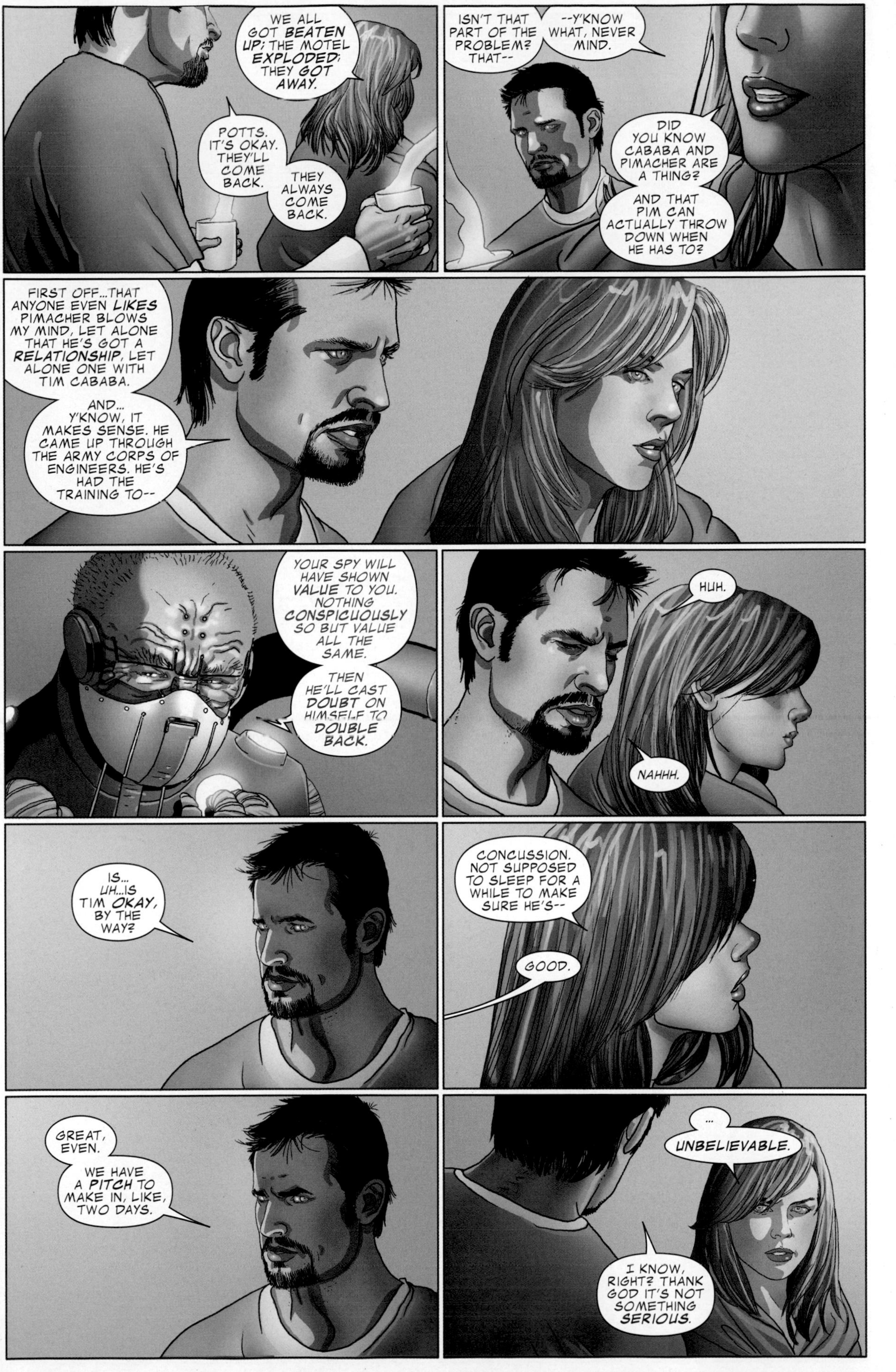
WE ALL GOT BEATEN UP; THE MOTEL EXPLODED; THEY GOT AWAY.
POTTS. IT'S OKAY. THEY'LL COME BACK.
THEY ALWAYS COME BACK.
ISN'T THAT PART OF THE PROBLEM? THAT--
--Y'KNOW WHAT, NEVER MIND.
DID YOU KNOW CABABA AND PIMACHER ARE A THING?
AND THAT PIM CAN ACTUALLY THROW DOWN WHEN HE HAS TO?
FIRST OFF...THAT ANYONE EVEN LIKES PIMACHER BLOWS MY MIND, LET ALONE THAT HE'S GOT A RELATIONSHIP, LET ALONE ONE WITH TIM CABABA.
AND... Y'KNOW, IT MAKES SENSE. HE CAME UP THROUGH THE ARMY CORPS OF ENGINEERS. HE'S HAD THE TRAINING TO--
YOUR SPY WILL HAVE SHOWN VALUE TO YOU. NOTHING CONSPICUOUSLY SO BUT VALUE ALL THE SAME.
THEN HE'LL CAST DOUBT ON HIMSELF TO DOUBLE BACK.
HUH.
NAHHH.
IS... UH...IS TIM OKAY, BY THE WAY?
CONCUSSION. NOT SUPPOSED TO SLEEP FOR A WHILE TO MAKE SURE HE'S--
GOOD.
GREAT, EVEN.
WE HAVE A PITCH TO MAKE IN, LIKE, TWO DAYS.
...
UNBELIEVABLE.
I KNOW, RIGHT? THANK GOD IT'S NOT SOMETHING SERIOUS.

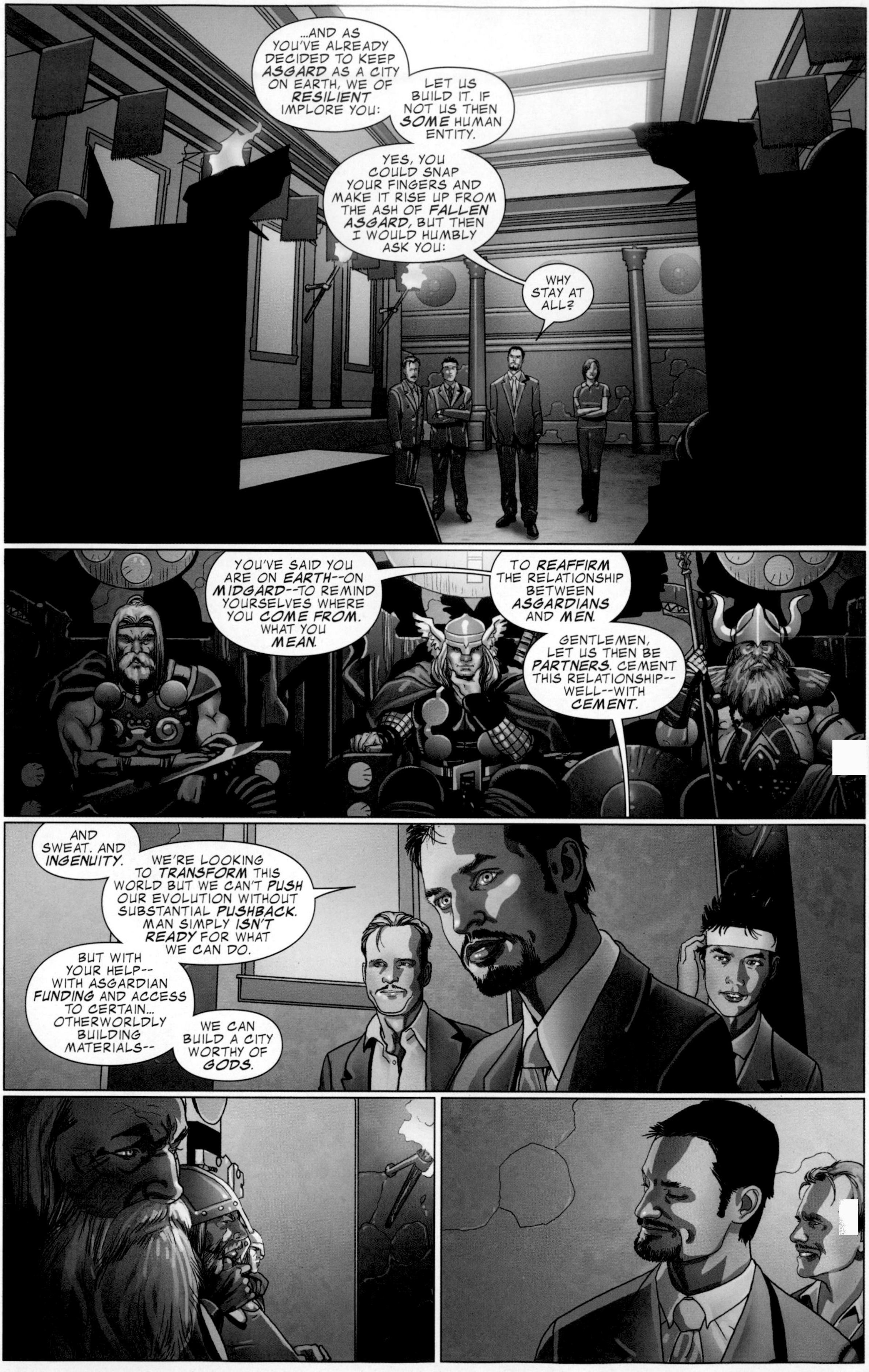
...AND AS YOU'VE ALREADY DECIDED TO KEEP ASGARD AS A CITY ON EARTH, WE OF RESILIENT IMPLORE YOU:
LET US BUILD IT. IF NOT US THEN SOME HUMAN ENTITY.
YES, YOU COULD SNAP YOUR FINGERS AND MAKE IT RISE UP FROM THE ASH OF FALLEN ASGARD, BUT THEN I WOULD HUMBLY ASK YOU:
WHY STAY AT ALL?
YOU'VE SAID YOU ARE ON EARTH--ON MIDGARD--TO REMIND YOURSELVES WHERE YOU COME FROM. WHAT YOU MEAN.
TO REAFFIRM THE RELATIONSHIP BETWEEN ASGARDIANS AND MEN.
GENTLEMEN, LET US THEN BE PARTNERS. CEMENT THIS RELATIONSHIP--WELL--WITH CEMENT.
AND SWEAT. AND INGENUITY.
WE'RE LOOKING TO TRANSFORM THIS WORLD BUT WE CAN'T PUSH OUR EVOLUTION WITHOUT SUBSTANTIAL PUSHBACK. MAN SIMPLY ISN'T READY FOR WHAT WE CAN DO.
BUT WITH YOUR HELP-- WITH ASGARDIAN FUNDING AND ACCESS TO CERTAIN... OTHERWORLDLY BUILDING MATERIALS--
WE CAN BUILD A CITY WORTHY OF GODS.

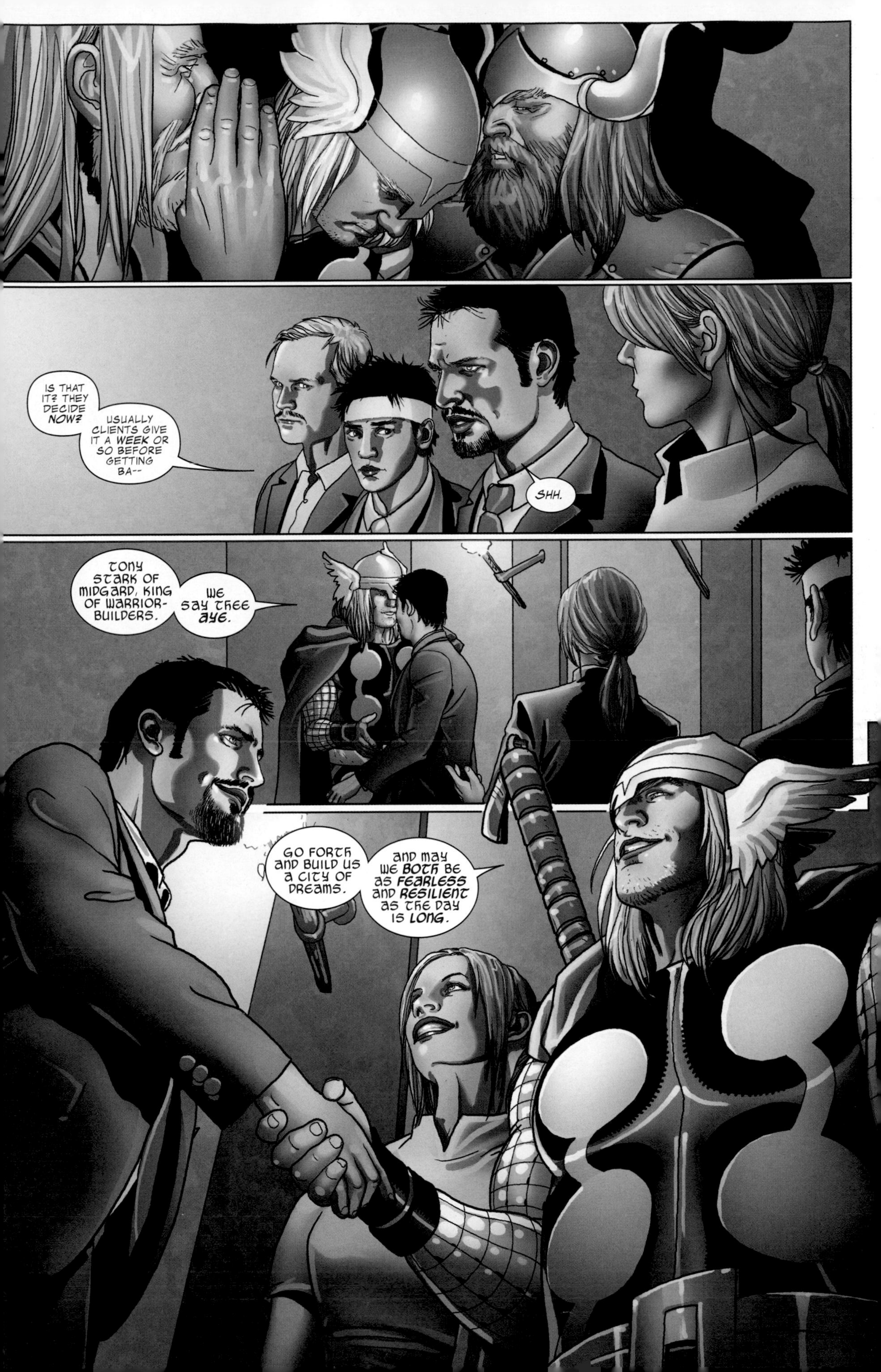
IS THAT IT? THEY DECIDE NOW?
USUALLY CLIENTS GIVE IT A WEEK OR SO BEFORE GETTING BA--
SHH.
TONY STARK OF MIDGARD, KING OF WARRIOR-BUILDERS.
WE SAY THEE AYE.
GO FORTH AND BUILD US A CITY OF DREAMS.
AND MAY WE BOTH BE AS FEARLESS AND RESILIENT AS THE DAY IS LONG.

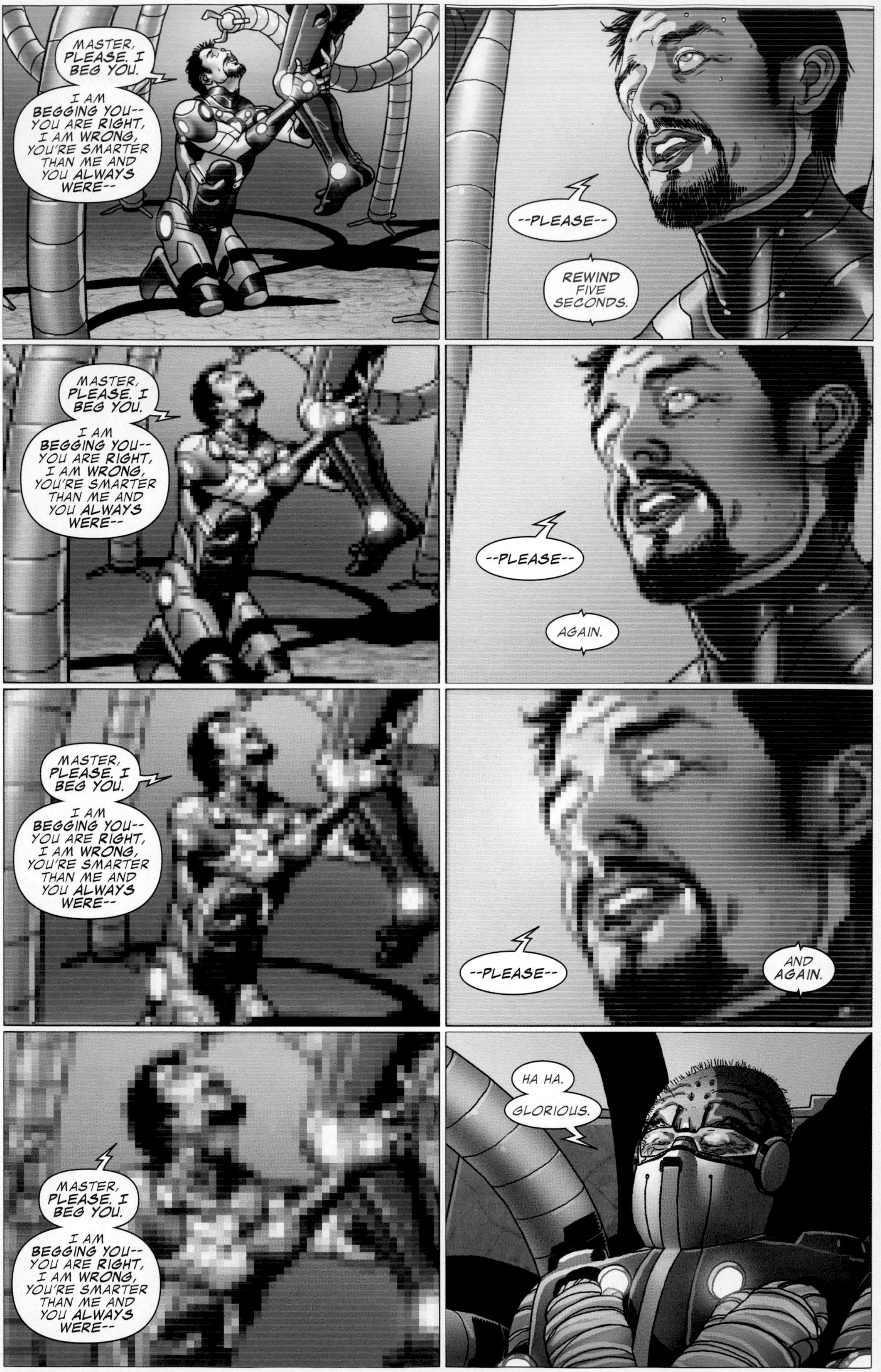
MASTER, PLEASE. I BEG YOU.
I AM BEGGING YOU-- YOU ARE RIGHT, I AM WRONG, YOU'RE SMARTER THAN ME AND YOU ALWAYS WERE--
--PLEASE--
REWIND FIVE SECONDS.
MASTER, PLEASE. I BEG YOU.
I AM BEGGING YOU-- YOU ARE RIGHT, I AM WRONG, YOU'RE SMARTER THAN ME AND YOU ALWAYS WERE--
--PLEASE--
AGAIN.
MASTER, PLEASE. I BEG YOU.
I AM BEGGING YOU-- YOU ARE RIGHT, I AM WRONG, YOU'RE SMARTER THAN ME AND YOU ALWAYS WERE--
--PLEASE--
AND AGAIN.
MASTER, PLEASE. I BEG YOU.
I AM BEGGING YOU-- YOU ARE RIGHT, I AM WRONG, YOU'RE SMARTER THAN ME AND YOU ALWAYS WERE--
HA HA.
GLORIOUS.

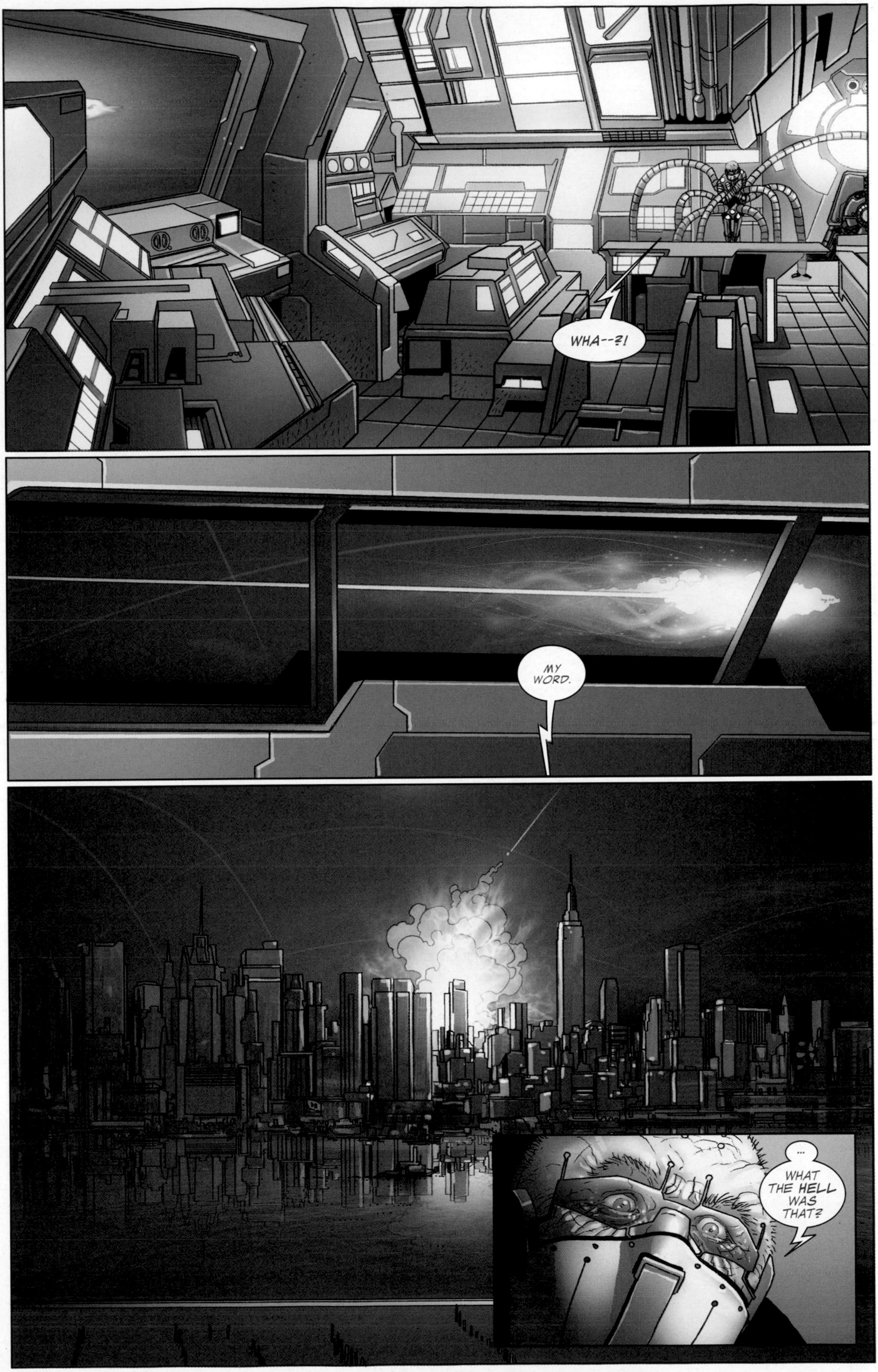
WHA--?!
MY WORD.
...
WHAT THE HELL WAS THAT?

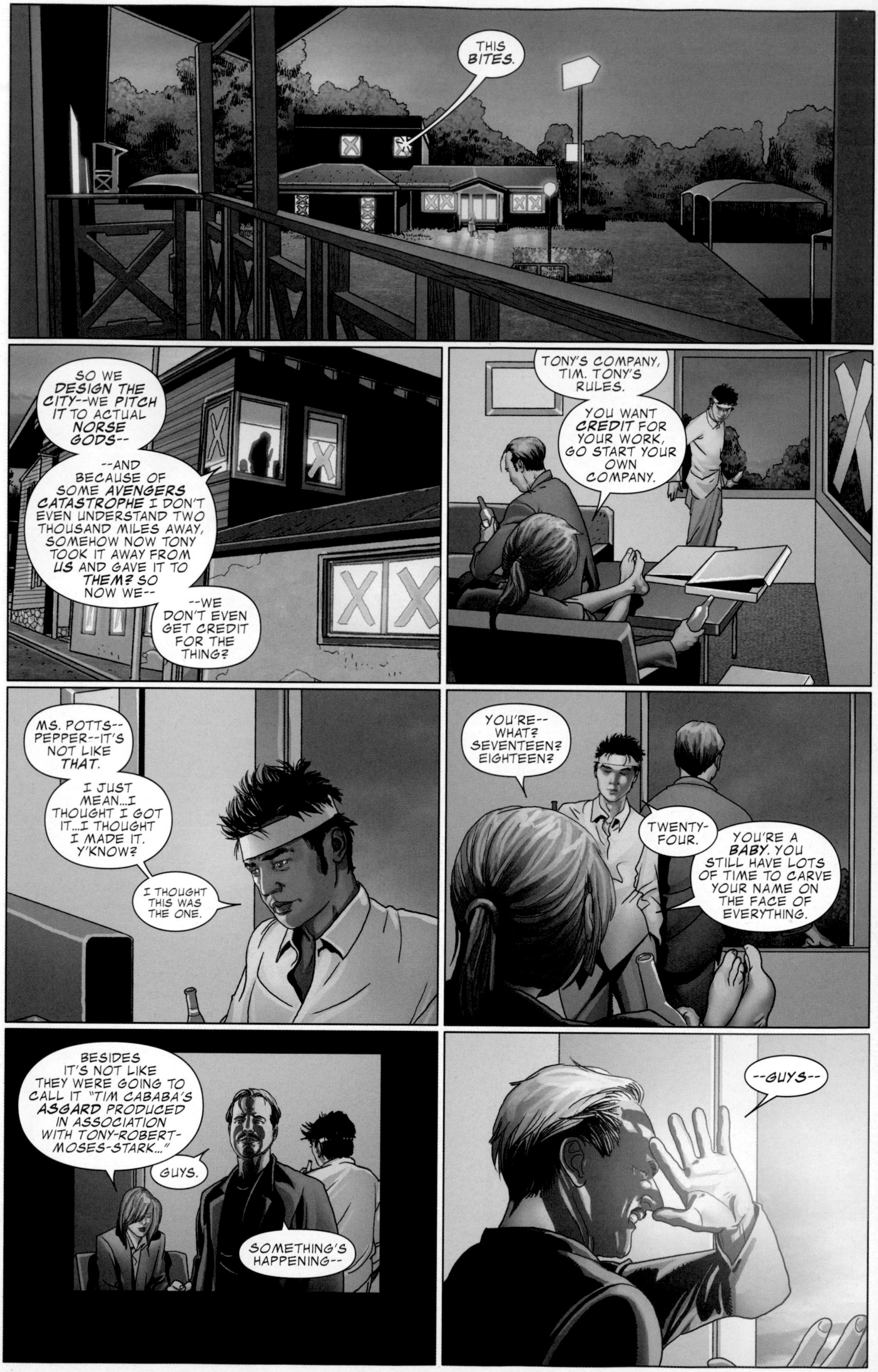
THIS BITES.
SO WE DESIGN THE CITY--WE PITCH IT TO ACTUAL NORSE GODS--
--AND BECAUSE OF SOME AVENGERS CATASTROPHE I DON'T EVEN UNDERSTAND TWO THOUSAND MILES AWAY, SOMEHOW NOW TONY TOOK IT AWAY FROM US AND GAVE IT TO THEM? SO NOW WE--
--WE DON'T EVEN GET CREDIT FOR THE THING?
TONY'S COMPANY, TIM. TONY'S RULES.
YOU WANT CREDIT FOR YOUR WORK, GO START YOUR OWN COMPANY.
MS. POTTS--PEPPER--IT'S NOT LIKE THAT.
I JUST MEAN...I THOUGHT I GOT IT...I THOUGHT I MADE IT. Y'KNOW?
I THOUGHT THIS WAS THE ONE.
YOU'RE--WHAT? SEVENTEEN? EIGHTEEN?
TWENTY-FOUR.
YOU'RE A BABY. YOU STILL HAVE LOTS OF TIME TO CARVE YOUR NAME ON THE FACE OF EVERYTHING.
BESIDES IT'S NOT LIKE THEY WERE GOING TO CALL IT "TIM CABABA'S ASGARD PRODUCED IN ASSOCIATION WITH TONY-ROBERT-MOSES-STARK..."
GUYS.
SOMETHING'S HAPPENING--
--GUYS--

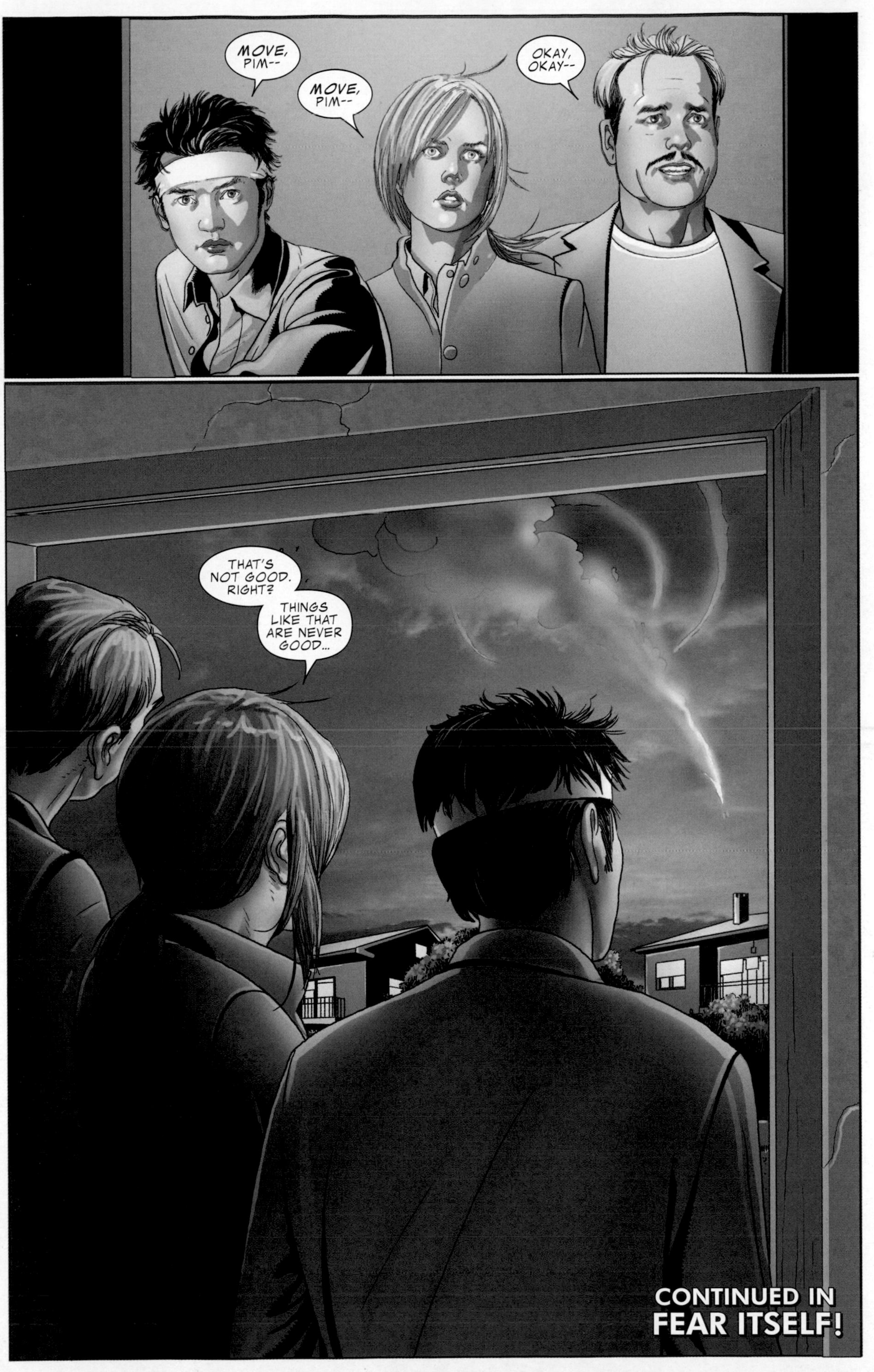
MOVE, PIM--
MOVE, PIM--
OKAY, OKAY--
THAT'S NOT GOOD. RIGHT?
THINGS LIKE THAT ARE NEVER GOOD...
CONTINUED IN FEAR ITSELF!

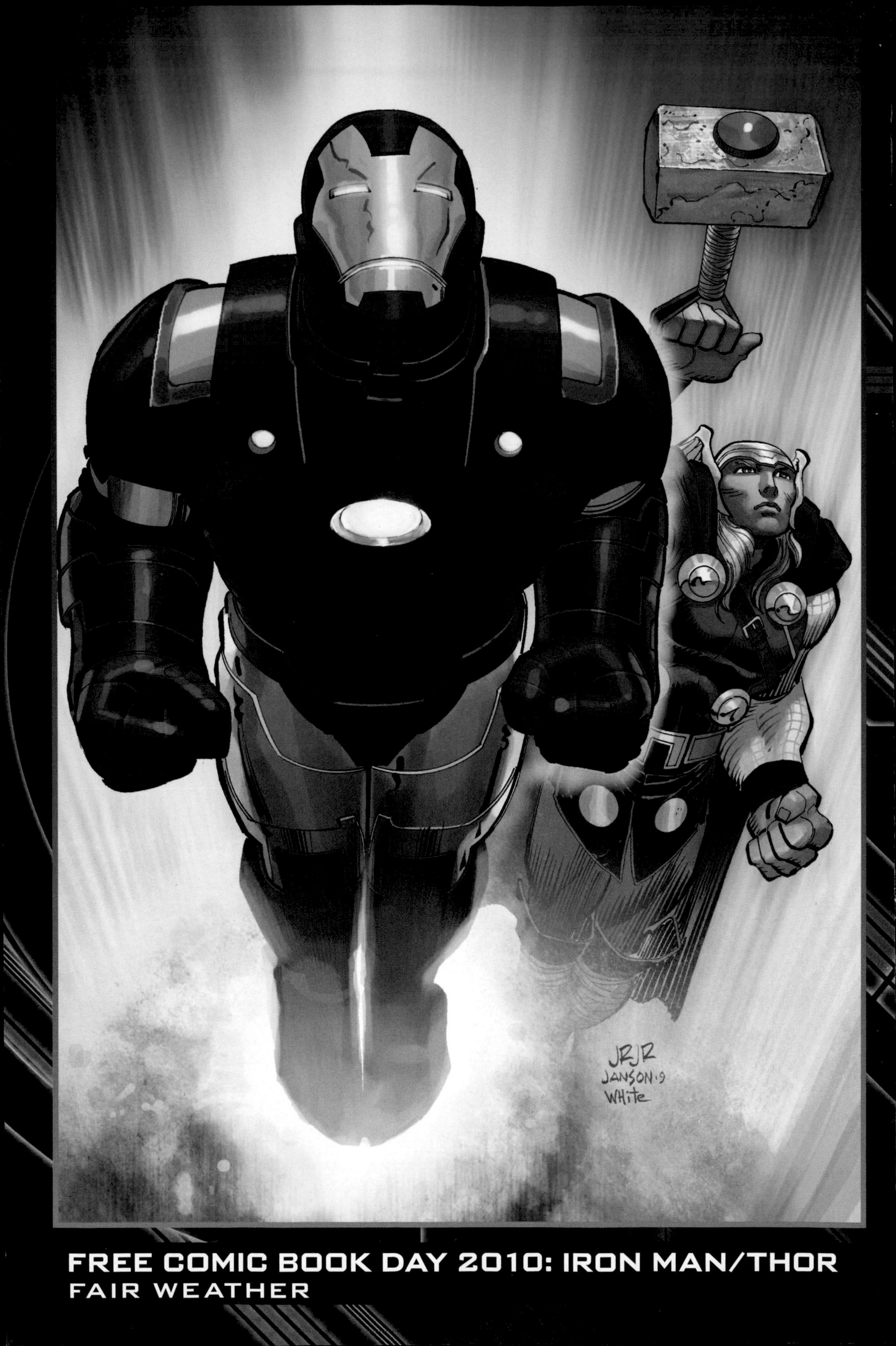
JRJR
JANSON '9
WHITE

FREE COMIC BOOK DAY 2010: IRON MAN/THOR
FAIR WEATHER

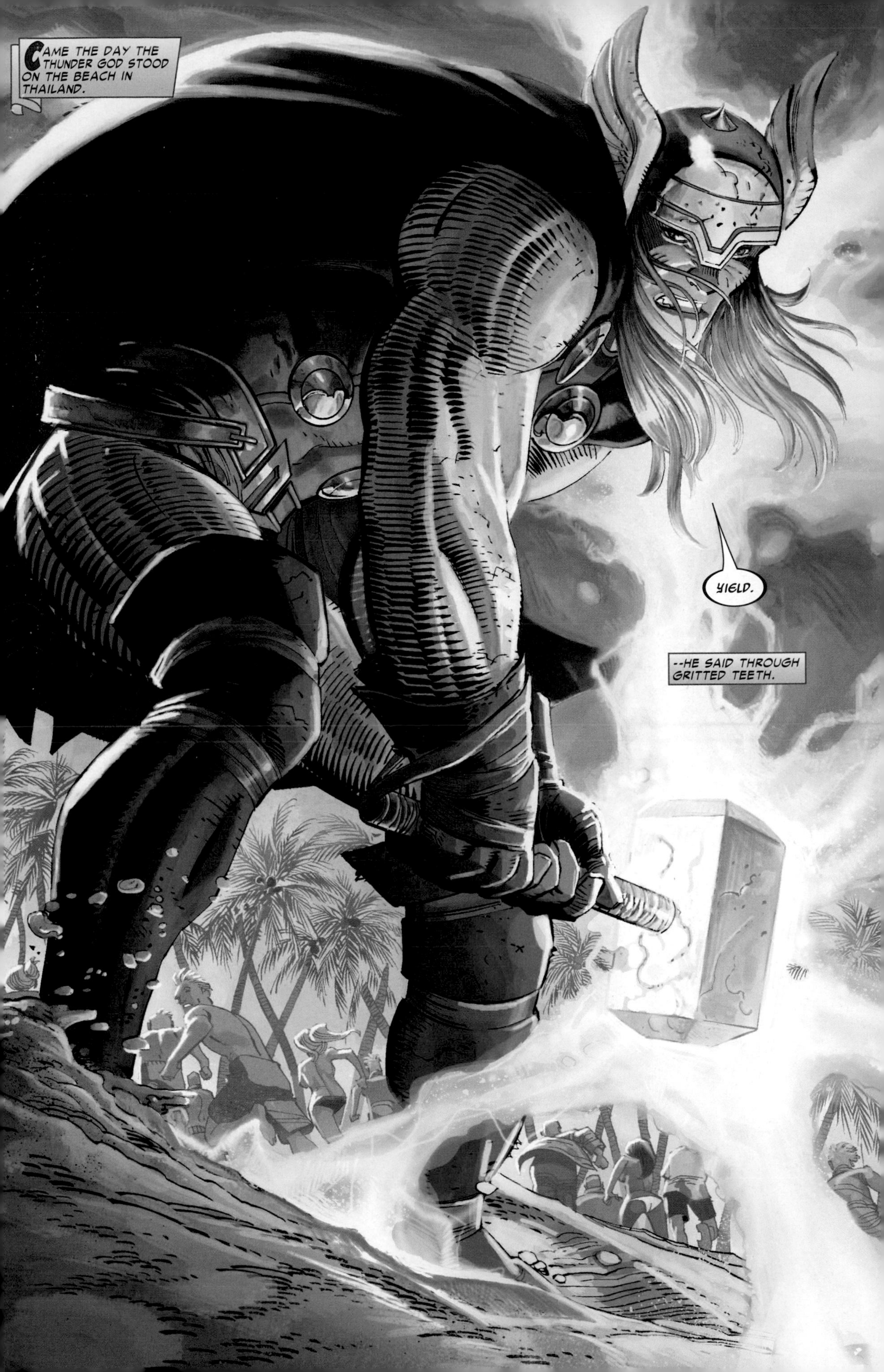
CAME THE DAY THE THUNDER GOD STOOD ON THE BEACH IN THAILAND.
YIELD.
--HE SAID THROUGH GRITTED TEETH.

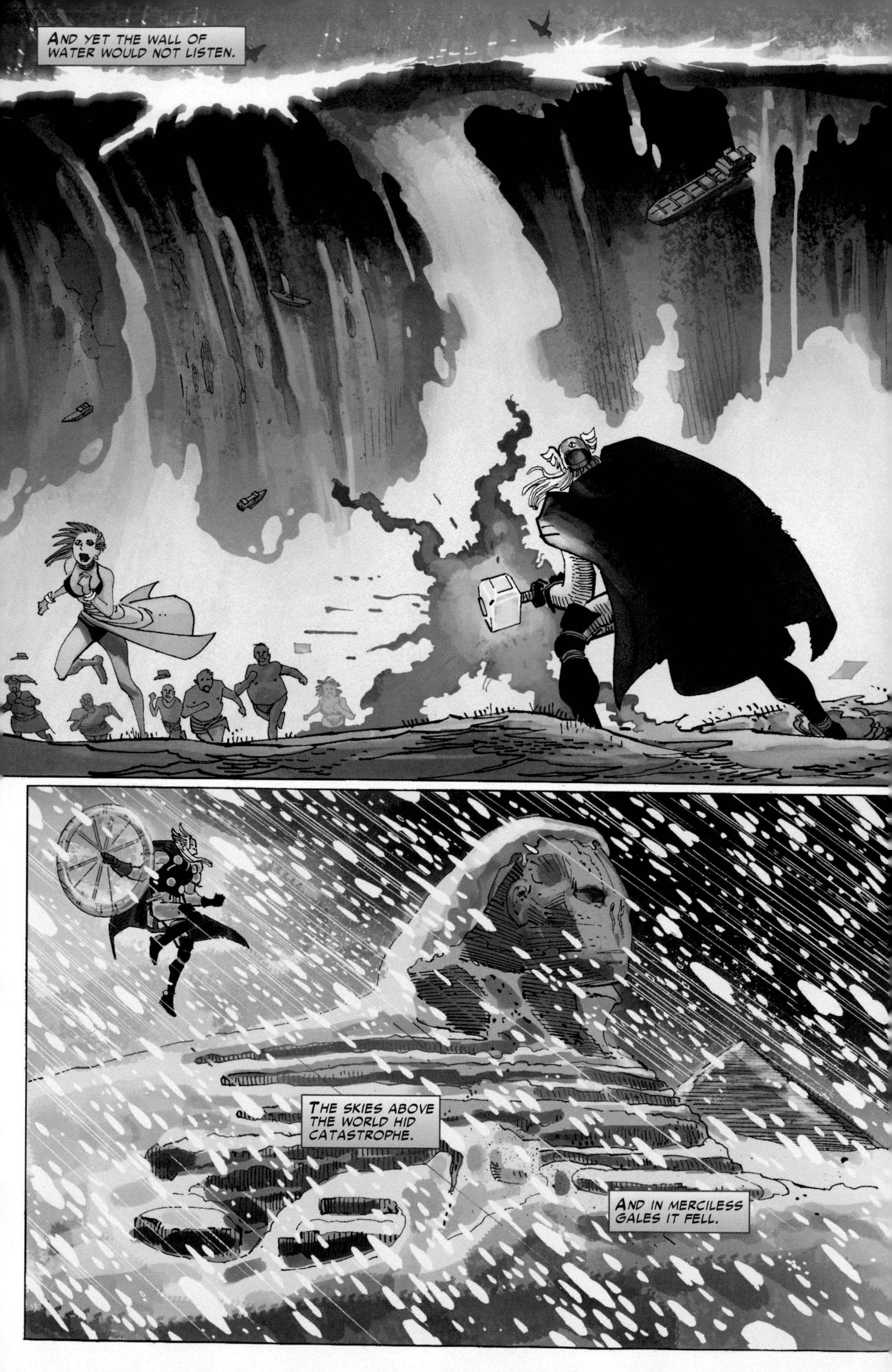
AND YET THE WALL OF WATER WOULD NOT LISTEN.
THE SKIES ABOVE THE WORLD HID CATASTROPHE.
AND IN MERCILESS GALES IT FELL.

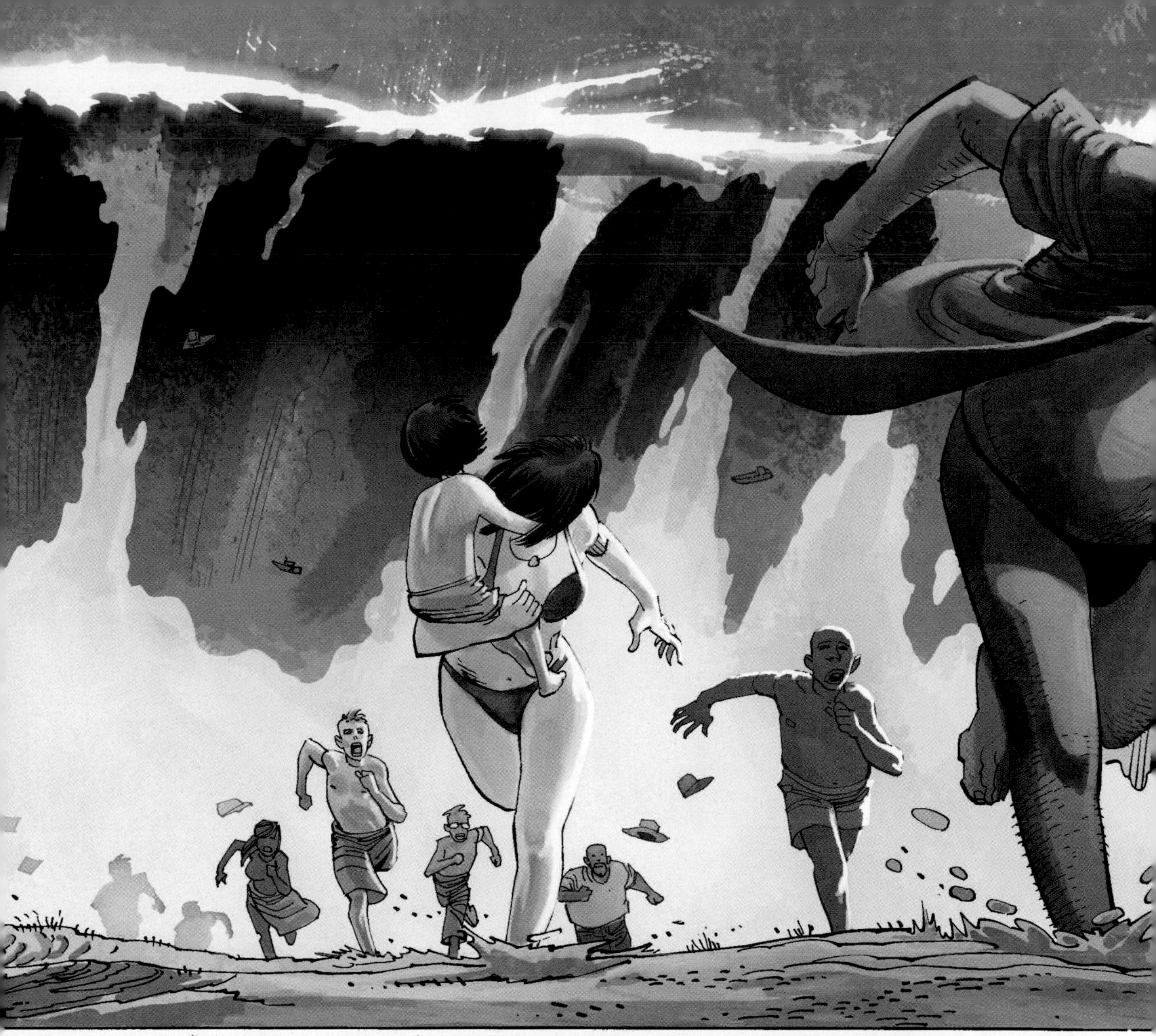

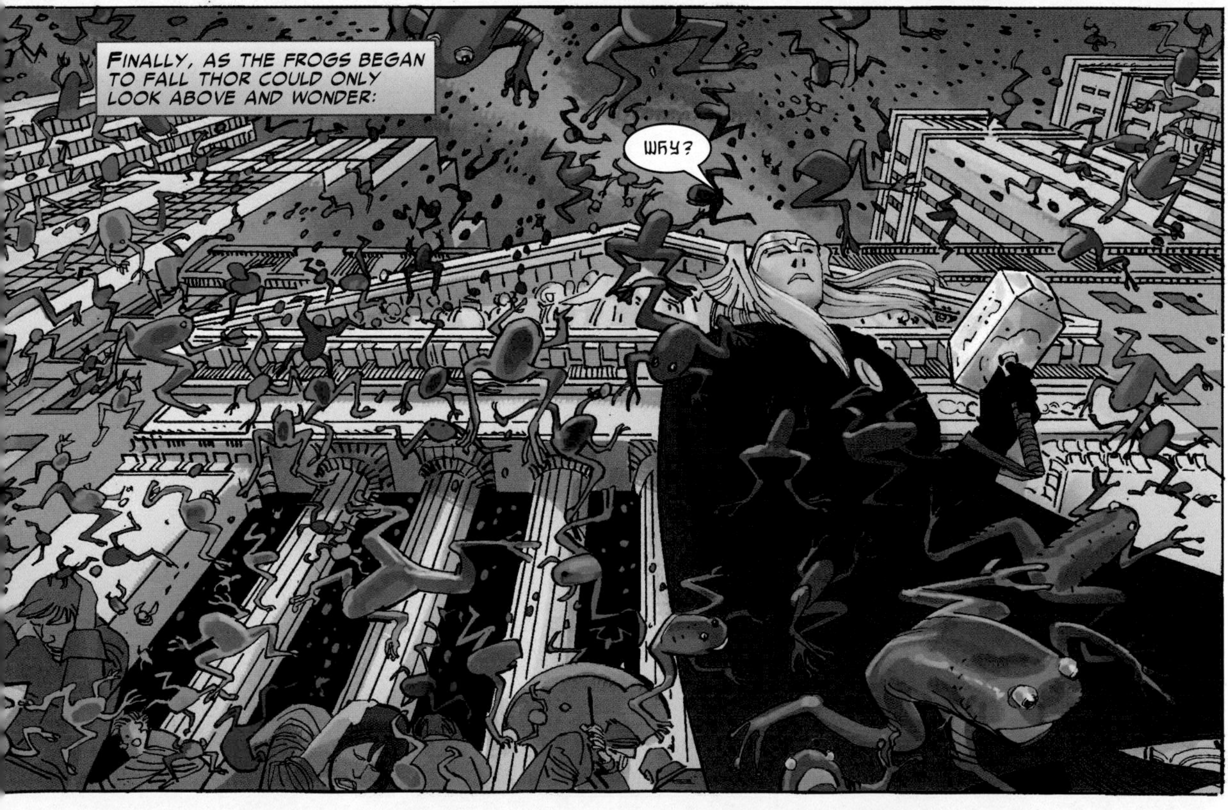
FINALLY, AS THE FROGS BEGAN TO FALL THOR COULD ONLY LOOK ABOVE AND WONDER:
WHY?

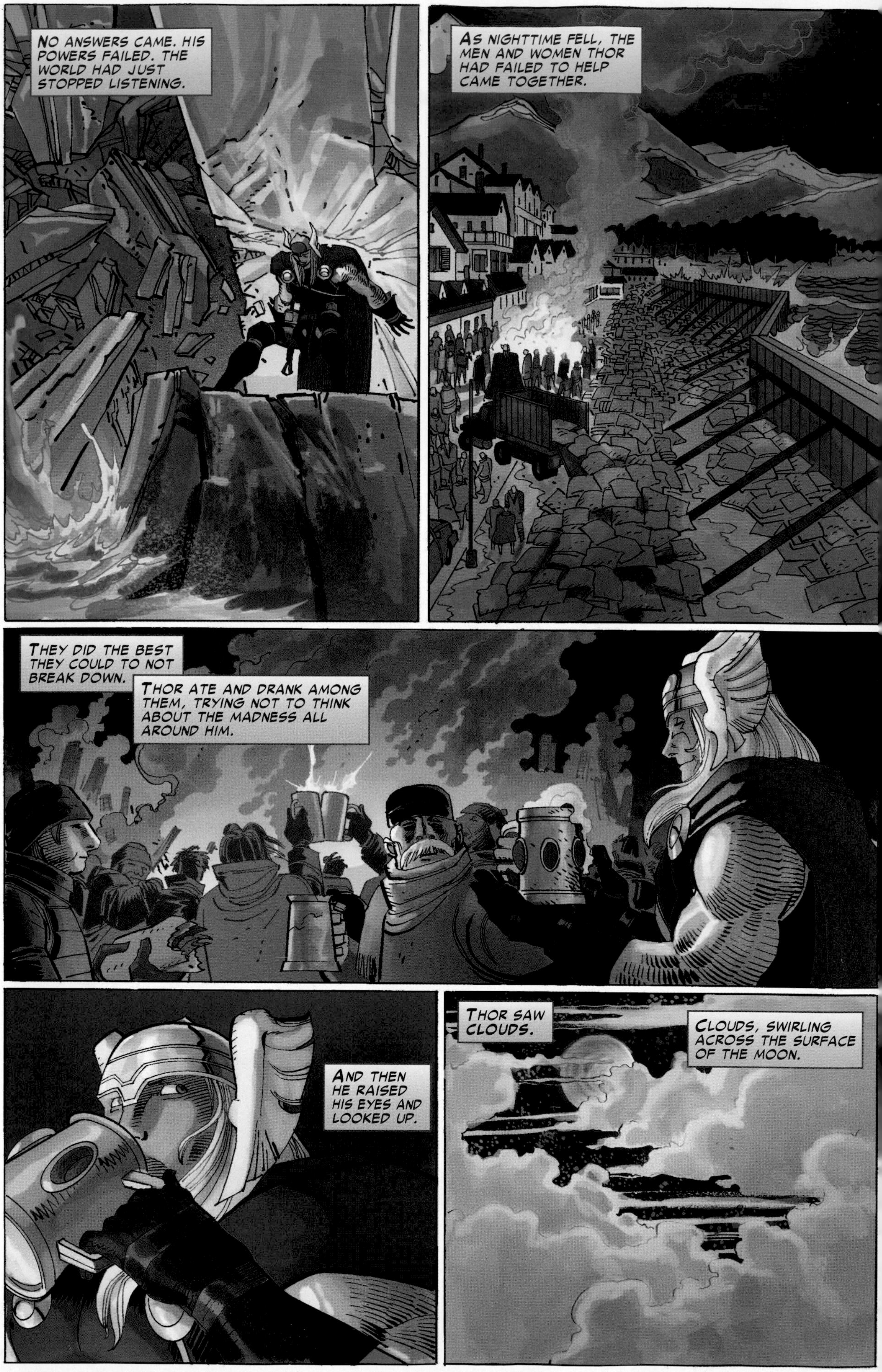
NO ANSWERS CAME. HIS POWERS FAILED. THE WORLD HAD JUST STOPPED LISTENING.
AS NIGHTTIME FELL, THE MEN AND WOMEN THOR HAD FAILED TO HELP CAME TOGETHER.
THEY DID THE BEST THEY COULD TO NOT BREAK DOWN.
THOR ATE AND DRANK AMONG THEM, TRYING NOT TO THINK ABOUT THE MADNESS ALL AROUND HIM.
AND THEN HE RAISED HIS EYES AND LOOKED UP.
THOR SAW CLOUDS.
CLOUDS, SWIRLING ACROSS THE SURFACE OF THE MOON.

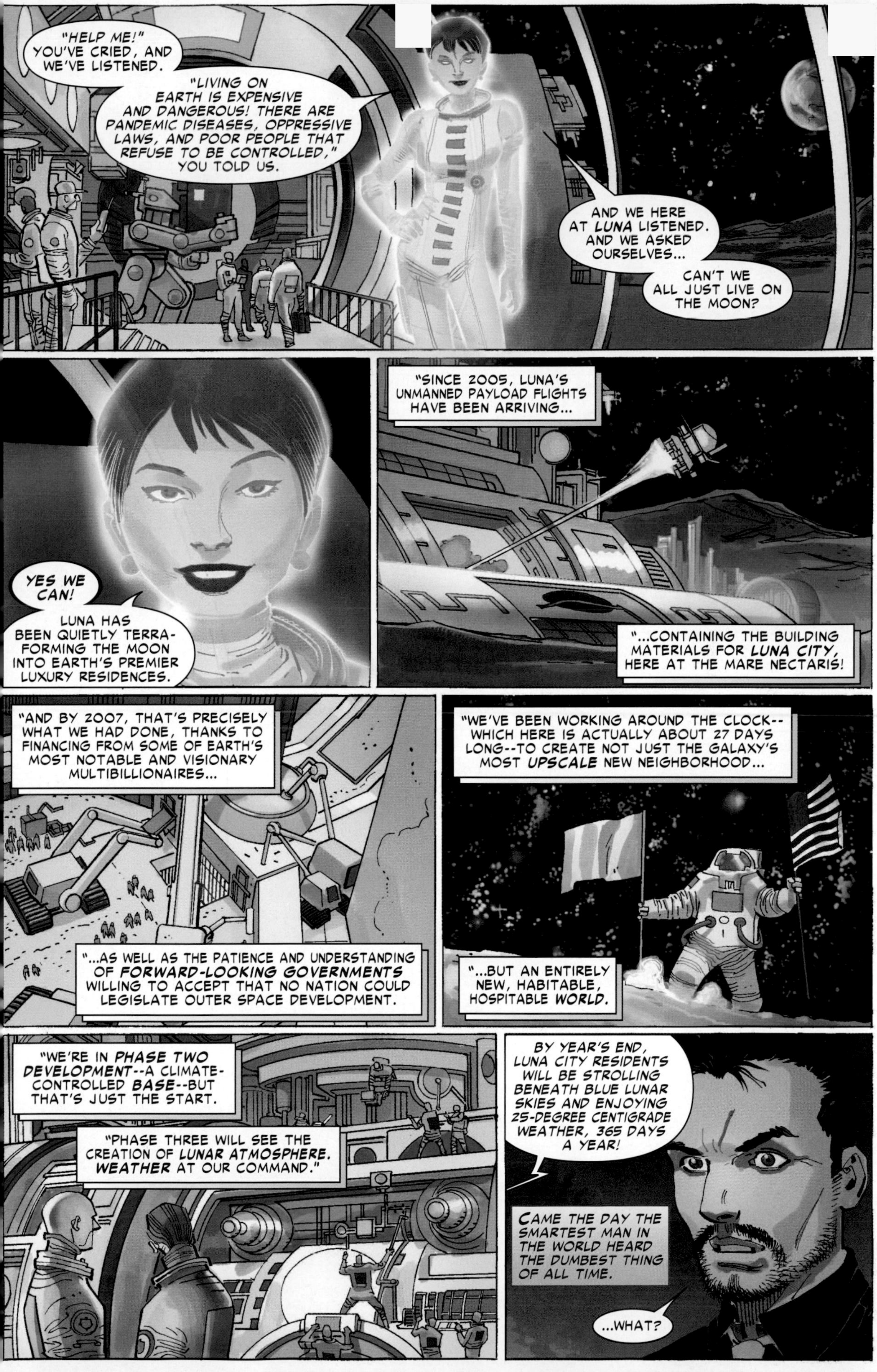
"HELP ME!" YOU'VE CRIED, AND WE'VE LISTENED.
"LIVING ON EARTH IS EXPENSIVE AND DANGEROUS! THERE ARE PANDEMIC DISEASES, OPPRESSIVE LAWS, AND POOR PEOPLE THAT REFUSE TO BE CONTROLLED," YOU TOLD US.
AND WE HERE AT LUNA LISTENED. AND WE ASKED OURSELVES...
CAN'T WE ALL JUST LIVE ON THE MOON?
YES WE CAN!
LUNA HAS BEEN QUIETLY TERRA-FORMING THE MOON INTO EARTH'S PREMIER LUXURY RESIDENCES.
"SINCE 2005, LUNA'S UNMANNED PAYLOAD FLIGHTS HAVE BEEN ARRIVING...
"...CONTAINING THE BUILDING MATERIALS FOR LUNA CITY, HERE AT THE MARE NECTARIS!
"AND BY 2007, THAT'S PRECISELY WHAT WE HAD DONE, THANKS TO FINANCING FROM SOME OF EARTH'S MOST NOTABLE AND VISIONARY MULTIBILLIONAIRES...
"...AS WELL AS THE PATIENCE AND UNDERSTANDING OF FORWARD-LOOKING GOVERNMENTS WILLING TO ACCEPT THAT NO NATION COULD LEGISLATE OUTER SPACE DEVELOPMENT.
"WE'VE BEEN WORKING AROUND THE CLOCK--WHICH HERE IS ACTUALLY ABOUT 27 DAYS LONG--TO CREATE NOT JUST THE GALAXY'S MOST UPSCALE NEW NEIGHBORHOOD...
"...BUT AN ENTIRELY NEW, HABITABLE, HOSPITABLE WORLD.
"WE'RE IN PHASE TWO DEVELOPMENT--A CLIMATE-CONTROLLED BASE--BUT THAT'S JUST THE START.
"PHASE THREE WILL SEE THE CREATION OF LUNAR ATMOSPHERE. WEATHER AT OUR COMMAND."
BY YEAR'S END, LUNA CITY RESIDENTS WILL BE STROLLING BENEATH BLUE LUNAR SKIES AND ENJOYING 25-DEGREE CENTIGRADE WEATHER, 365 DAYS A YEAR!
CAME THE DAY THE SMARTEST MAN IN THE WORLD HEARD THE DUMBEST THING OF ALL TIME.
...WHAT?

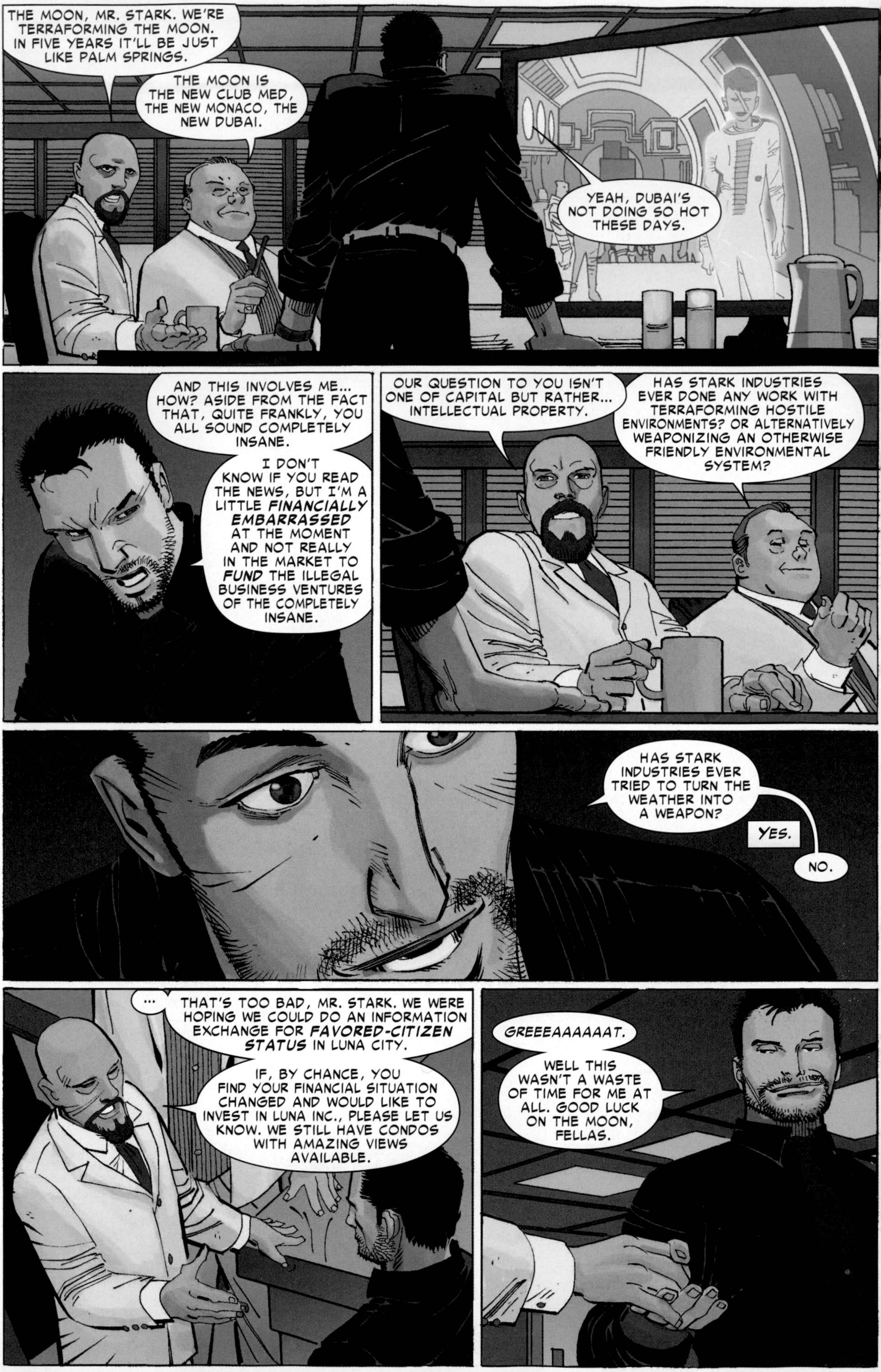
THE MOON, MR. STARK. WE'RE TERRAFORMING THE MOON. IN FIVE YEARS IT'LL BE JUST LIKE PALM SPRINGS.
THE MOON IS THE NEW CLUB MED, THE NEW MONACO, THE NEW DUBAI.
YEAH, DUBAI'S NOT DOING SO HOT THESE DAYS.
AND THIS INVOLVES ME... HOW? ASIDE FROM THE FACT THAT, QUITE FRANKLY, YOU ALL SOUND COMPLETELY INSANE.
I DON'T KNOW IF YOU READ THE NEWS, BUT I'M A LITTLE *FINANCIALLY EMBARRASSED* AT THE MOMENT AND NOT REALLY IN THE MARKET TO *FUND* THE ILLEGAL BUSINESS VENTURES OF THE COMPLETELY INSANE.
OUR QUESTION TO YOU ISN'T ONE OF CAPITAL BUT RATHER... INTELLECTUAL PROPERTY.
HAS STARK INDUSTRIES EVER DONE ANY WORK WITH TERRAFORMING HOSTILE ENVIRONMENTS? OR ALTERNATIVELY WEAPONIZING AN OTHERWISE FRIENDLY ENVIRONMENTAL SYSTEM?
HAS STARK INDUSTRIES EVER TRIED TO TURN THE WEATHER INTO A WEAPON?
YES.
NO.
...
THAT'S TOO BAD, MR. STARK. WE WERE HOPING WE COULD DO AN INFORMATION EXCHANGE FOR *FAVORED-CITIZEN STATUS* IN LUNA CITY.
IF, BY CHANCE, YOU FIND YOUR FINANCIAL SITUATION CHANGED AND WOULD LIKE TO INVEST IN LUNA INC., PLEASE LET US KNOW. WE STILL HAVE CONDOS WITH AMAZING VIEWS AVAILABLE.
GREEEAAAAAAT.
WELL THIS WASN'T A WASTE OF TIME FOR ME AT ALL. GOOD LUCK ON THE MOON, FELLAS.

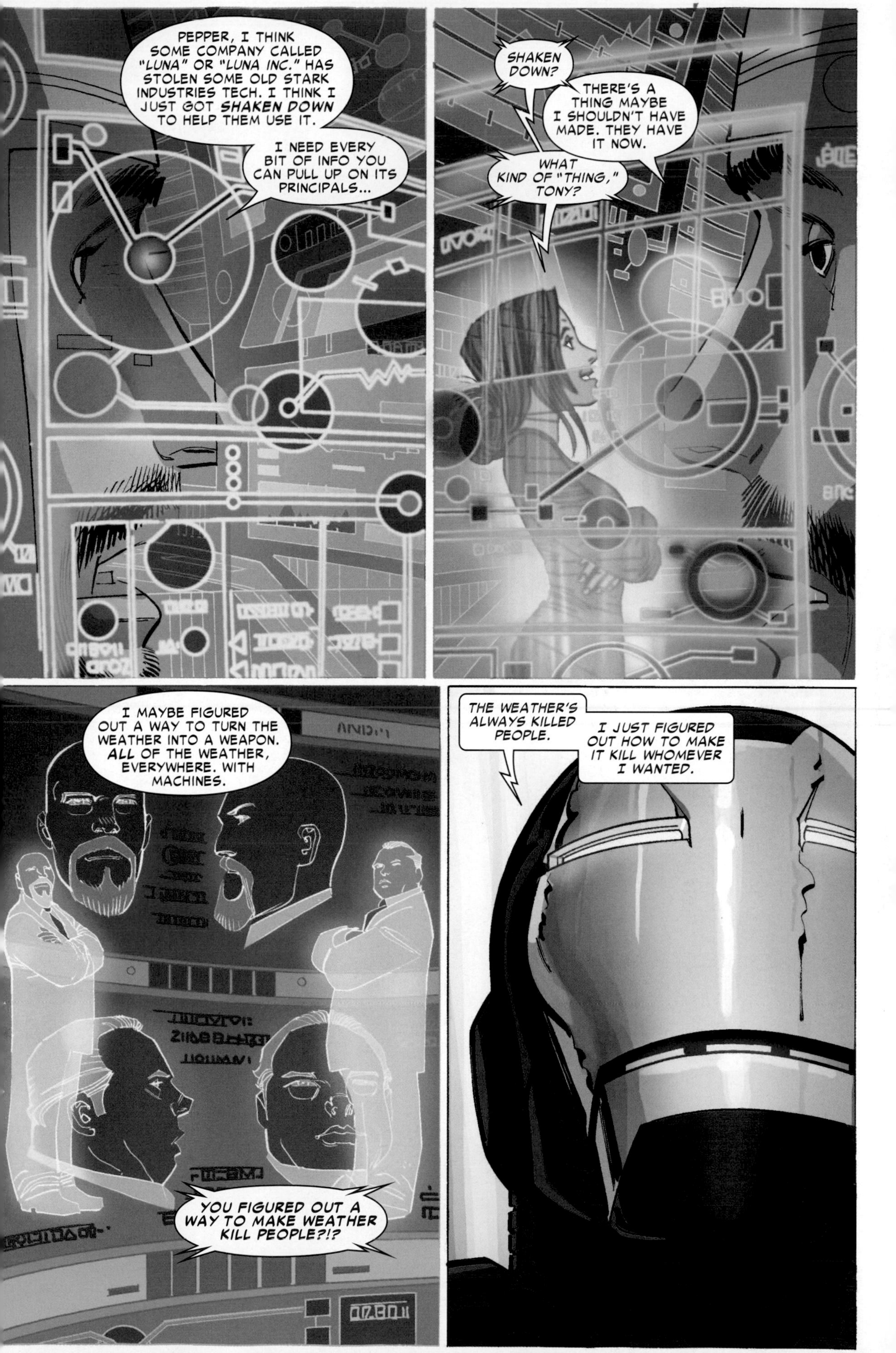
PEPPER, I THINK SOME COMPANY CALLED "LUNA" OR "LUNA INC." HAS STOLEN SOME OLD STARK INDUSTRIES TECH. I THINK I JUST GOT SHAKEN DOWN TO HELP THEM USE IT.
I NEED EVERY BIT OF INFO YOU CAN PULL UP ON ITS PRINCIPALS...
SHAKEN DOWN?
THERE'S A THING MAYBE I SHOULDN'T HAVE MADE. THEY HAVE IT NOW.
WHAT KIND OF "THING," TONY?
I MAYBE FIGURED OUT A WAY TO TURN THE WEATHER INTO A WEAPON. ALL OF THE WEATHER, EVERYWHERE. WITH MACHINES.
YOU FIGURED OUT A WAY TO MAKE WEATHER KILL PEOPLE?!?
THE WEATHER'S ALWAYS KILLED PEOPLE.
I JUST FIGURED OUT HOW TO MAKE IT KILL WHOMEVER I WANTED.

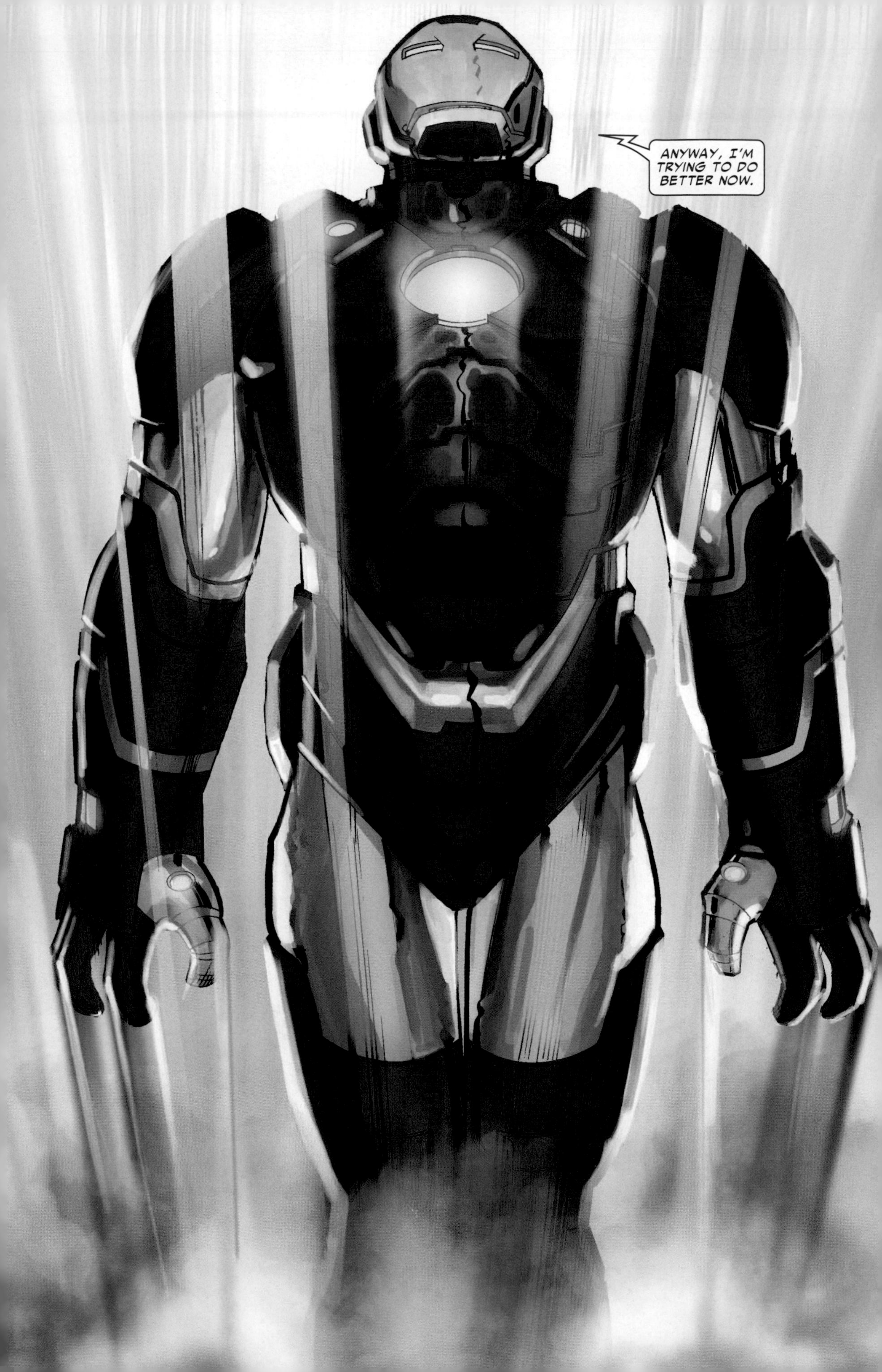
ANYWAY, I'M TRYING TO DO BETTER NOW.

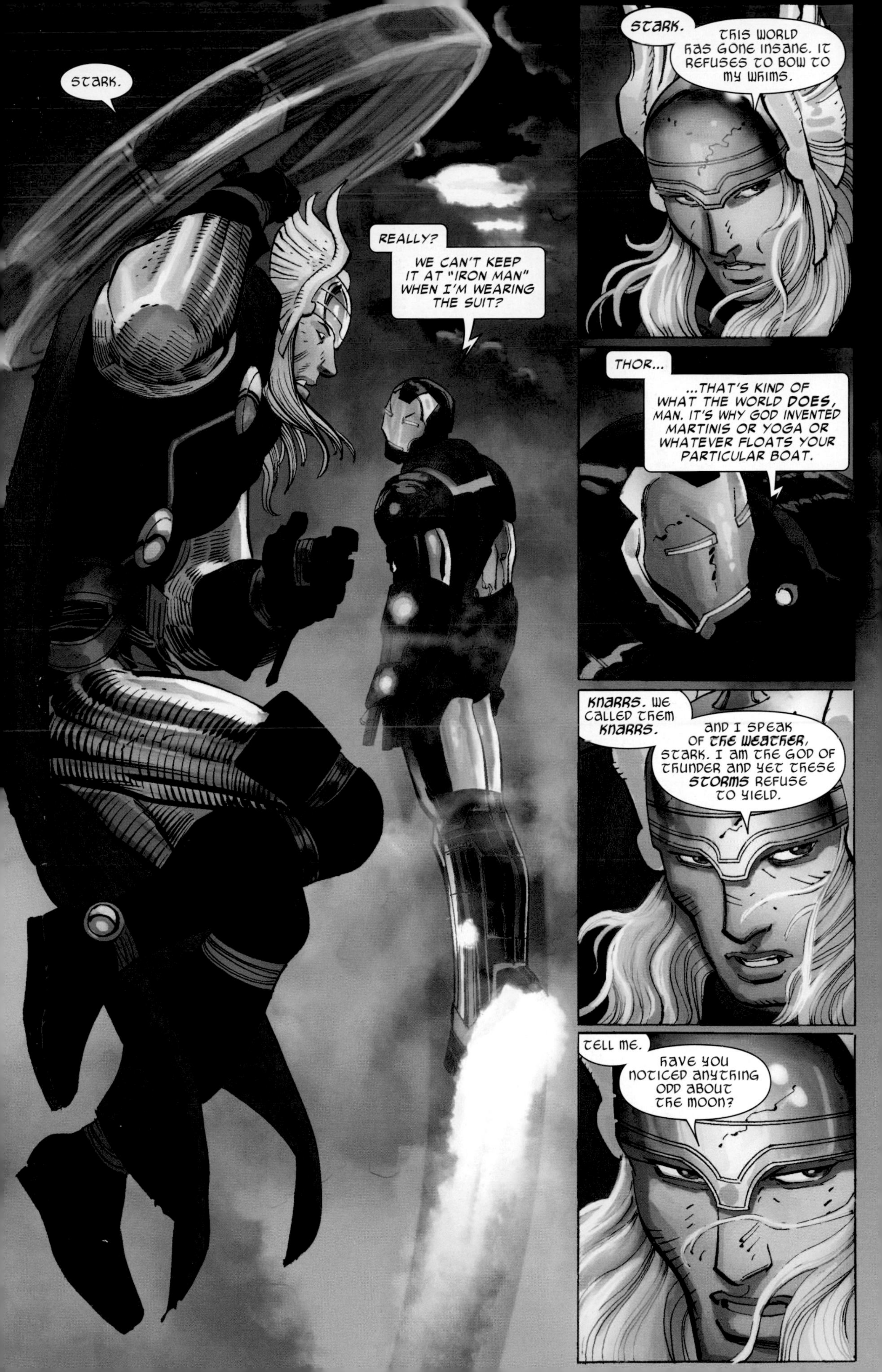
STARK.
REALLY?
WE CAN'T KEEP IT AT "IRON MAN" WHEN I'M WEARING THE SUIT?
STARK.
THIS WORLD HAS GONE INSANE. IT REFUSES TO BOW TO MY WHIMS.
THOR...
...THAT'S KIND OF WHAT THE WORLD DOES, MAN. IT'S WHY GOD INVENTED MARTINIS OR YOGA OR WHATEVER FLOATS YOUR PARTICULAR BOAT.
KNARRS. WE CALLED THEM KNARRS.
AND I SPEAK OF THE WEATHER, STARK. I AM THE GOD OF THUNDER AND YET THESE STORMS REFUSE TO YIELD.
TELL ME.
HAVE YOU NOTICED ANYTHING ODD ABOUT THE MOON?

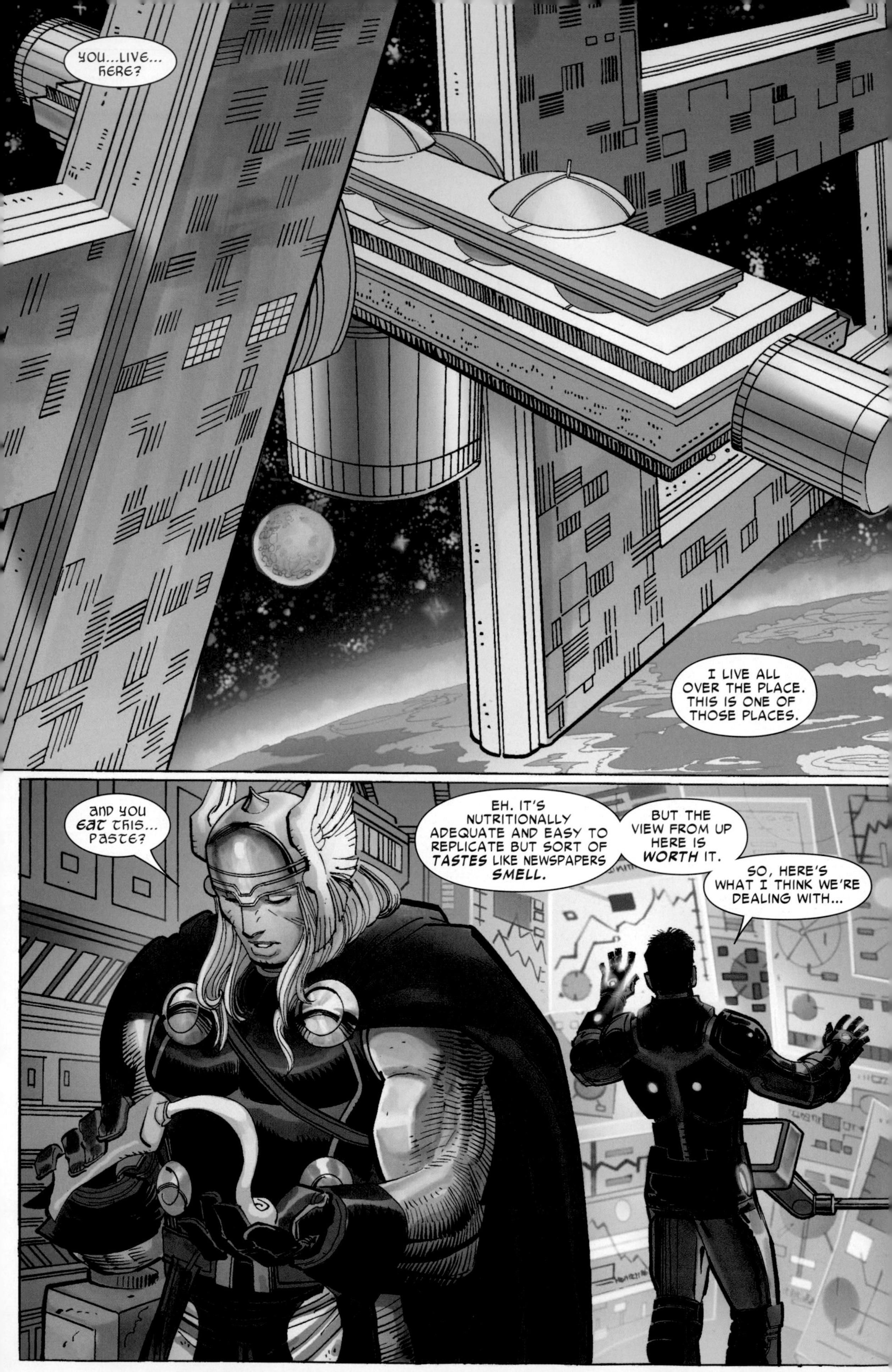

YOU...LIVE... HERE?
I LIVE ALL OVER THE PLACE. THIS IS ONE OF THOSE PLACES.
AND YOU EAT THIS... PASTE?
EH. IT'S NUTRITIONALLY ADEQUATE AND EASY TO REPLICATE BUT SORT OF TASTES LIKE NEWSPAPERS SMELL.
BUT THE VIEW FROM UP HERE IS WORTH IT.
SO, HERE'S WHAT I THINK WE'RE DEALING WITH...

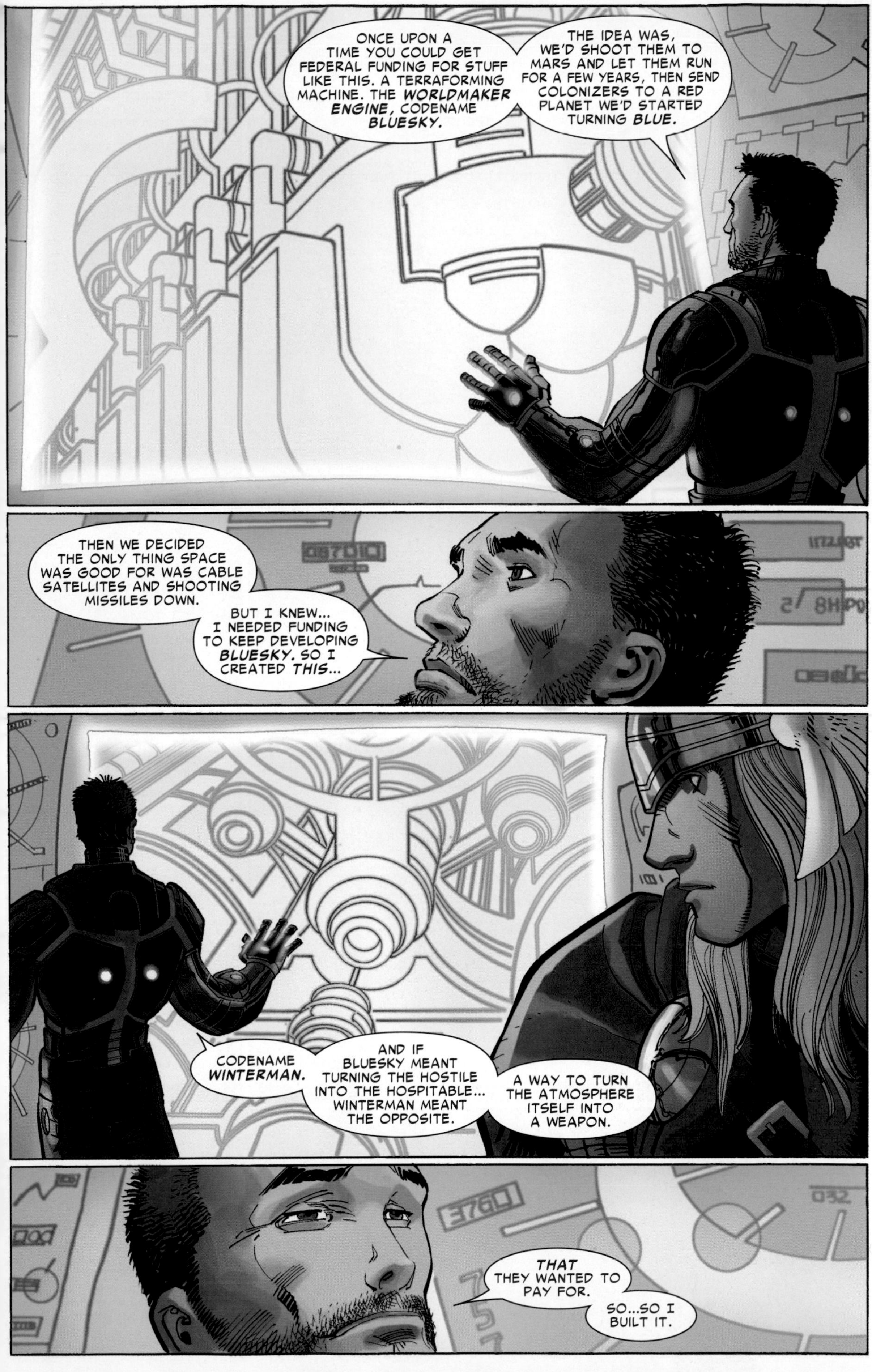
ONCE UPON A TIME YOU COULD GET FEDERAL FUNDING FOR STUFF LIKE THIS. A TERRAFORMING MACHINE. THE *WORLDMAKER ENGINE*, CODENAME *BLUESKY.*
THE IDEA WAS, WE'D SHOOT THEM TO MARS AND LET THEM RUN FOR A FEW YEARS, THEN SEND COLONIZERS TO A RED PLANET WE'D STARTED TURNING *BLUE*.
THEN WE DECIDED THE ONLY THING SPACE WAS GOOD FOR WAS CABLE SATELLITES AND SHOOTING MISSILES DOWN.
BUT I KNEW... I NEEDED FUNDING TO KEEP DEVELOPING *BLUESKY*. SO I CREATED *THIS*...
CODENAME *WINTERMAN.*
AND IF BLUESKY MEANT TURNING THE HOSTILE INTO THE HOSPITABLE... WINTERMAN MEANT THE OPPOSITE.
A WAY TO TURN THE ATMOSPHERE ITSELF INTO A WEAPON.
THAT THEY WANTED TO PAY FOR.
SO...SO I BUILT IT.

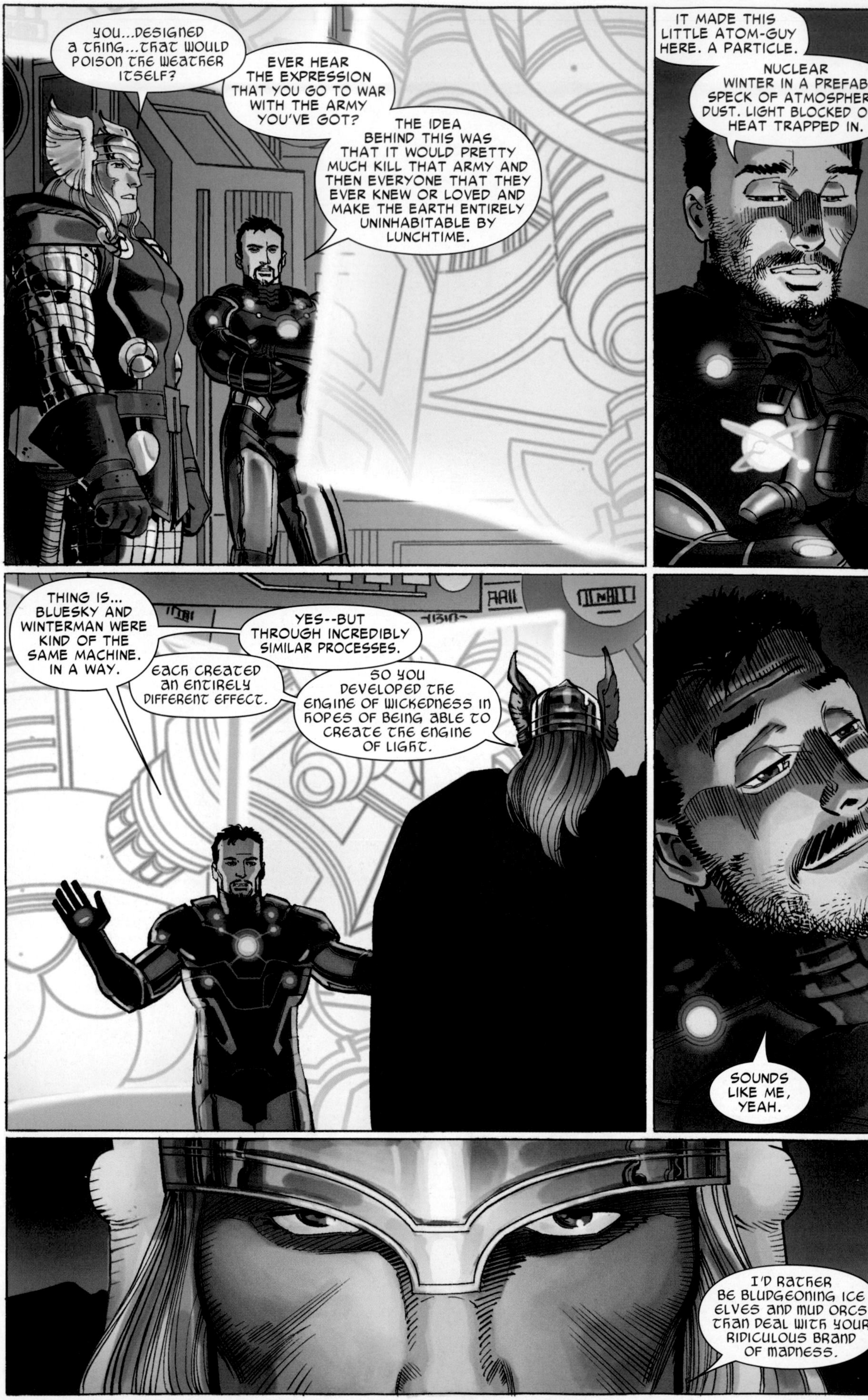
YOU...DESIGNED A THING...THAT WOULD POISON THE WEATHER ITSELF?
EVER HEAR THE EXPRESSION THAT YOU GO TO WAR WITH THE ARMY YOU'VE GOT?
THE IDEA BEHIND THIS WAS THAT IT WOULD PRETTY MUCH KILL THAT ARMY AND THEN EVERYONE THAT THEY EVER KNEW OR LOVED AND MAKE THE EARTH ENTIRELY UNINHABITABLE BY LUNCHTIME.
IT MADE THIS LITTLE ATOM-GUY HERE. A PARTICLE.
NUCLEAR WINTER IN A PREFAB SPECK OF ATMOSPHERIC DUST. LIGHT BLOCKED OUT; HEAT TRAPPED IN.
THING IS... BLUESKY AND WINTERMAN WERE KIND OF THE SAME MACHINE. IN A WAY.
EACH CREATED AN ENTIRELY DIFFERENT EFFECT.
YES--BUT THROUGH INCREDIBLY SIMILAR PROCESSES.
SO YOU DEVELOPED THE ENGINE OF WICKEDNESS IN HOPES OF BEING ABLE TO CREATE THE ENGINE OF LIGHT.
SOUNDS LIKE ME, YEAH.
I'D RATHER BE BLUDGEONING ICE ELVES AND MUD ORCS THAN DEAL WITH YOUR RIDICULOUS BRAND OF MADNESS.

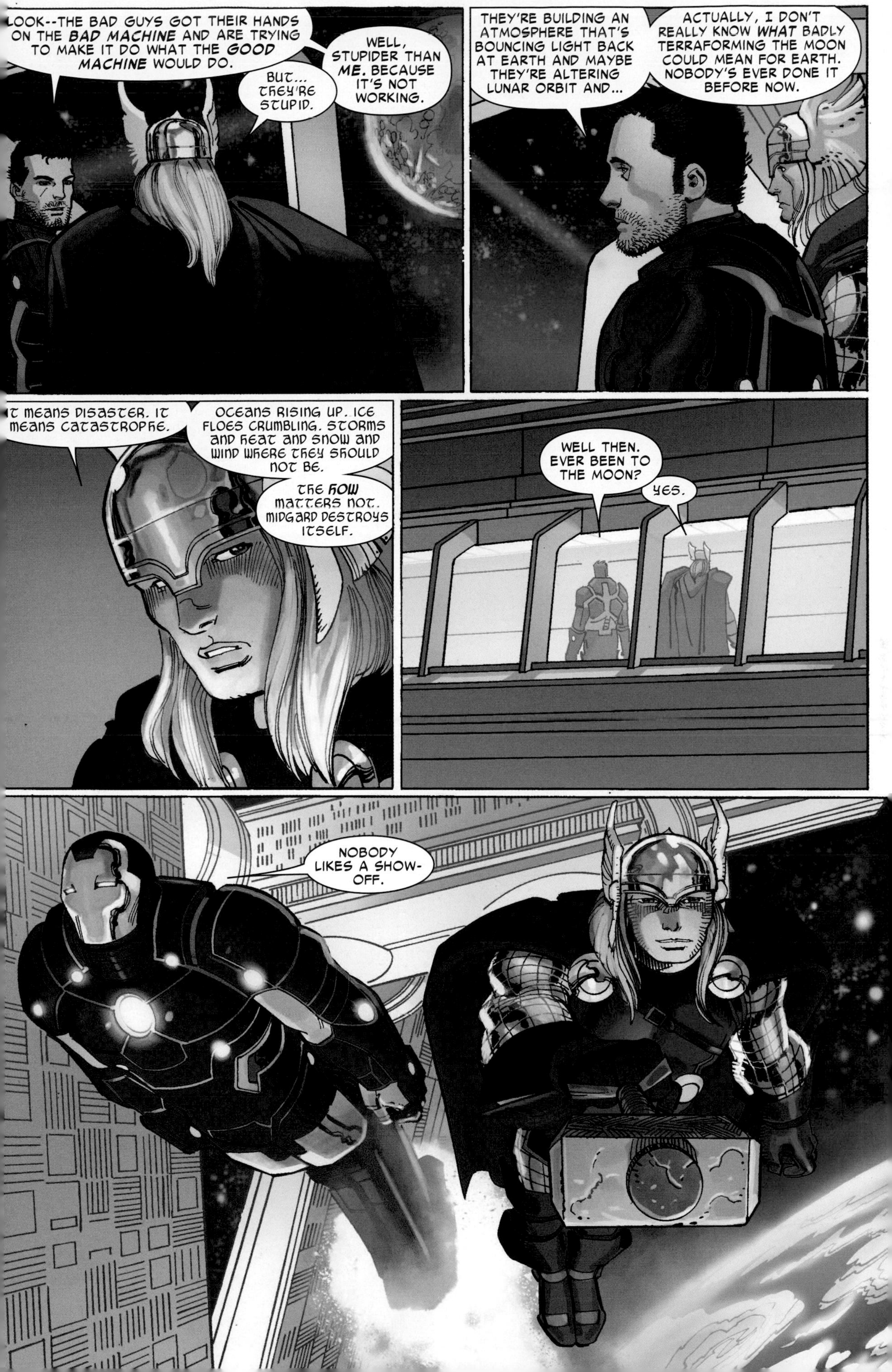
LOOK--THE BAD GUYS GOT THEIR HANDS ON THE BAD MACHINE AND ARE TRYING TO MAKE IT DO WHAT THE GOOD MACHINE WOULD DO.
BUT... THEY'RE STUPID.
WELL, STUPIDER THAN ME. BECAUSE IT'S NOT WORKING.
THEY'RE BUILDING AN ATMOSPHERE THAT'S BOUNCING LIGHT BACK AT EARTH AND MAYBE THEY'RE ALTERING LUNAR ORBIT AND...
ACTUALLY, I DON'T REALLY KNOW WHAT BADLY TERRAFORMING THE MOON COULD MEAN FOR EARTH. NOBODY'S EVER DONE IT BEFORE NOW.
IT MEANS DISASTER. IT MEANS CATASTROPHE.
OCEANS RISING UP. ICE FLOES CRUMBLING. STORMS AND HEAT AND SNOW AND WIND WHERE THEY SHOULD NOT BE.
THE HOW MATTERS NOT. MIDGARD DESTROYS ITSELF.
WELL THEN. EVER BEEN TO THE MOON?
YES.
NOBODY LIKES A SHOW-OFF.

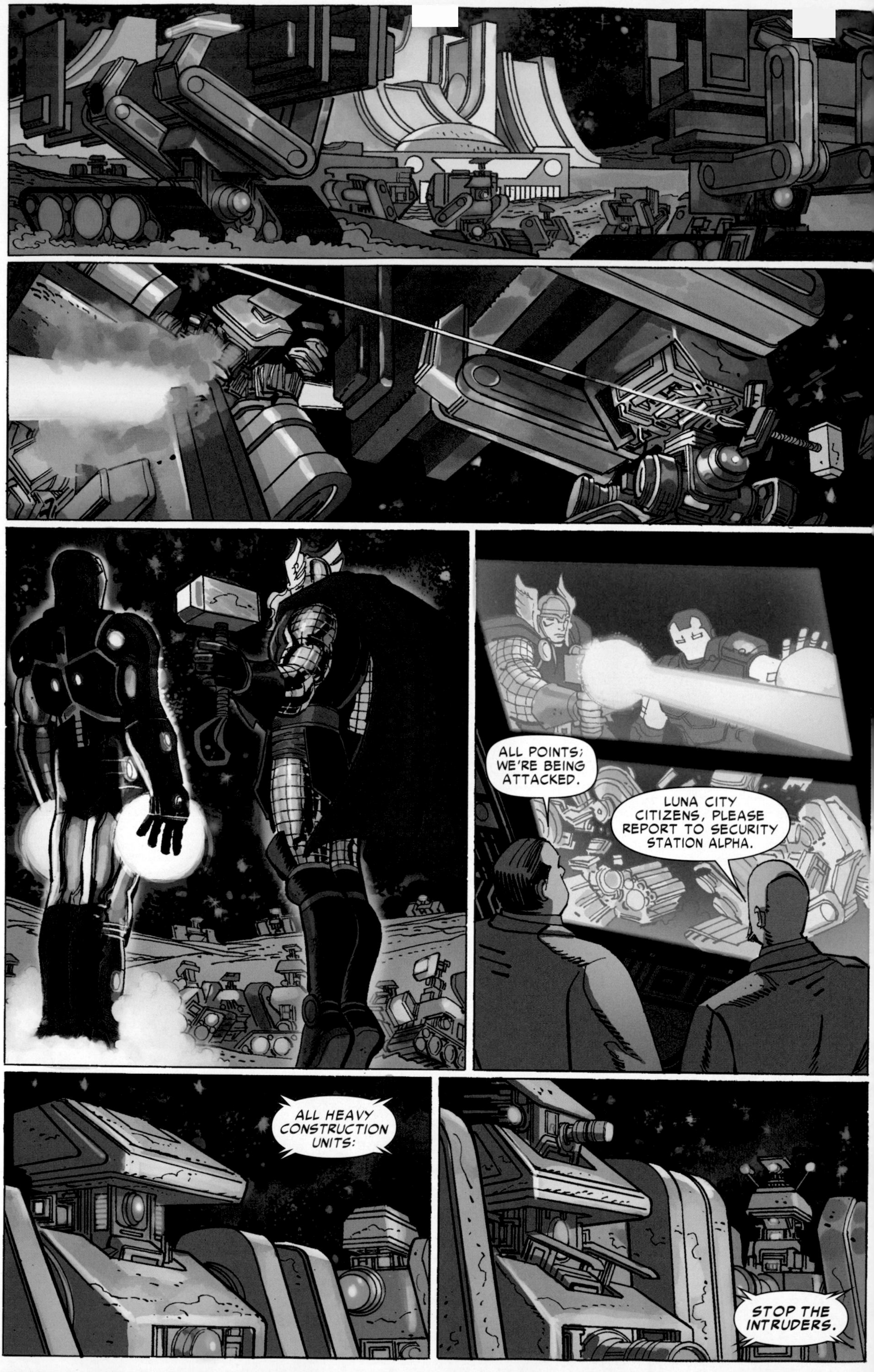
ALL POINTS; WE'RE BEING ATTACKED.
LUNA CITY CITIZENS, PLEASE REPORT TO SECURITY STATION ALPHA.
ALL HEAVY CONSTRUCTION UNITS:
STOP THE INTRUDERS.

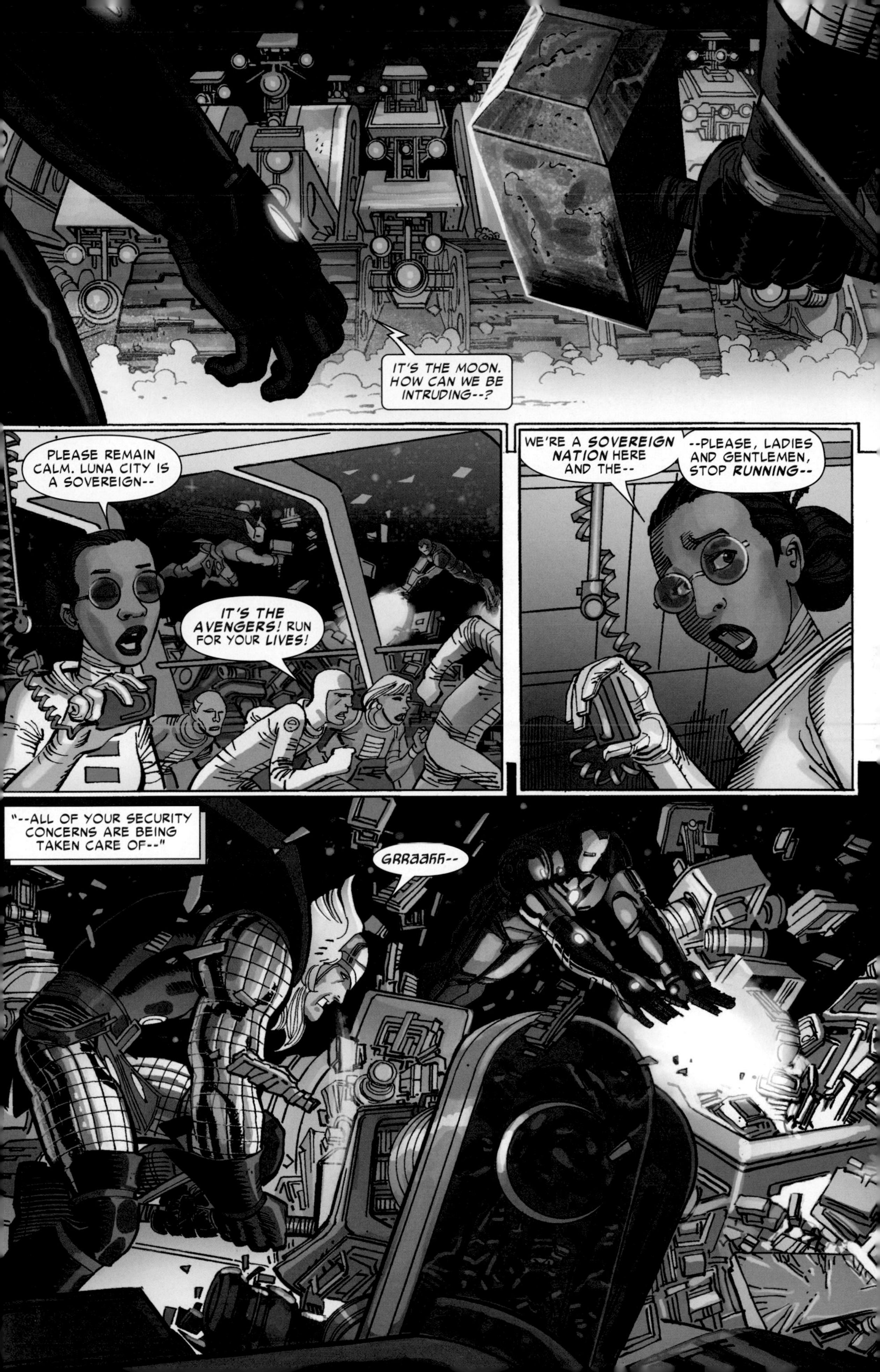
IT'S THE MOON. HOW CAN WE BE INTRUDING--?
PLEASE REMAIN CALM. LUNA CITY IS A SOVEREIGN--
IT'S THE AVENGERS! RUN FOR YOUR LIVES!
WE'RE A SOVEREIGN NATION HERE AND THE--
--PLEASE, LADIES AND GENTLEMEN, STOP RUNNING--
"--ALL OF YOUR SECURITY CONCERNS ARE BEING TAKEN CARE OF--"
GRRAAHH--

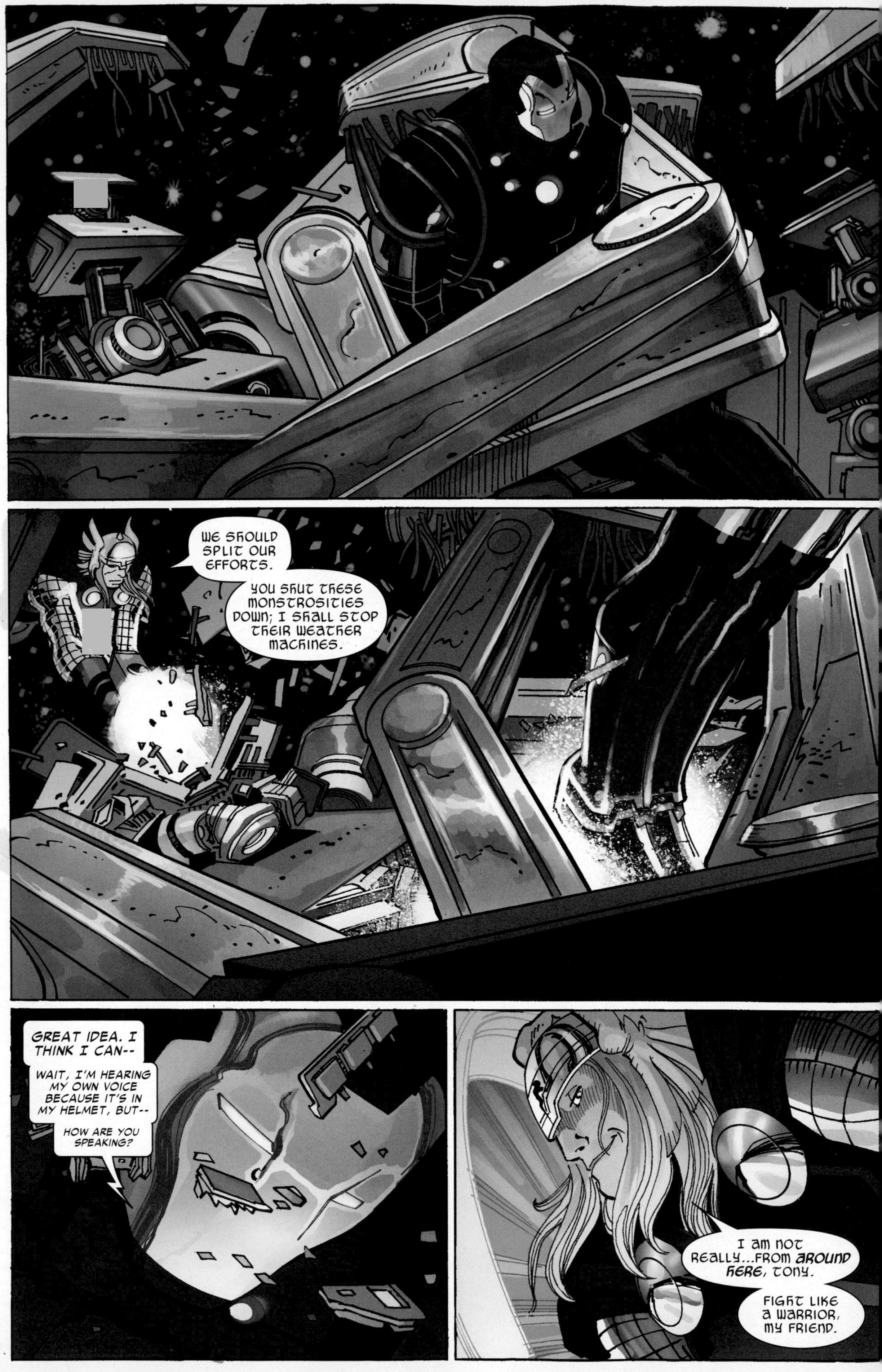

WE SHOULD SPLIT OUR EFFORTS.
YOU SHUT THESE MONSTROSITIES DOWN; I SHALL STOP THEIR WEATHER MACHINES.
GREAT IDEA. I THINK I CAN--
WAIT, I'M HEARING MY OWN VOICE BECAUSE IT'S IN MY HELMET, BUT--
HOW ARE YOU SPEAKING?
I AM NOT REALLY...FROM AROUND HERE, TONY.
FIGHT LIKE A WARRIOR, MY FRIEND.

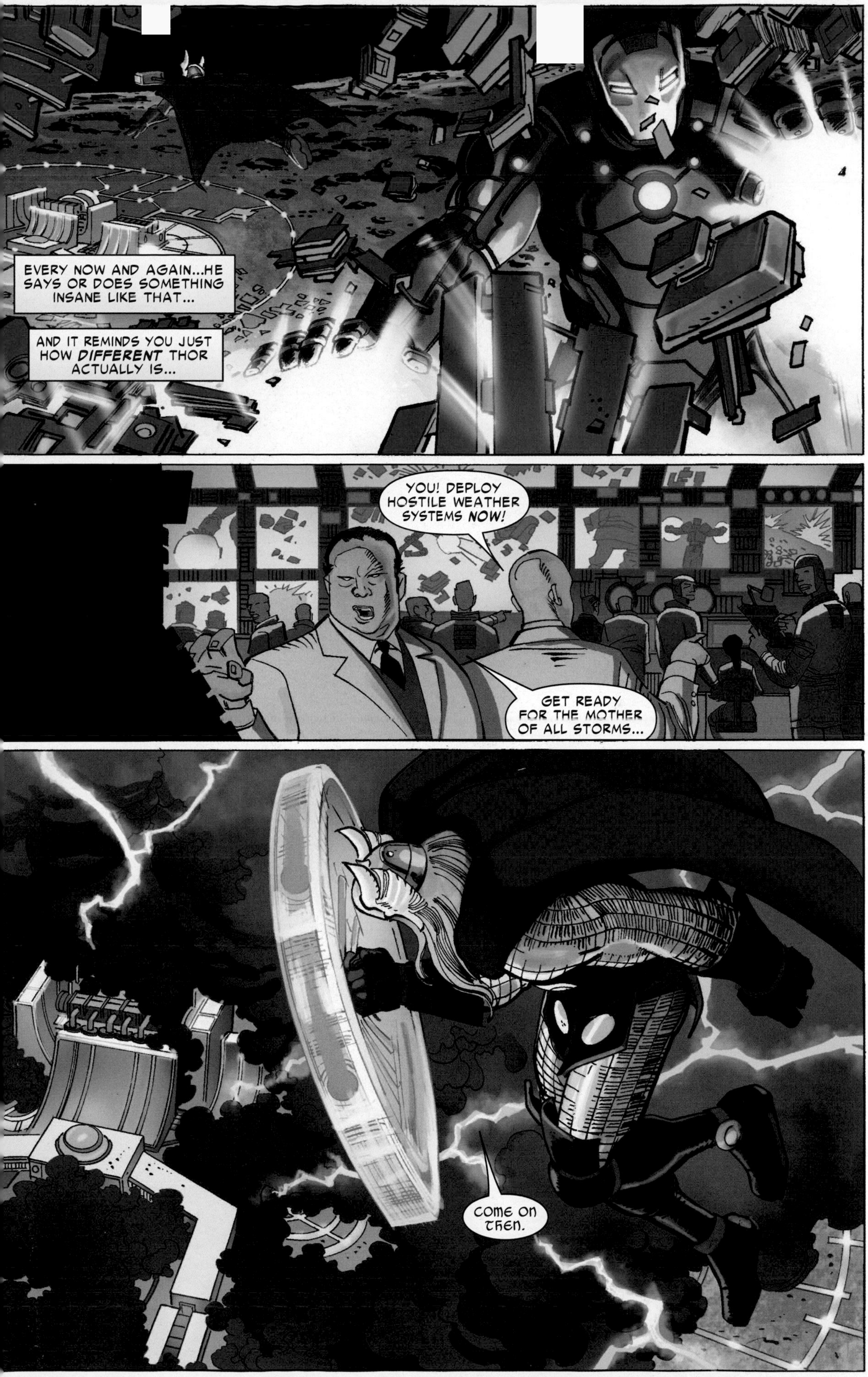
EVERY NOW AND AGAIN...HE SAYS OR DOES SOMETHING INSANE LIKE THAT...
AND IT REMINDS YOU JUST HOW *DIFFERENT* THOR ACTUALLY IS...
YOU! DEPLOY HOSTILE WEATHER SYSTEMS *NOW!*
GET READY FOR THE MOTHER OF ALL STORMS...
COME ON THEN.

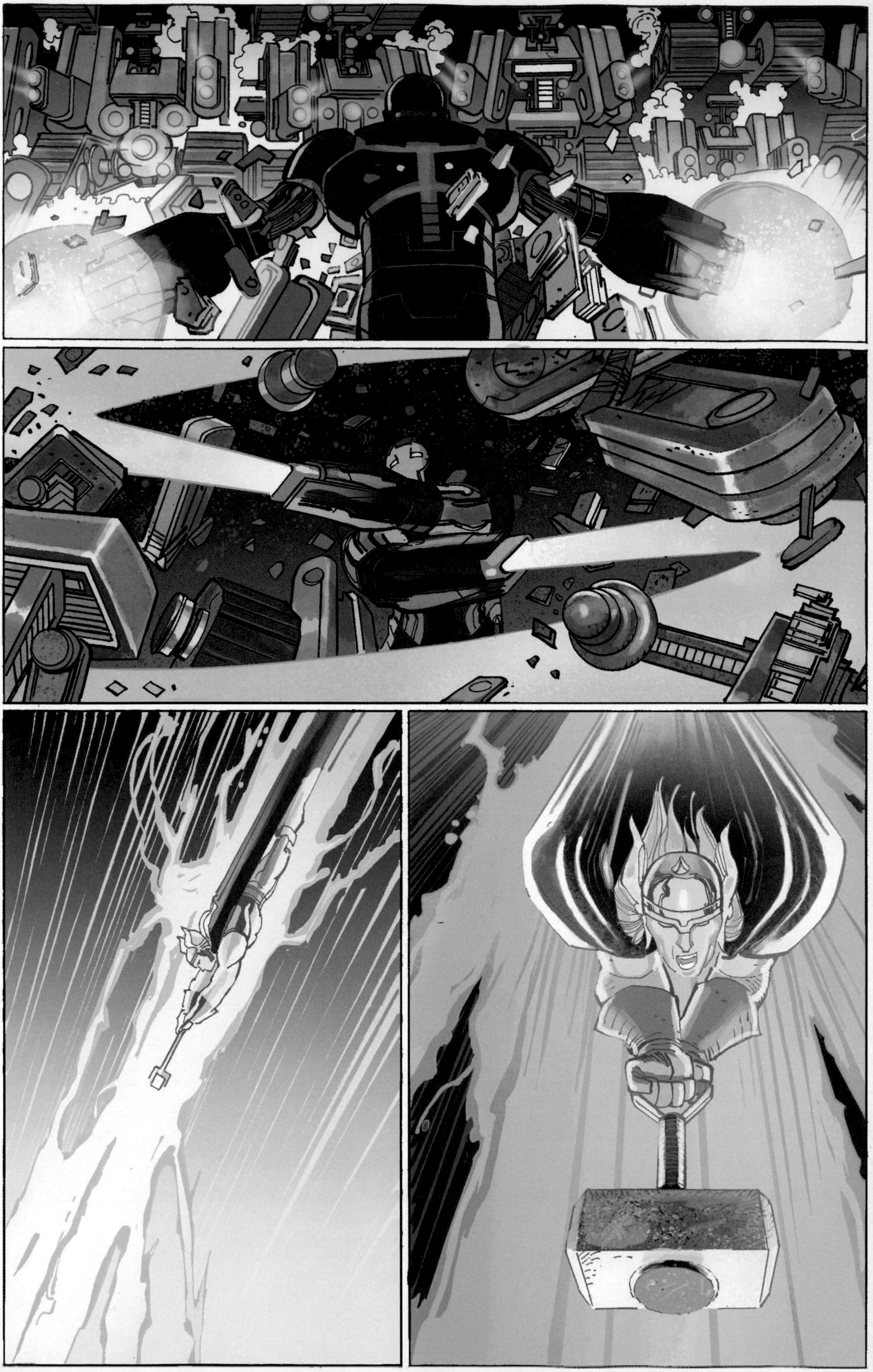

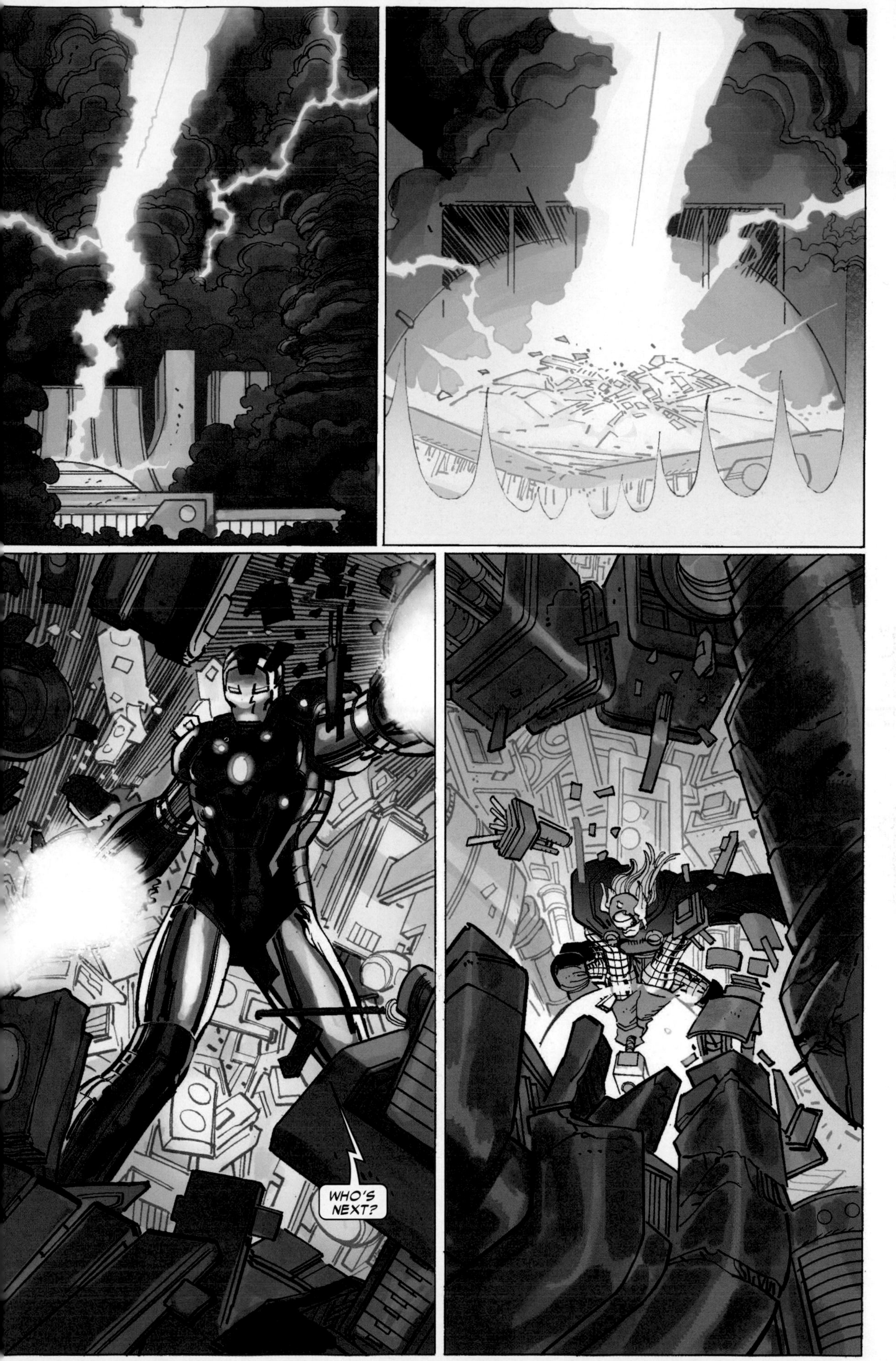
WHO'S NEXT?

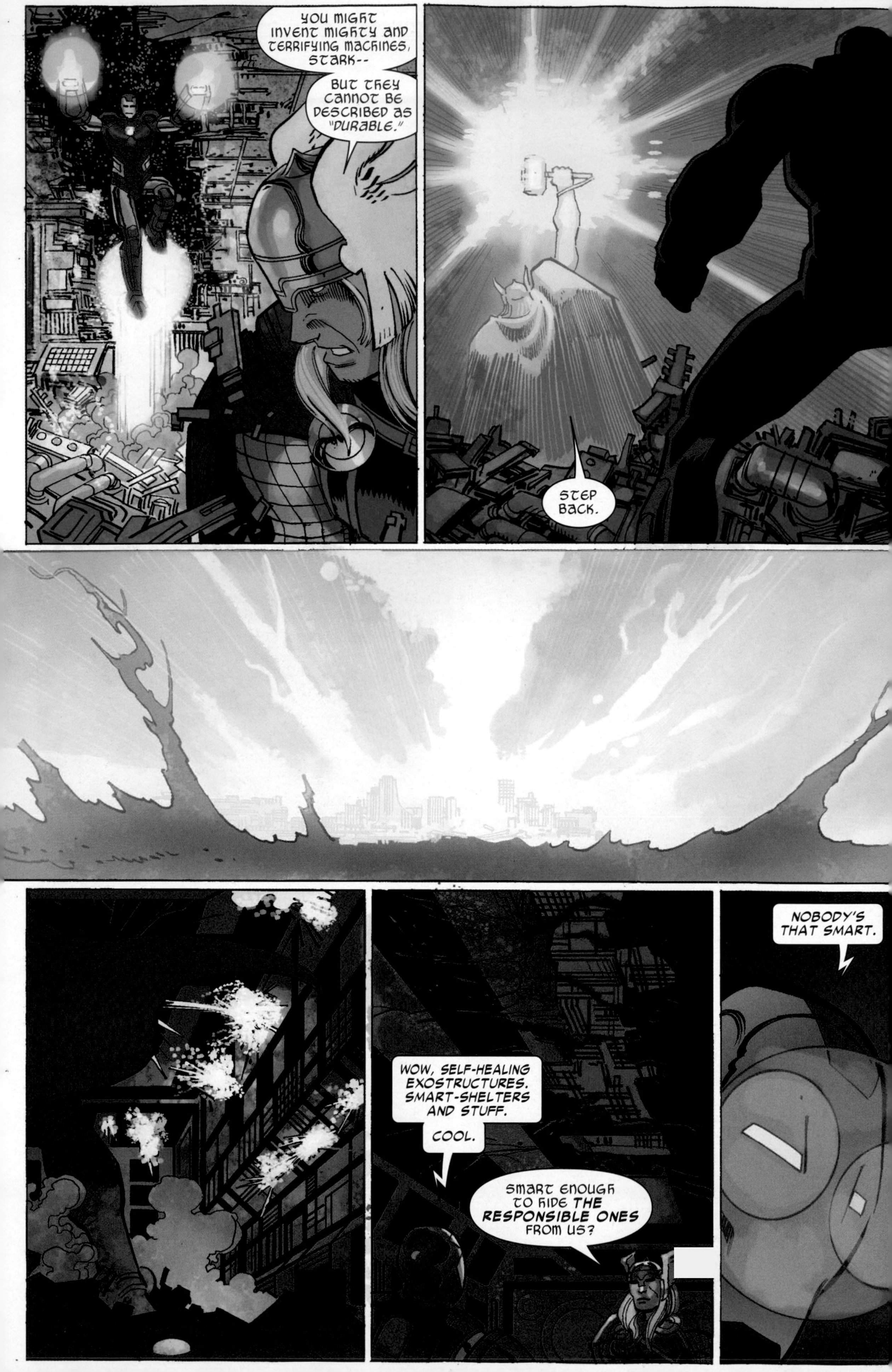
YOU MIGHT INVENT MIGHTY AND TERRIFYING MACHINES, STARK--
BUT THEY CANNOT BE DESCRIBED AS "DURABLE."
STEP BACK.
WOW, SELF-HEALING EXOSTRUCTURES. SMART-SHELTERS AND STUFF.
COOL.
SMART ENOUGH TO HIDE THE RESPONSIBLE ONES FROM US?
NOBODY'S THAT SMART.

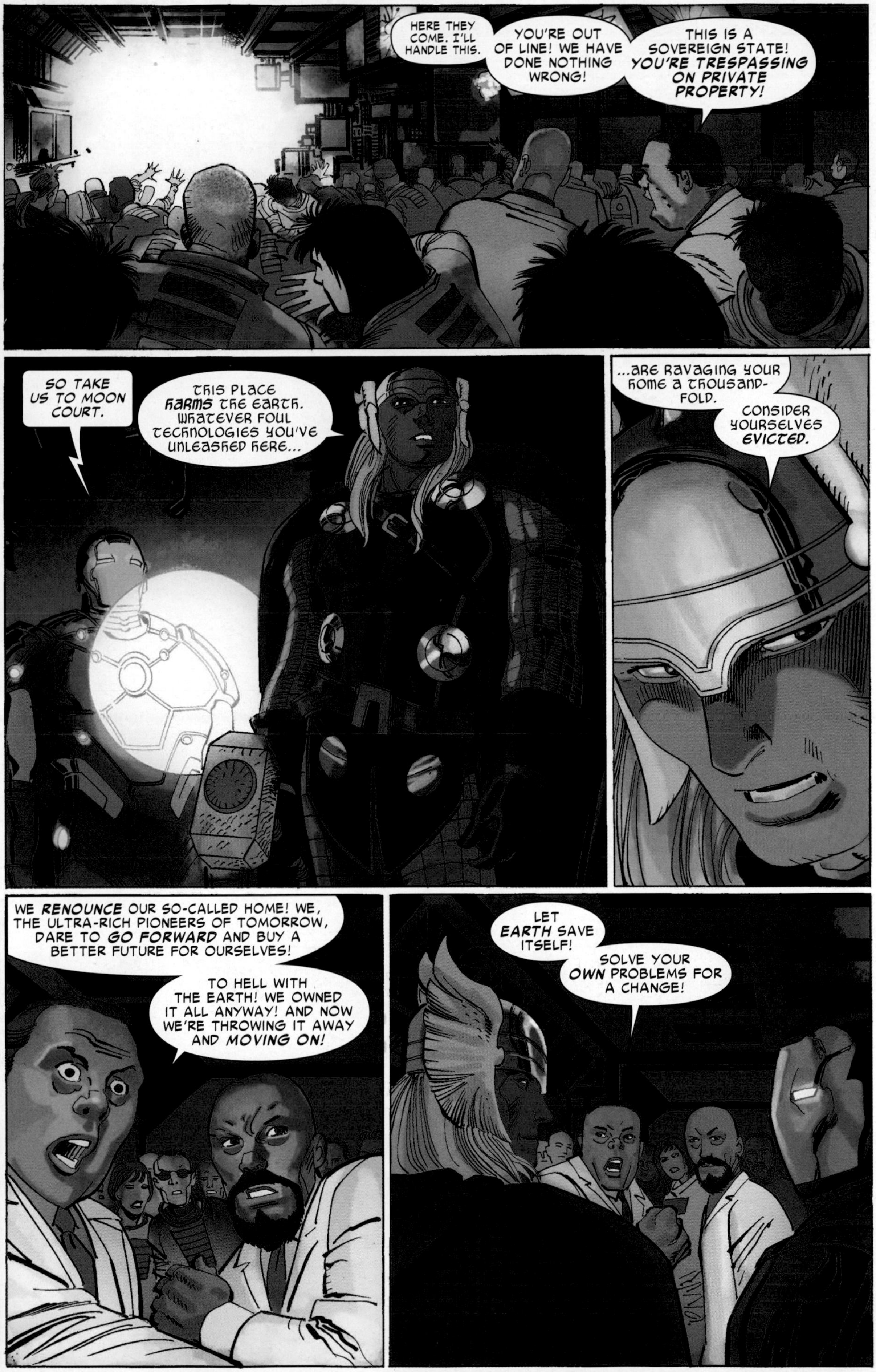
HERE THEY COME. I'LL HANDLE THIS.
YOU'RE OUT OF LINE! WE HAVE DONE NOTHING WRONG!
THIS IS A SOVEREIGN STATE! YOU'RE TRESPASSING ON PRIVATE PROPERTY!
SO TAKE US TO MOON COURT.
THIS PLACE HARMS THE EARTH. WHATEVER FOUL TECHNOLOGIES YOU'VE UNLEASHED HERE...
...ARE RAVAGING YOUR HOME A THOUSAND-FOLD.
CONSIDER YOURSELVES EVICTED.
WE RENOUNCE OUR SO-CALLED HOME! WE, THE ULTRA-RICH PIONEERS OF TOMORROW, DARE TO GO FORWARD AND BUY A BETTER FUTURE FOR OURSELVES!
TO HELL WITH THE EARTH! WE OWNED IT ALL ANYWAY! AND NOW WE'RE THROWING IT AWAY AND MOVING ON!
LET EARTH SAVE ITSELF!
SOLVE YOUR OWN PROBLEMS FOR A CHANGE!

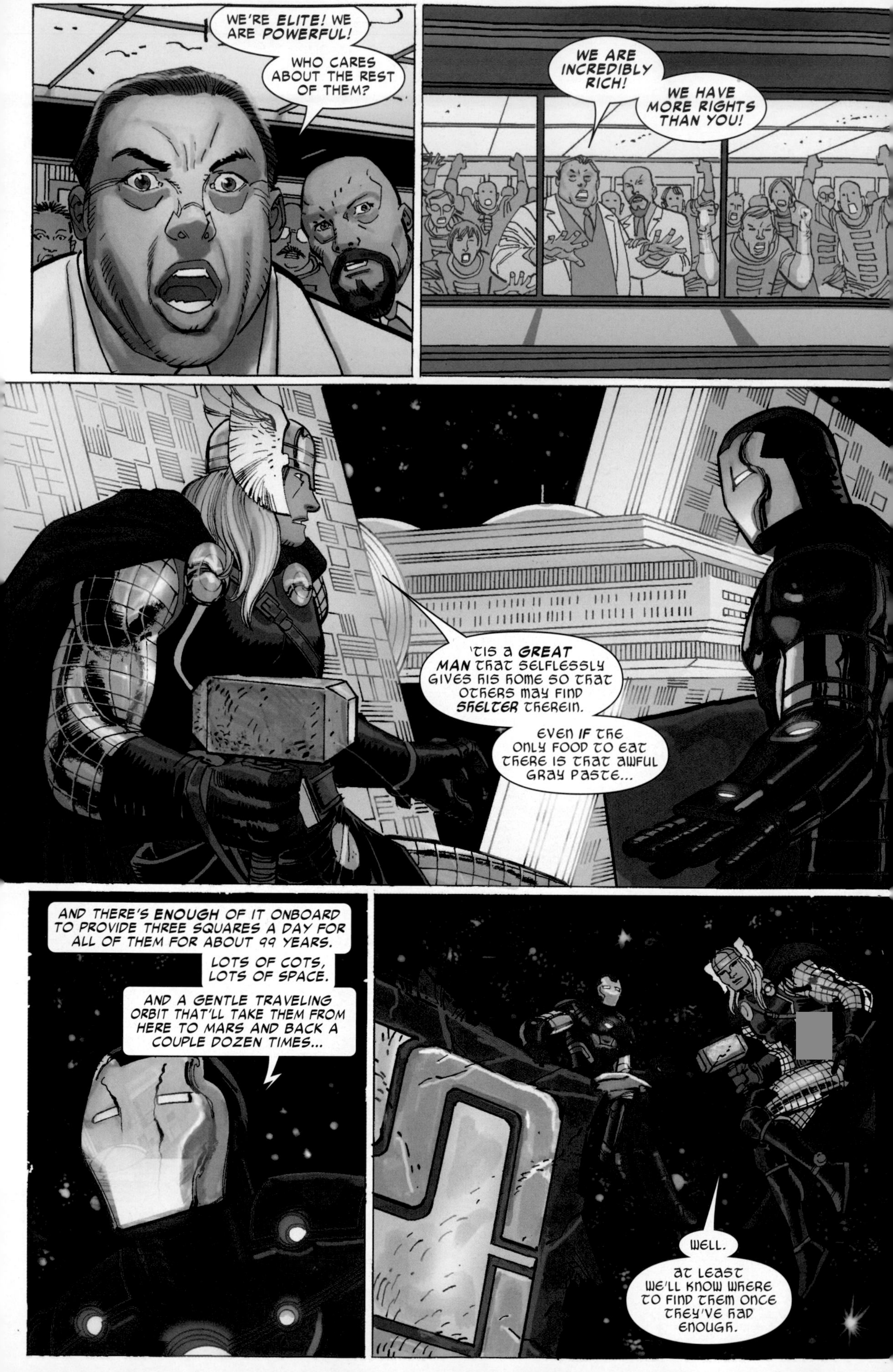
WE'RE ELITE! WE ARE POWERFUL!
WHO CARES ABOUT THE REST OF THEM?
WE ARE INCREDIBLY RICH!
WE HAVE MORE RIGHTS THAN YOU!
'TIS A GREAT MAN THAT SELFLESSLY GIVES HIS HOME SO THAT OTHERS MAY FIND SHELTER THEREIN.
EVEN IF THE ONLY FOOD TO EAT THERE IS THAT AWFUL GRAY PASTE...
AND THERE'S ENOUGH OF IT ONBOARD TO PROVIDE THREE SQUARES A DAY FOR ALL OF THEM FOR ABOUT 99 YEARS.
LOTS OF COTS, LOTS OF SPACE.
AND A GENTLE TRAVELING ORBIT THAT'LL TAKE THEM FROM HERE TO MARS AND BACK A COUPLE DOZEN TIMES...
WELL.
AT LEAST WE'LL KNOW WHERE TO FIND THEM ONCE THEY'VE HAD ENOUGH.

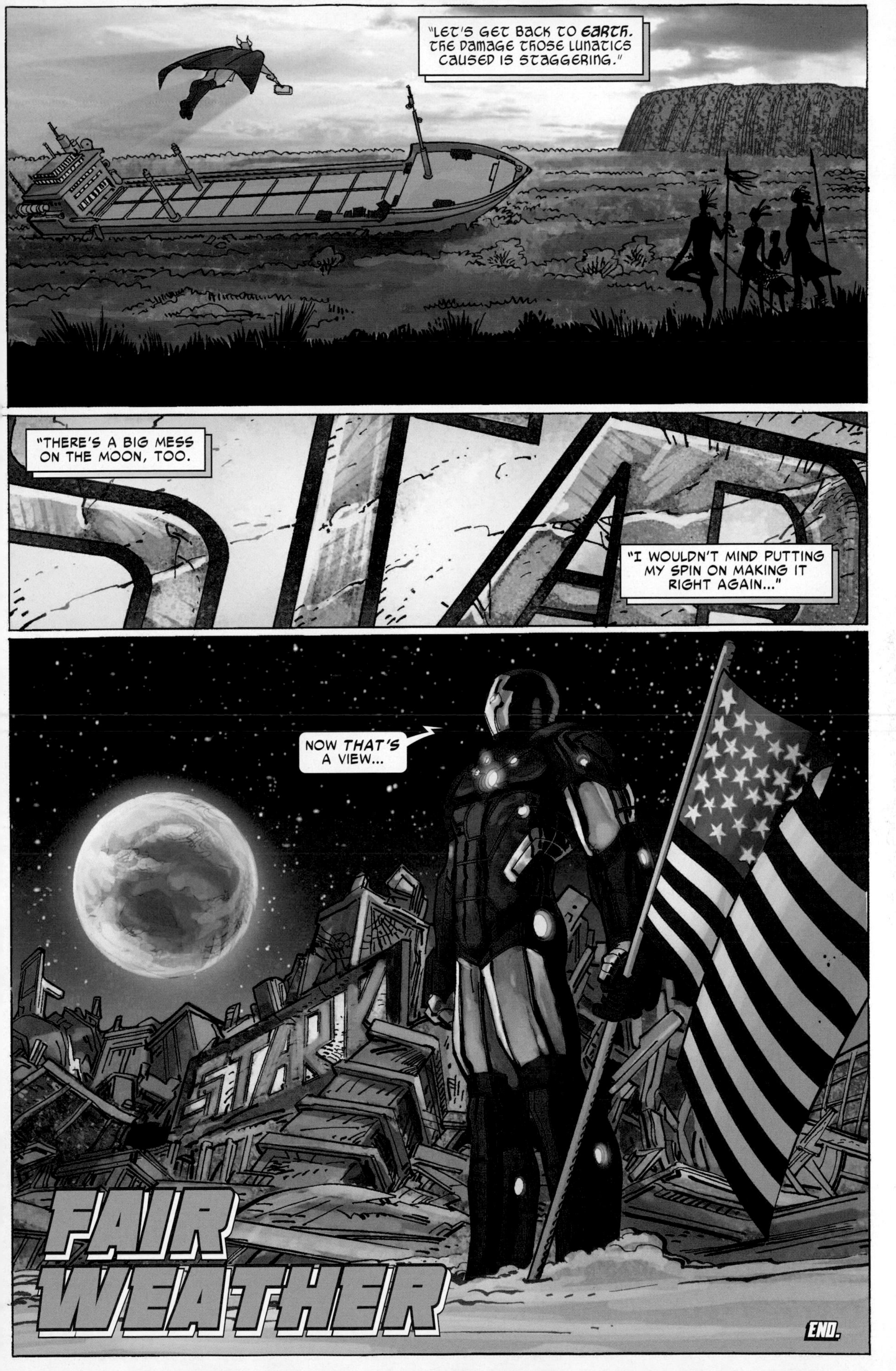
"LET'S GET BACK TO EARTH. THE DAMAGE THOSE LUNATICS CAUSED IS STAGGERING."
"THERE'S A BIG MESS ON THE MOON, TOO.
"I WOULDN'T MIND PUTTING MY SPIN ON MAKING IT RIGHT AGAIN..."
NOW THAT'S A VIEW...
STARK
FAIR WEATHER
END.

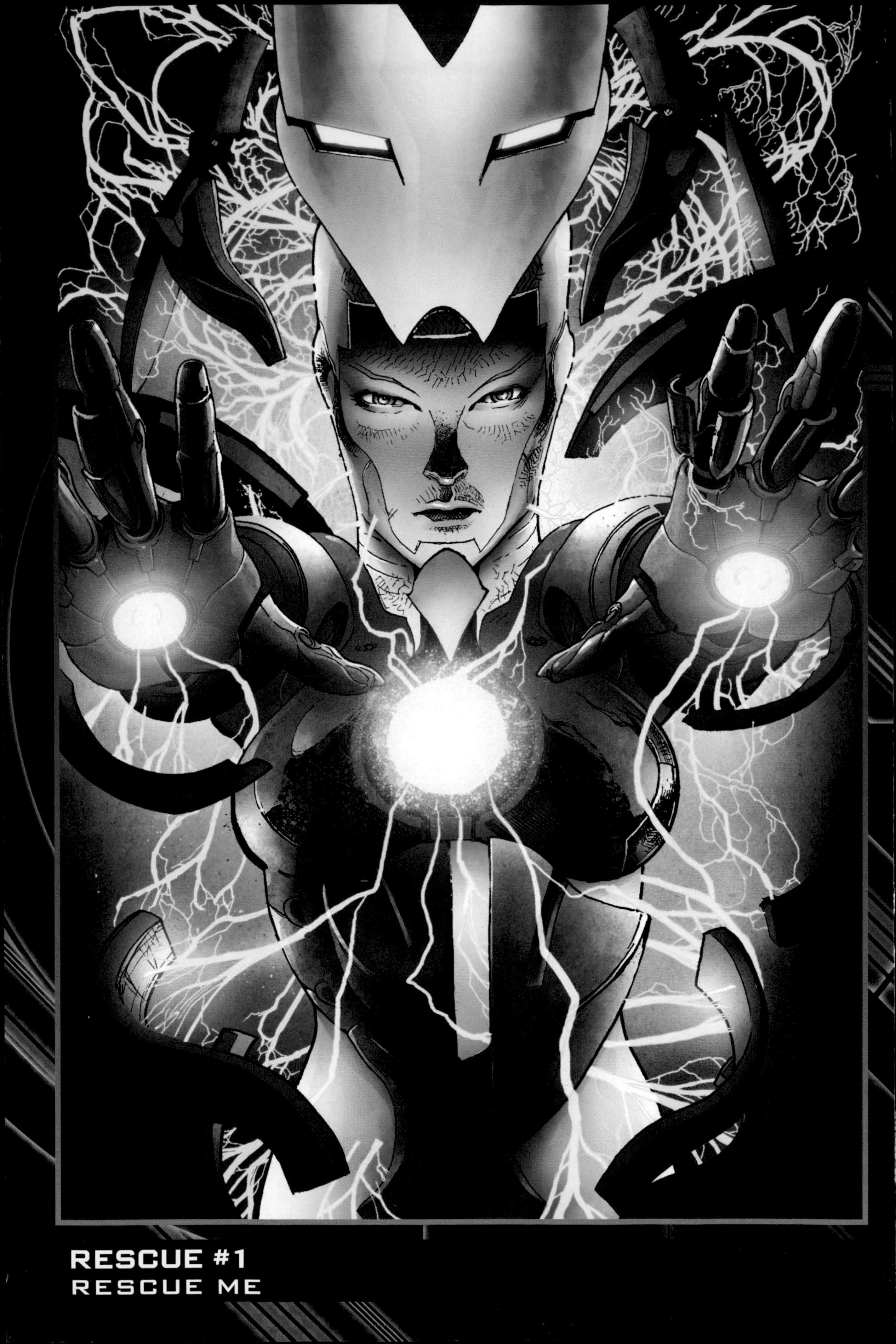

RESCUE #1
RESCUE ME

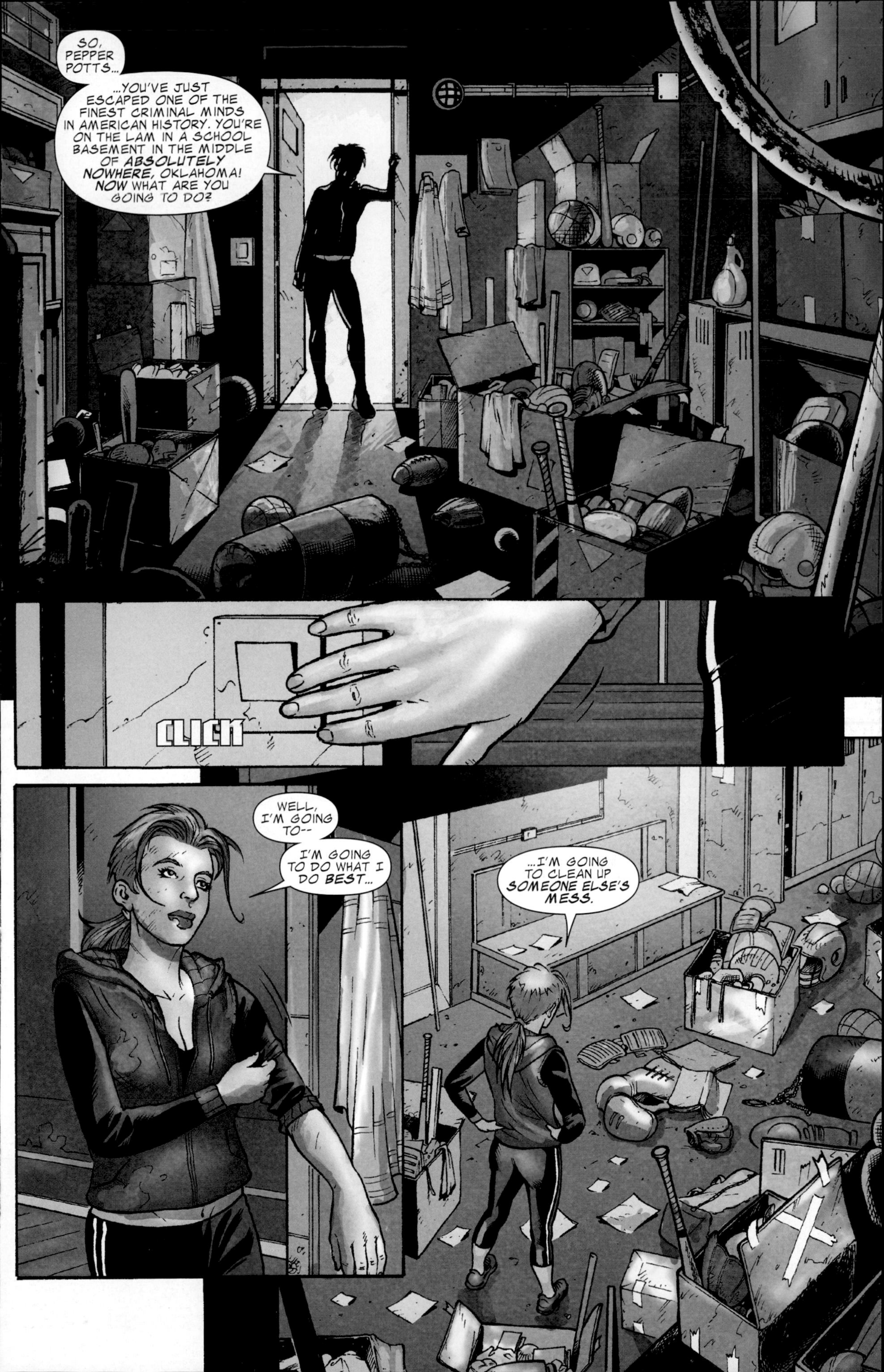
SO, PEPPER POTTS...
...YOU'VE JUST ESCAPED ONE OF THE FINEST CRIMINAL MINDS IN AMERICAN HISTORY. YOU'RE ON THE LAM IN A SCHOOL BASEMENT IN THE MIDDLE OF ABSOLUTELY NOWHERE, OKLAHOMA! NOW WHAT ARE YOU GOING TO DO?
CLICK
WELL, I'M GOING TO--
I'M GOING TO DO WHAT I DO BEST...
...I'M GOING TO CLEAN UP SOMEONE ELSE'S MESS.

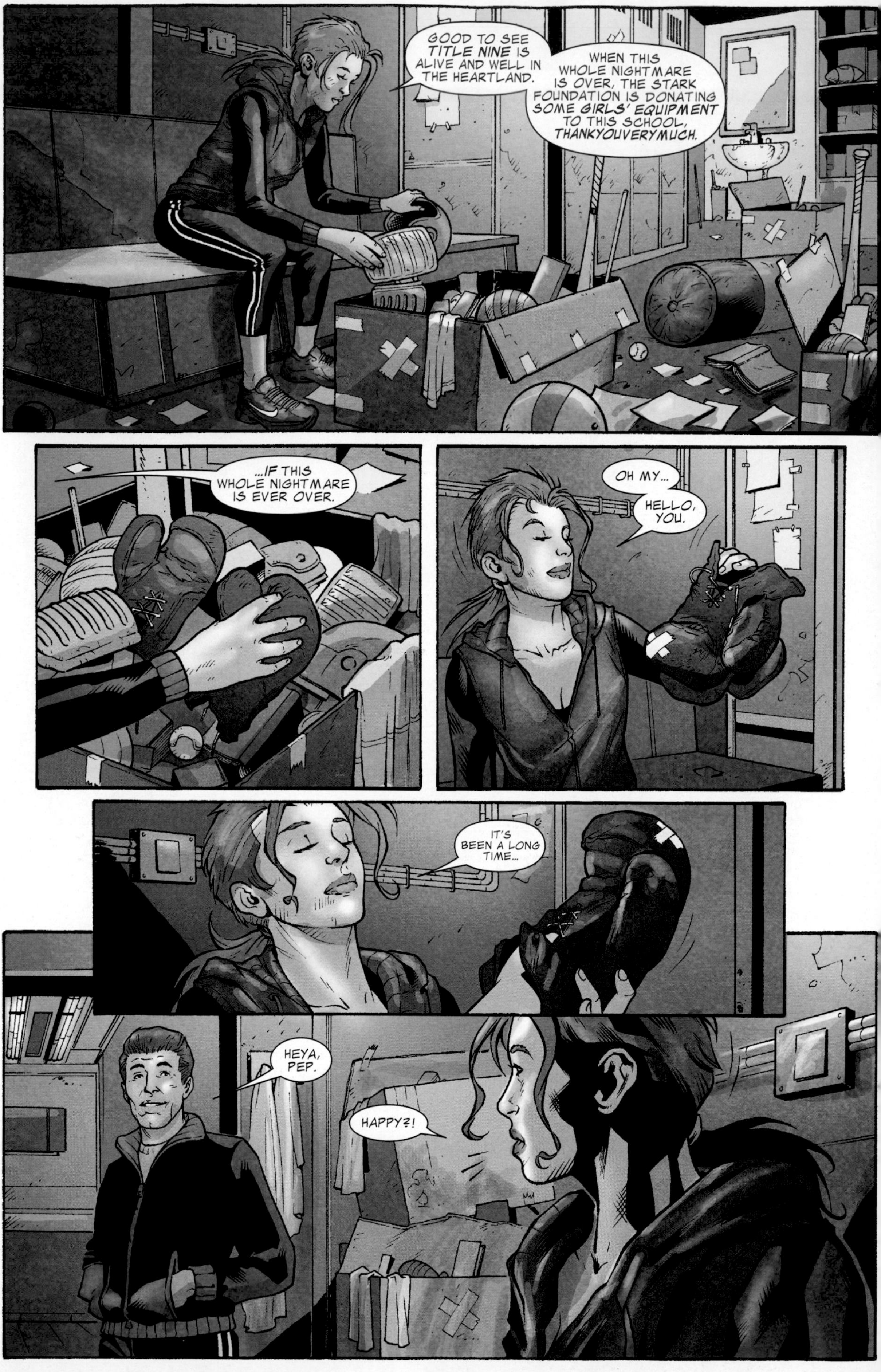
GOOD TO SEE TITLE NINE IS ALIVE AND WELL IN THE HEARTLAND.
WHEN THIS WHOLE NIGHTMARE IS OVER, THE STARK FOUNDATION IS DONATING SOME GIRLS' EQUIPMENT TO THIS SCHOOL, THANKYOUVERYMUCH.
...IF THIS WHOLE NIGHTMARE IS EVER OVER.
OH MY...
HELLO, YOU.
IT'S BEEN A LONG TIME...
HEYA, PEP.
HAPPY?!

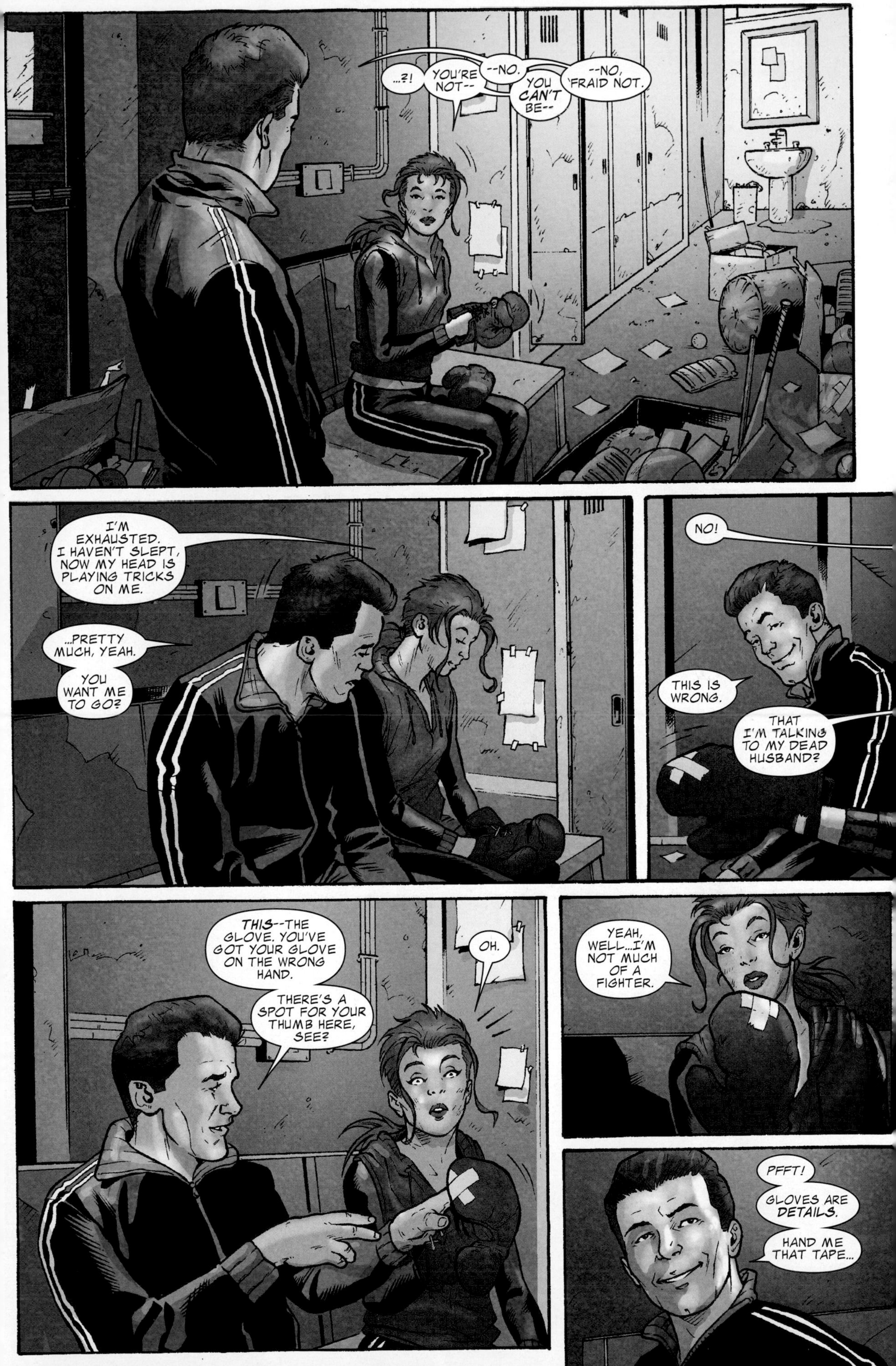

...?!
YOU'RE NOT--
--NO.
YOU CAN'T BE--
--NO, 'FRAID NOT.
I'M EXHAUSTED. I HAVEN'T SLEPT, NOW MY HEAD IS PLAYING TRICKS ON ME.
...PRETTY MUCH, YEAH.
YOU WANT ME TO GO?
NO!
THIS IS WRONG.
THAT I'M TALKING TO MY DEAD HUSBAND?
THIS--THE GLOVE. YOU'VE GOT YOUR GLOVE ON THE WRONG HAND.
THERE'S A SPOT FOR YOUR THUMB HERE, SEE?
OH.
YEAH, WELL...I'M NOT MUCH OF A FIGHTER.
PFFT!
GLOVES ARE DETAILS.
HAND ME THAT TAPE...

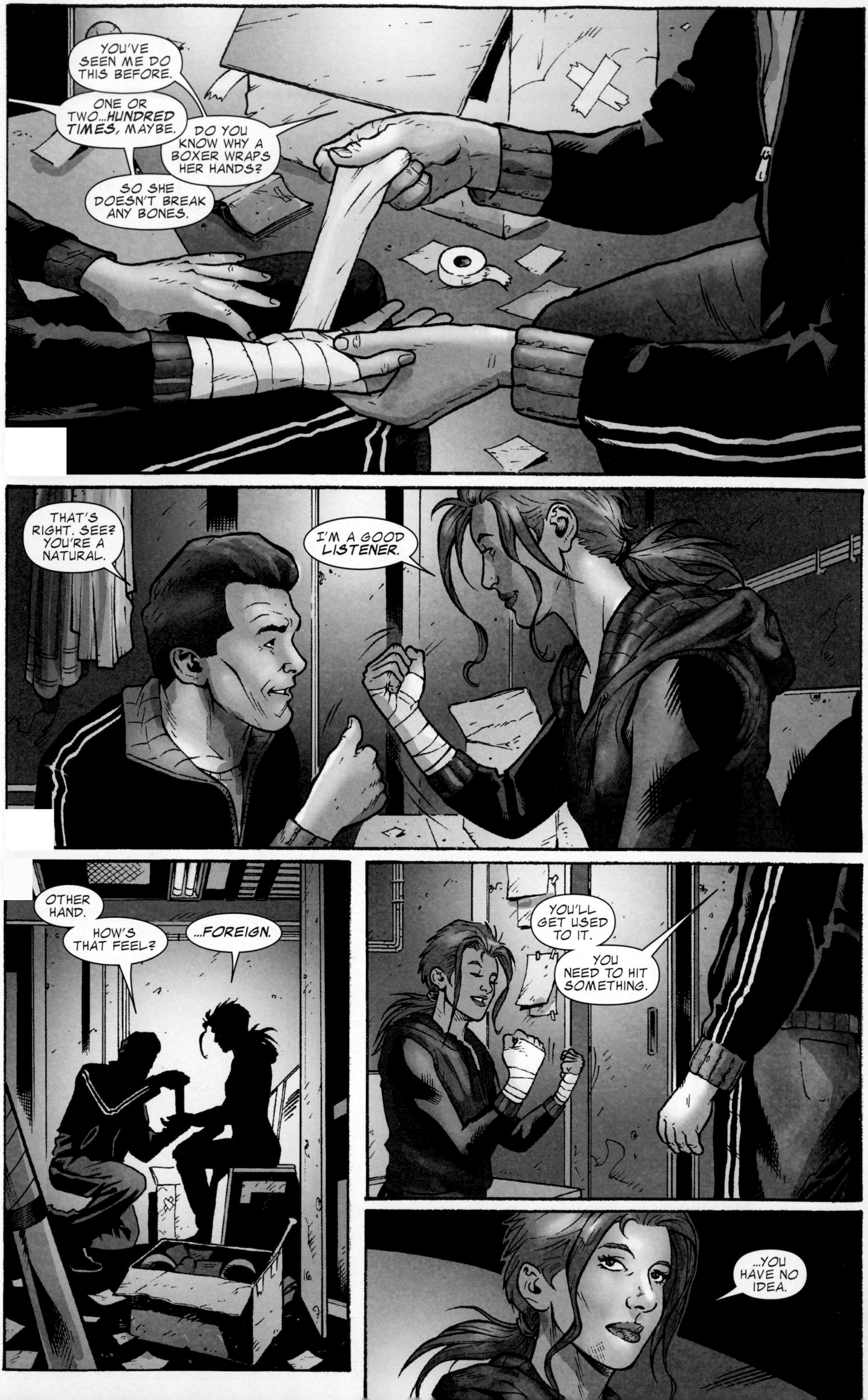

YOU'VE SEEN ME DO THIS BEFORE.
ONE OR TWO...HUNDRED TIMES, MAYBE.
DO YOU KNOW WHY A BOXER WRAPS HER HANDS?
SO SHE DOESN'T BREAK ANY BONES.
THAT'S RIGHT. SEE? YOU'RE A NATURAL.
I'M A GOOD LISTENER.
OTHER HAND.
HOW'S THAT FEEL?
...FOREIGN.
YOU'LL GET USED TO IT.
YOU NEED TO HIT SOMETHING.
...YOU HAVE NO IDEA.

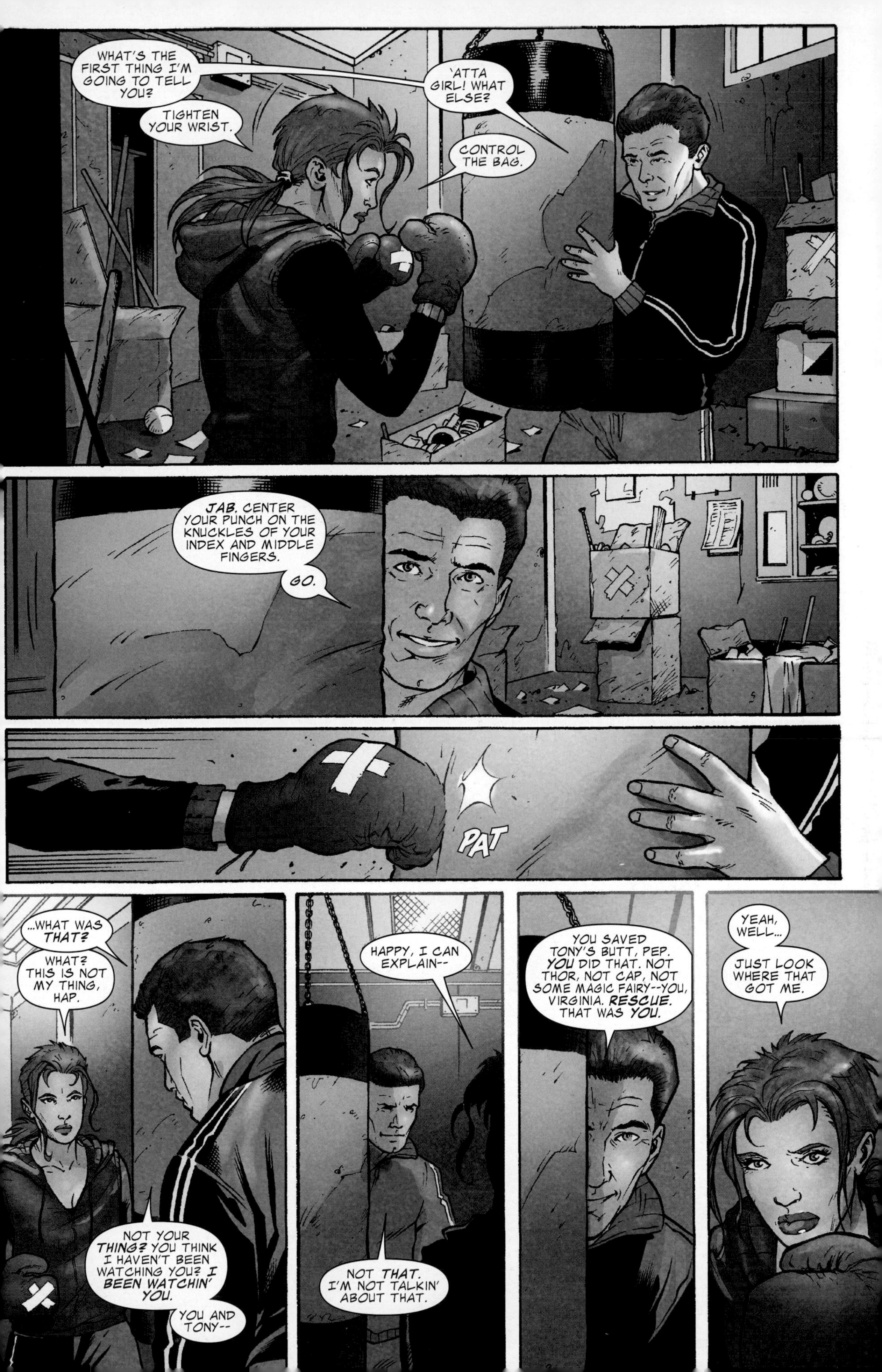

WHAT'S THE FIRST THING I'M GOING TO TELL YOU?
TIGHTEN YOUR WRIST.
'ATTA GIRL! WHAT ELSE?
CONTROL THE BAG.
JAB. CENTER YOUR PUNCH ON THE KNUCKLES OF YOUR INDEX AND MIDDLE FINGERS.
GO.
PAT
...WHAT WAS THAT?
WHAT? THIS IS NOT MY THING, HAP.
NOT YOUR THING? YOU THINK I HAVEN'T BEEN WATCHING YOU? I BEEN WATCHIN' YOU.
YOU AND TONY--
HAPPY, I CAN EXPLAIN--
NOT THAT. I'M NOT TALKIN' ABOUT THAT.
YOU SAVED TONY'S BUTT, PEP. YOU DID THAT. NOT THOR, NOT CAP, NOT SOME MAGIC FAIRY--YOU, VIRGINIA. RESCUE. THAT WAS YOU.
YEAH, WELL...
JUST LOOK WHERE THAT GOT ME.

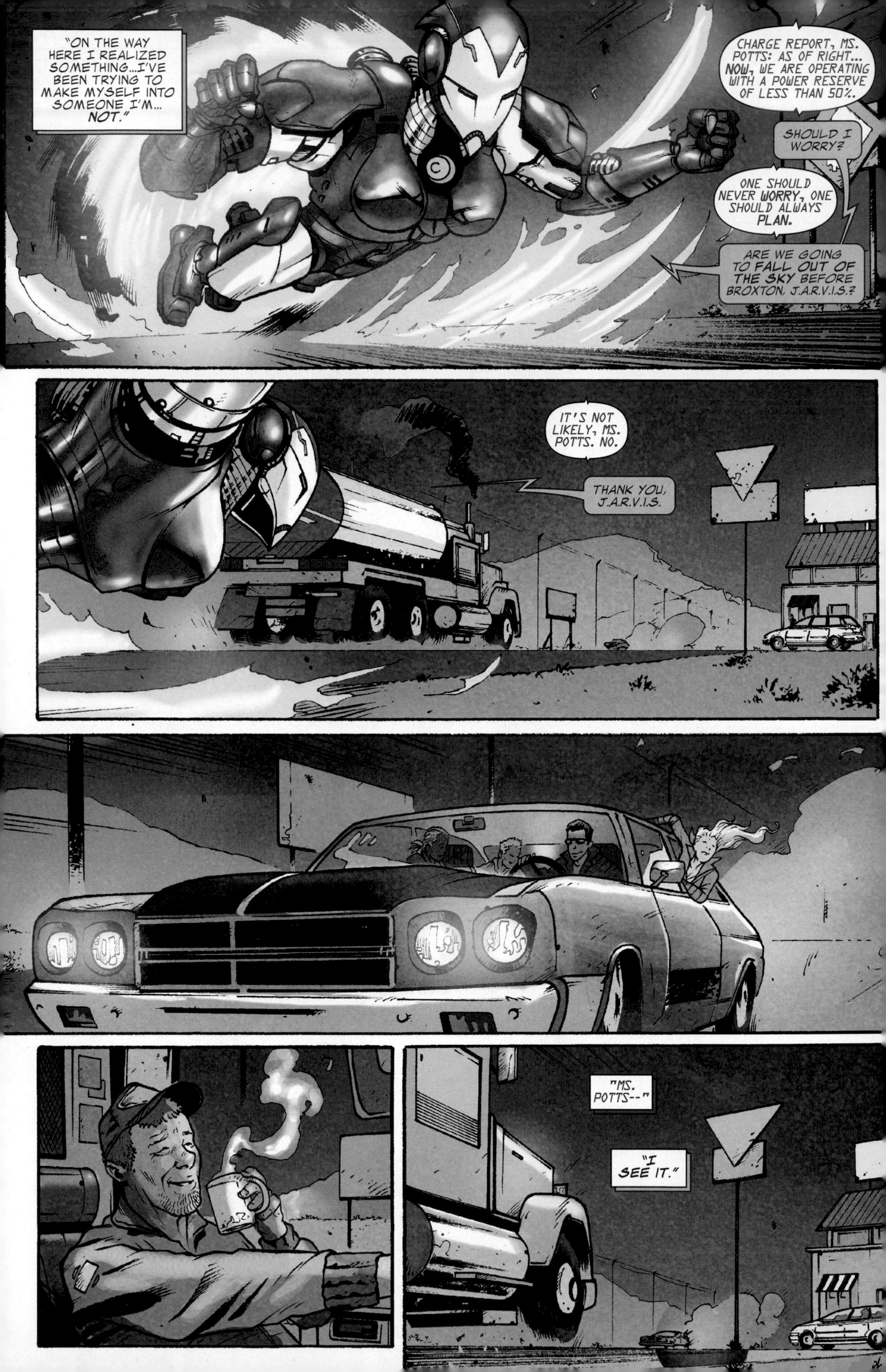
"ON THE WAY HERE I REALIZED SOMETHING...I'VE BEEN TRYING TO MAKE MYSELF INTO SOMEONE I'M... NOT."
CHARGE REPORT, MS. POTTS: AS OF RIGHT... NOW, WE ARE OPERATING WITH A POWER RESERVE OF LESS THAN 50%.
SHOULD I WORRY?
ONE SHOULD NEVER WORRY, ONE SHOULD ALWAYS PLAN.
ARE WE GOING TO FALL OUT OF THE SKY BEFORE BROXTON, J.A.R.V.I.S.?
IT'S NOT LIKELY, MS. POTTS. NO.
THANK YOU, J.A.R.V.I.S.
"MS. POTTS--"
"I SEE IT."

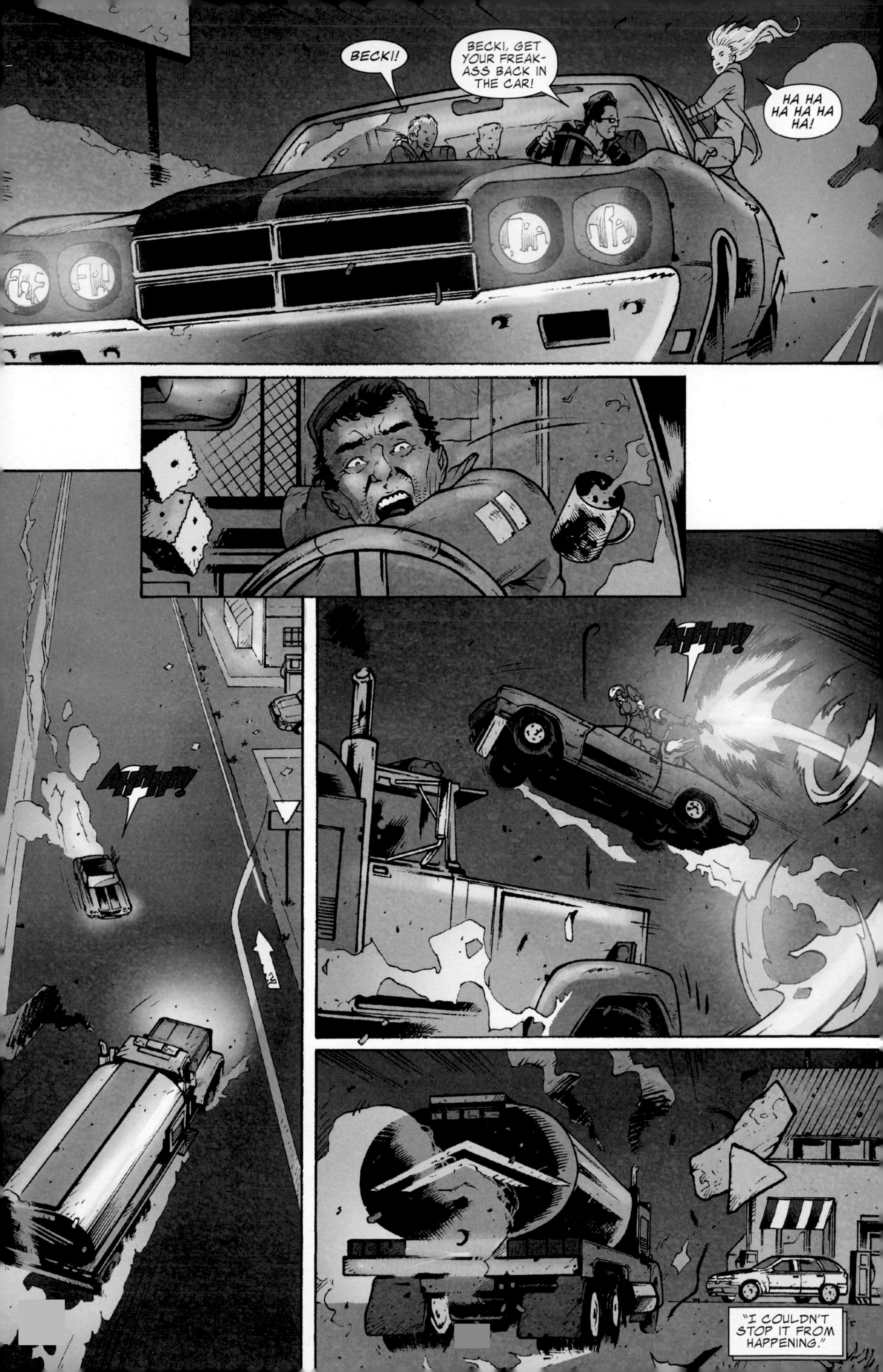
BECKI!
BECKI, GET YOUR FREAK-ASS BACK IN THE CAR!
HA HA HA HA HA HA!
"I COULDN'T STOP IT FROM HAPPENING."

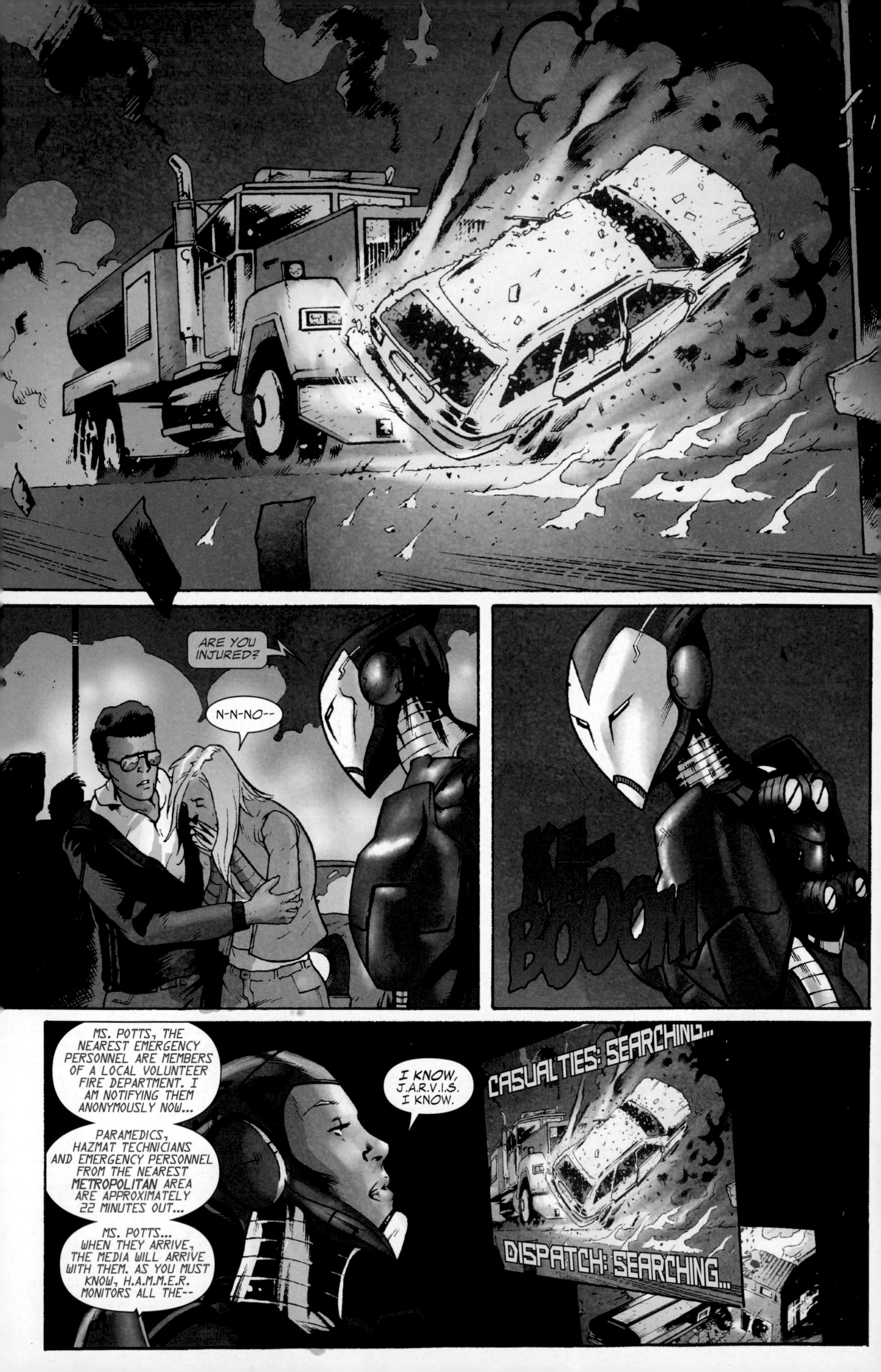
ARE YOU INJURED?
N-N-NO--
KA-BOOM
MS. POTTS, THE NEAREST EMERGENCY PERSONNEL ARE MEMBERS OF A LOCAL VOLUNTEER FIRE DEPARTMENT. I AM NOTIFYING THEM ANONYMOUSLY NOW...
PARAMEDICS, HAZMAT TECHNICIANS AND EMERGENCY PERSONNEL FROM THE NEAREST METROPOLITAN AREA ARE APPROXIMATELY 22 MINUTES OUT...
MS. POTTS... WHEN THEY ARRIVE, THE MEDIA WILL ARRIVE WITH THEM. AS YOU MUST KNOW, H.A.M.M.E.R. MONITORS ALL THE--
I KNOW, J.A.R.V.I.S. I KNOW.
CASUALTIES: SEARCHING...
DISPATCH: SEARCHING...

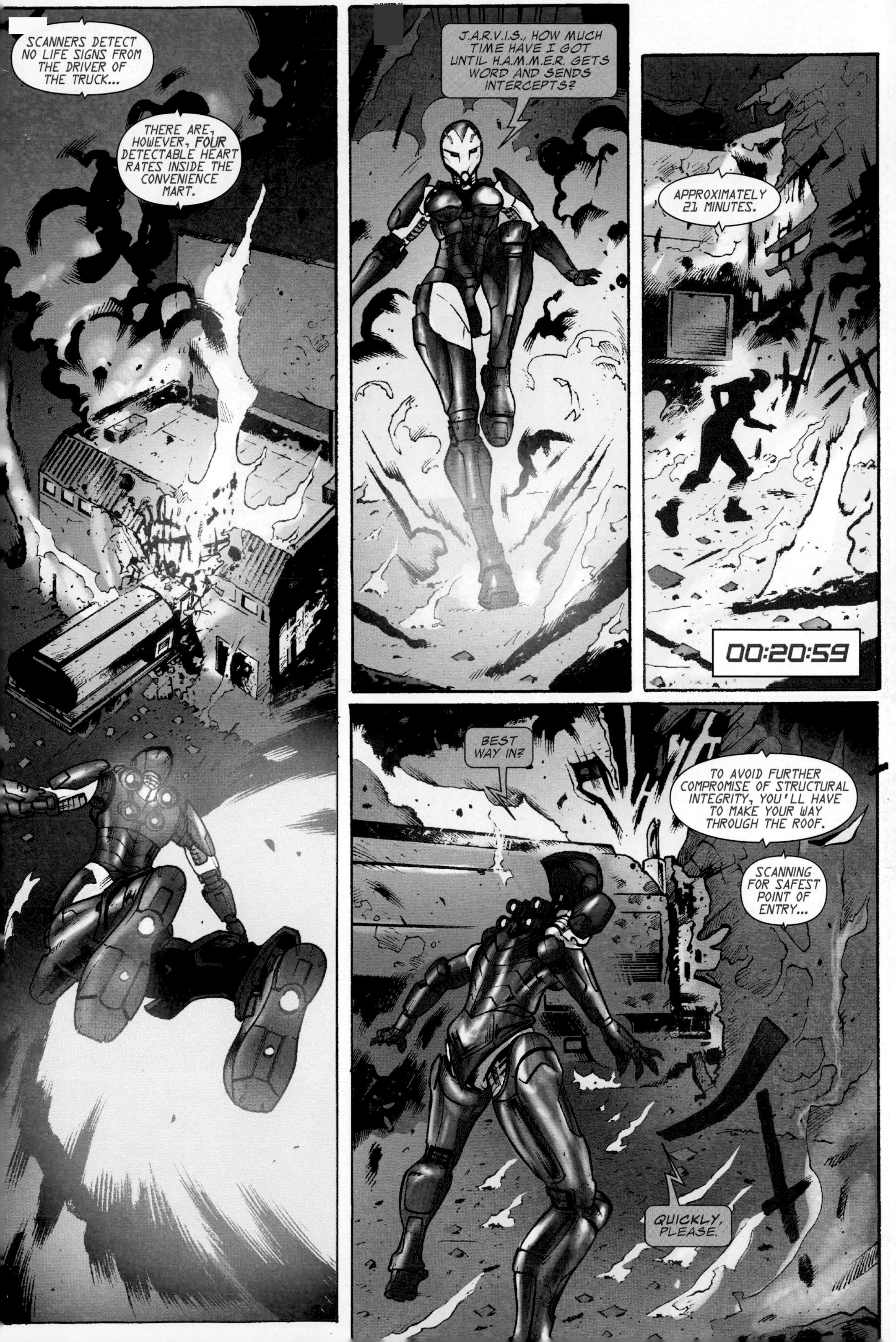
SCANNERS DETECT NO LIFE SIGNS FROM THE DRIVER OF THE TRUCK...
THERE ARE, HOWEVER, FOUR DETECTABLE HEART RATES INSIDE THE CONVENIENCE MART.
J.A.R.V.I.S., HOW MUCH TIME HAVE I GOT UNTIL H.A.M.M.E.R. GETS WORD AND SENDS INTERCEPTS?
APPROXIMATELY 21 MINUTES.
00:20:59
BEST WAY IN?
TO AVOID FURTHER COMPROMISE OF STRUCTURAL INTEGRITY, YOU'LL HAVE TO MAKE YOUR WAY THROUGH THE ROOF.
SCANNING FOR SAFEST POINT OF ENTRY...
QUICKLY, PLEASE.

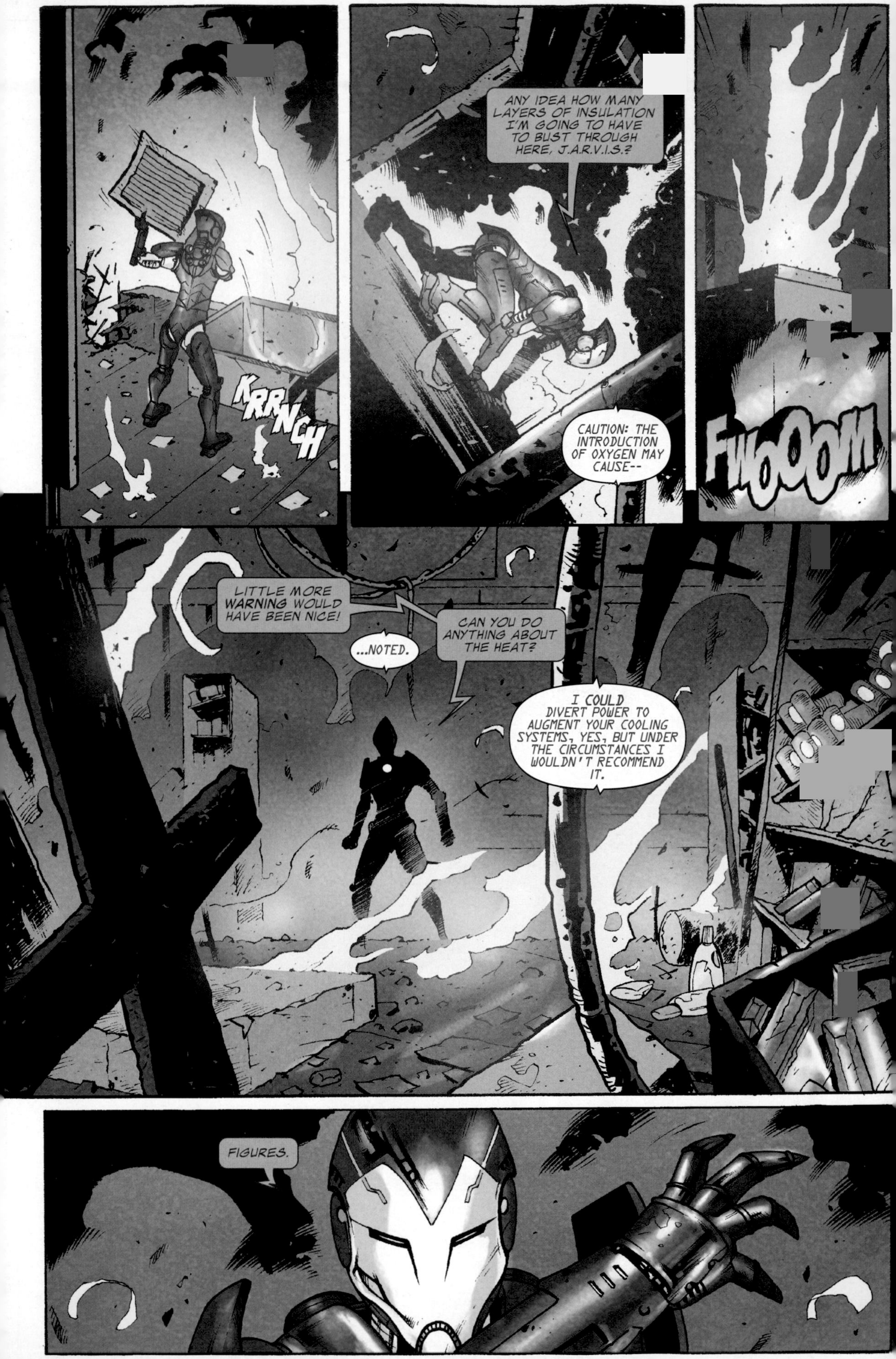

KRRNCH
ANY IDEA HOW MANY LAYERS OF INSULATION I'M GOING TO HAVE TO BUST THROUGH HERE, J.A.R.V.I.S.?
CAUTION: THE INTRODUCTION OF OXYGEN MAY CAUSE--
FWOOOM
LITTLE MORE WARNING WOULD HAVE BEEN NICE!
...NOTED.
CAN YOU DO ANYTHING ABOUT THE HEAT?
I COULD DIVERT POWER TO AUGMENT YOUR COOLING SYSTEMS, YES, BUT UNDER THE CIRCUMSTANCES I WOULDN'T RECOMMEND IT.
FIGURES.

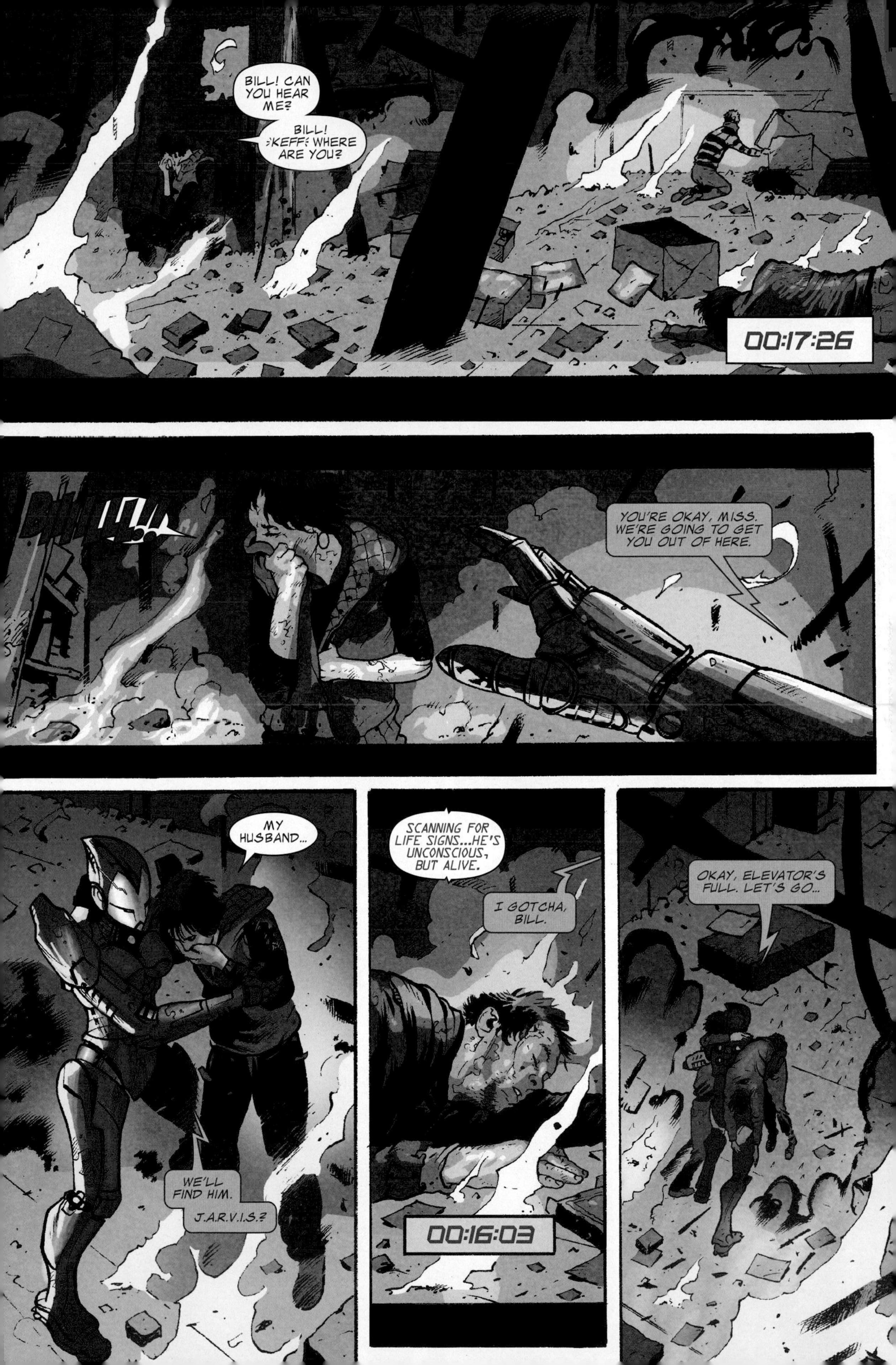
BILL! CAN YOU HEAR ME?
BILL! KEFF WHERE ARE YOU?
00:17:26
YOU'RE OKAY, MISS. WE'RE GOING TO GET YOU OUT OF HERE.
MY HUSBAND...
WE'LL FIND HIM.
J.A.R.V.I.S.?
SCANNING FOR LIFE SIGNS...HE'S UNCONSCIOUS, BUT ALIVE.
I GOTCHA, BILL.
00:16:03
OKAY, ELEVATOR'S FULL. LET'S GO...

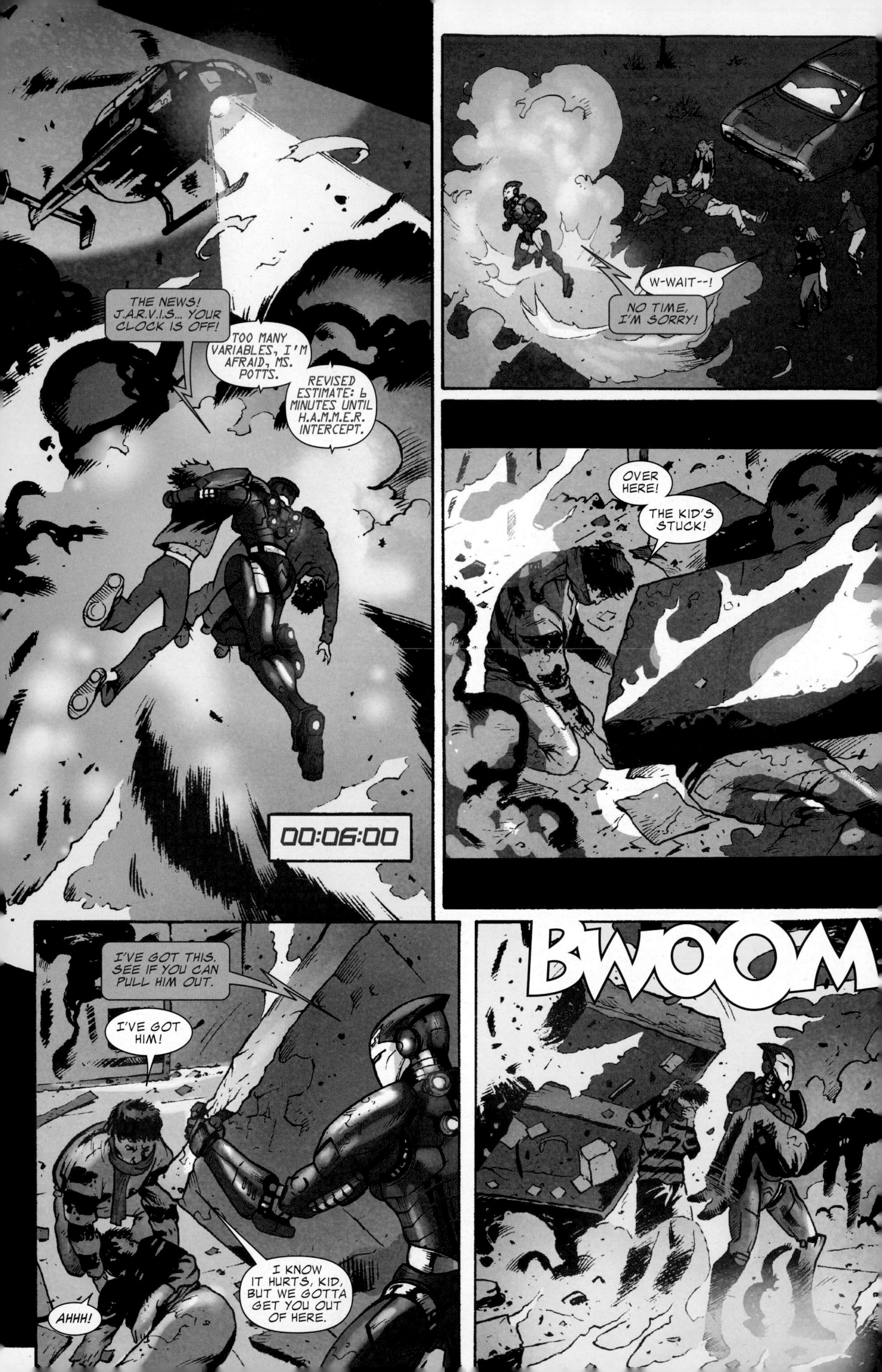
THE NEWS! J.A.R.V.I.S... YOUR CLOCK IS OFF!
TOO MANY VARIABLES, I'M AFRAID, MS. POTTS.
REVISED ESTIMATE: 6 MINUTES UNTIL H.A.M.M.E.R. INTERCEPT.
00:06:00
W-WAIT--!
NO TIME, I'M SORRY!
OVER HERE!
THE KID'S STUCK!
I'VE GOT THIS. SEE IF YOU CAN PULL HIM OUT.
I'VE GOT HIM!
I KNOW IT HURTS, KID, BUT WE GOTTA GET YOU OUT OF HERE.
AHHH!
BWOOM

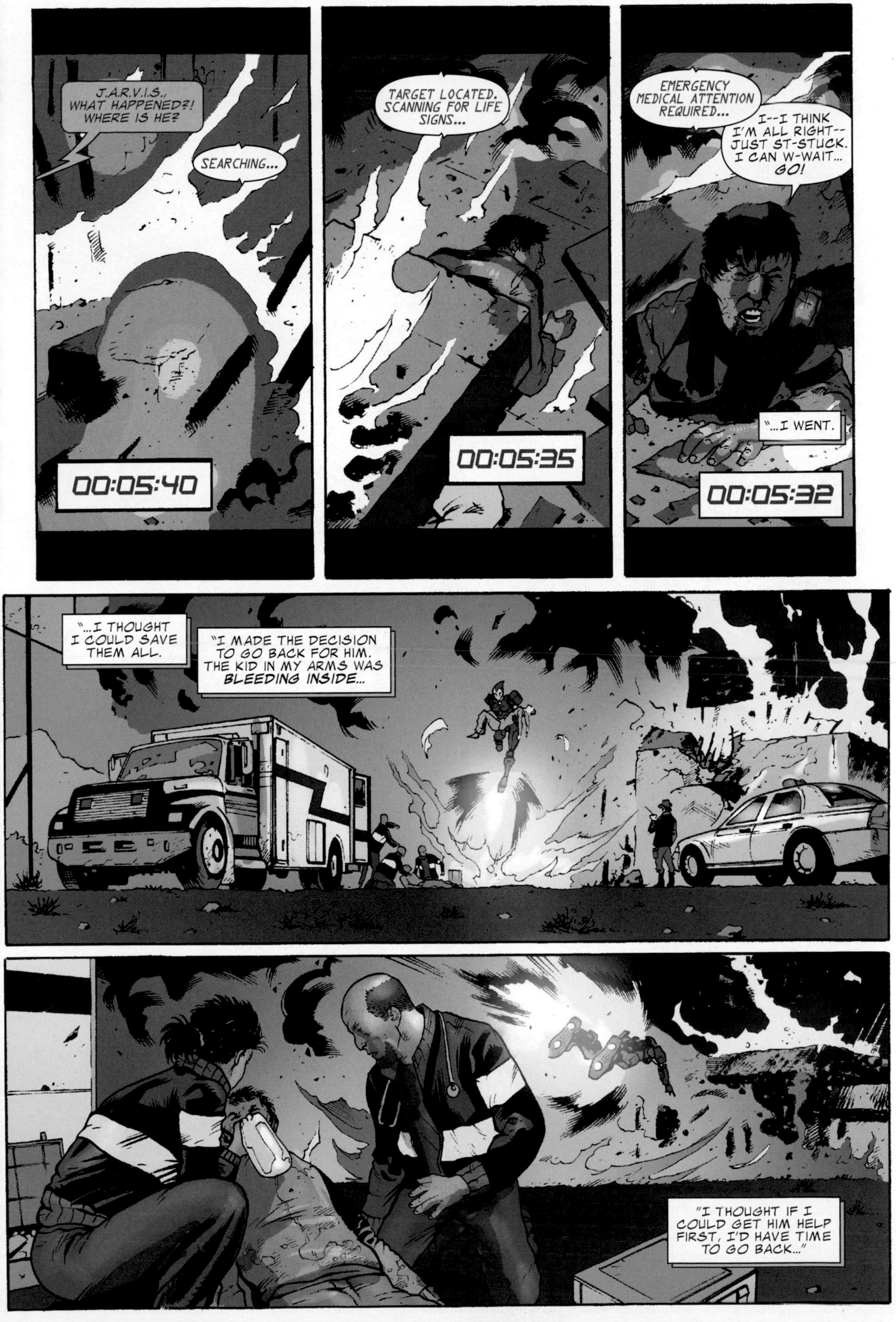
J.A.R.V.I.S., WHAT HAPPENED?! WHERE IS HE?
SEARCHING...
00:05:40
TARGET LOCATED. SCANNING FOR LIFE SIGNS...
00:05:35
EMERGENCY MEDICAL ATTENTION REQUIRED...
I--I THINK I'M ALL RIGHT-- JUST ST-STUCK. I CAN W-WAIT... GO!
"...I WENT.
00:05:32
"...I THOUGHT I COULD SAVE THEM ALL.
"I MADE THE DECISION TO GO BACK FOR HIM. THE KID IN MY ARMS WAS BLEEDING INSIDE...
"I THOUGHT IF I COULD GET HIM HELP FIRST, I'D HAVE TIME TO GO BACK..."

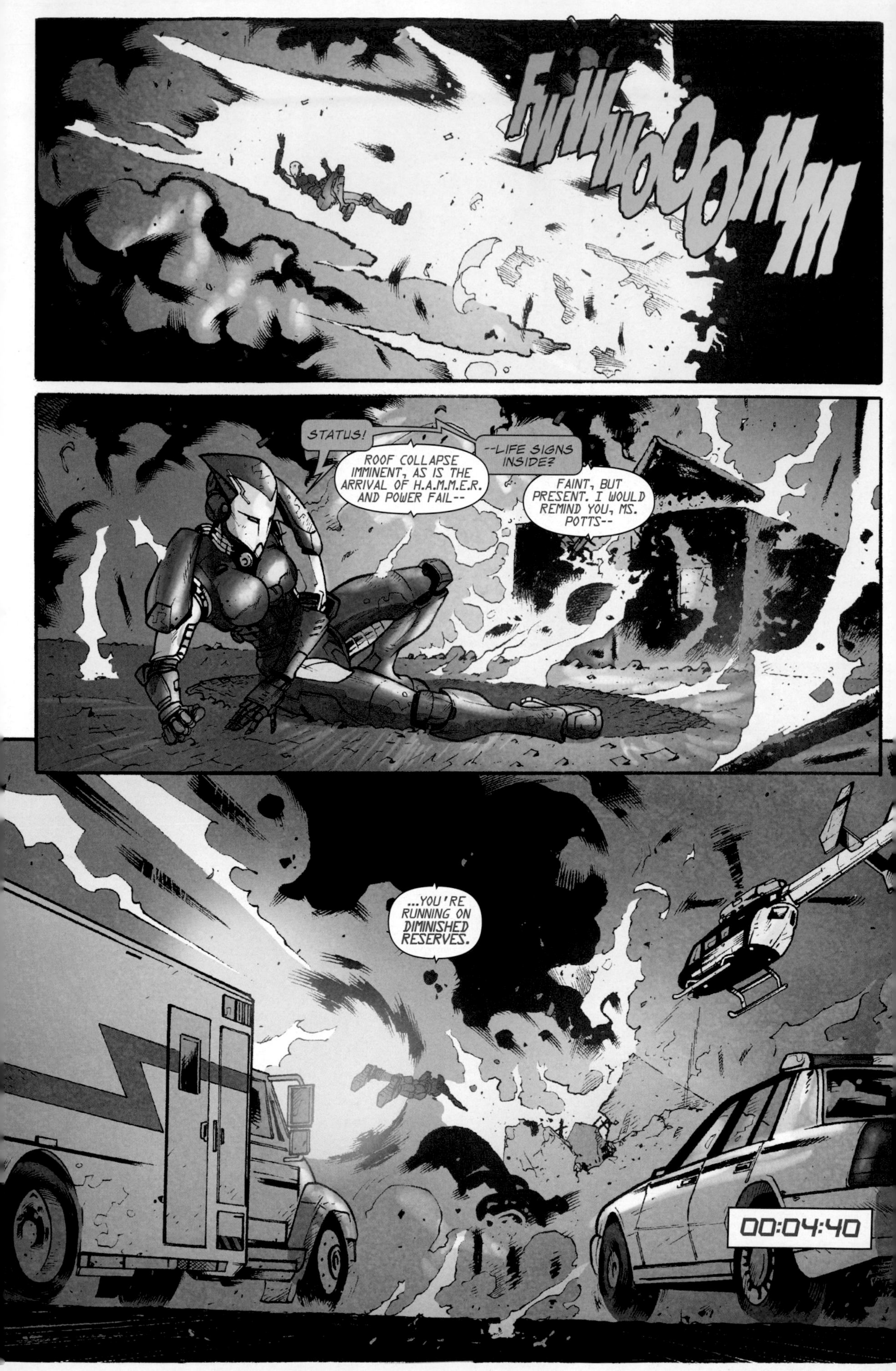
FWWWOOOMMM
STATUS!
--LIFE SIGNS INSIDE?
ROOF COLLAPSE IMMINENT, AS IS THE ARRIVAL OF H.A.M.M.E.R. AND POWER FAIL--
FAINT, BUT PRESENT. I WOULD REMIND YOU, MS. POTTS--
...YOU'RE RUNNING ON DIMINISHED RESERVES.
00:04:40

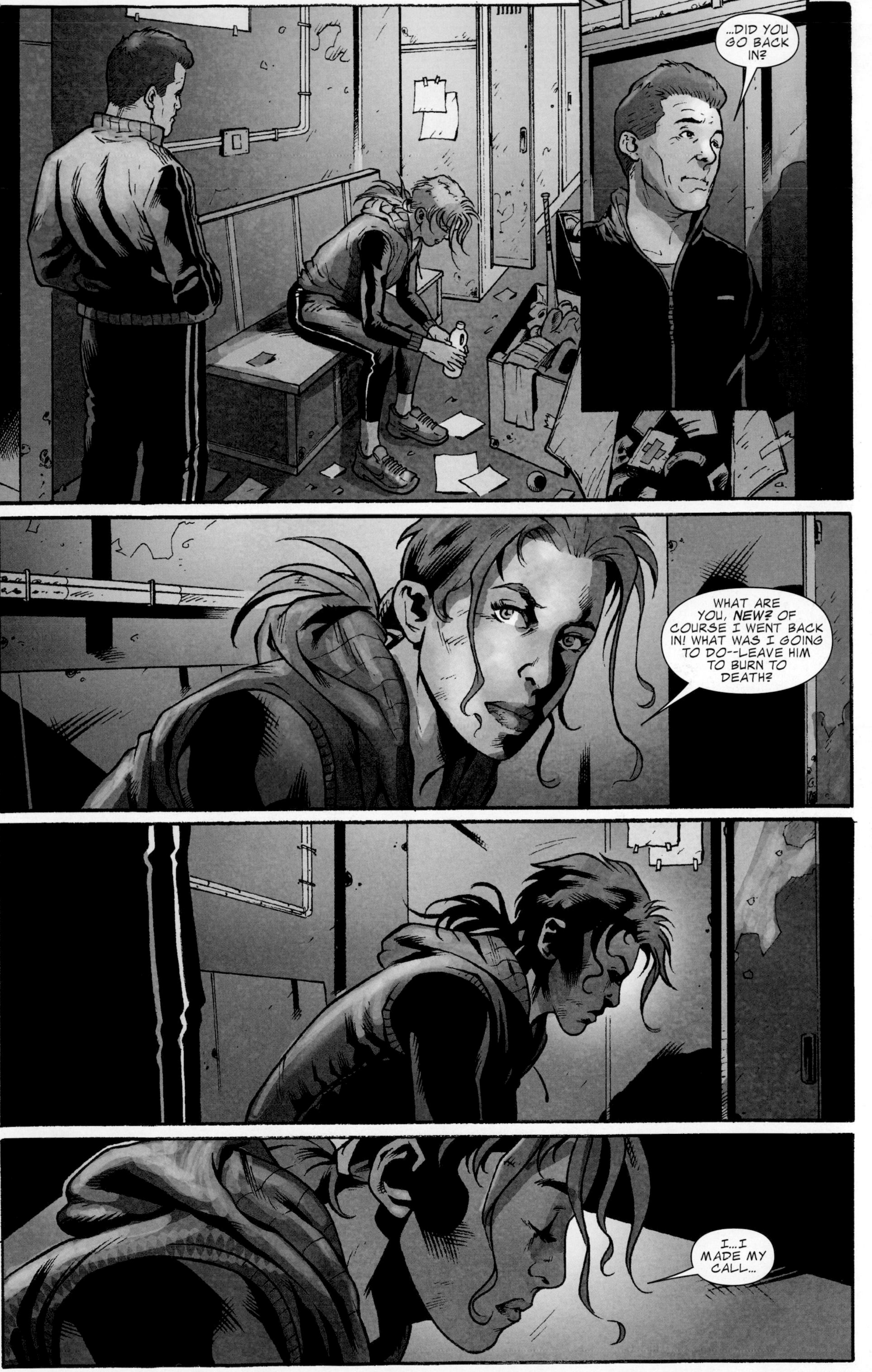
...DID YOU GO BACK IN?
WHAT ARE YOU, NEW? OF COURSE I WENT BACK IN! WHAT WAS I GOING TO DO--LEAVE HIM TO BURN TO DEATH?
I...I MADE MY CALL...

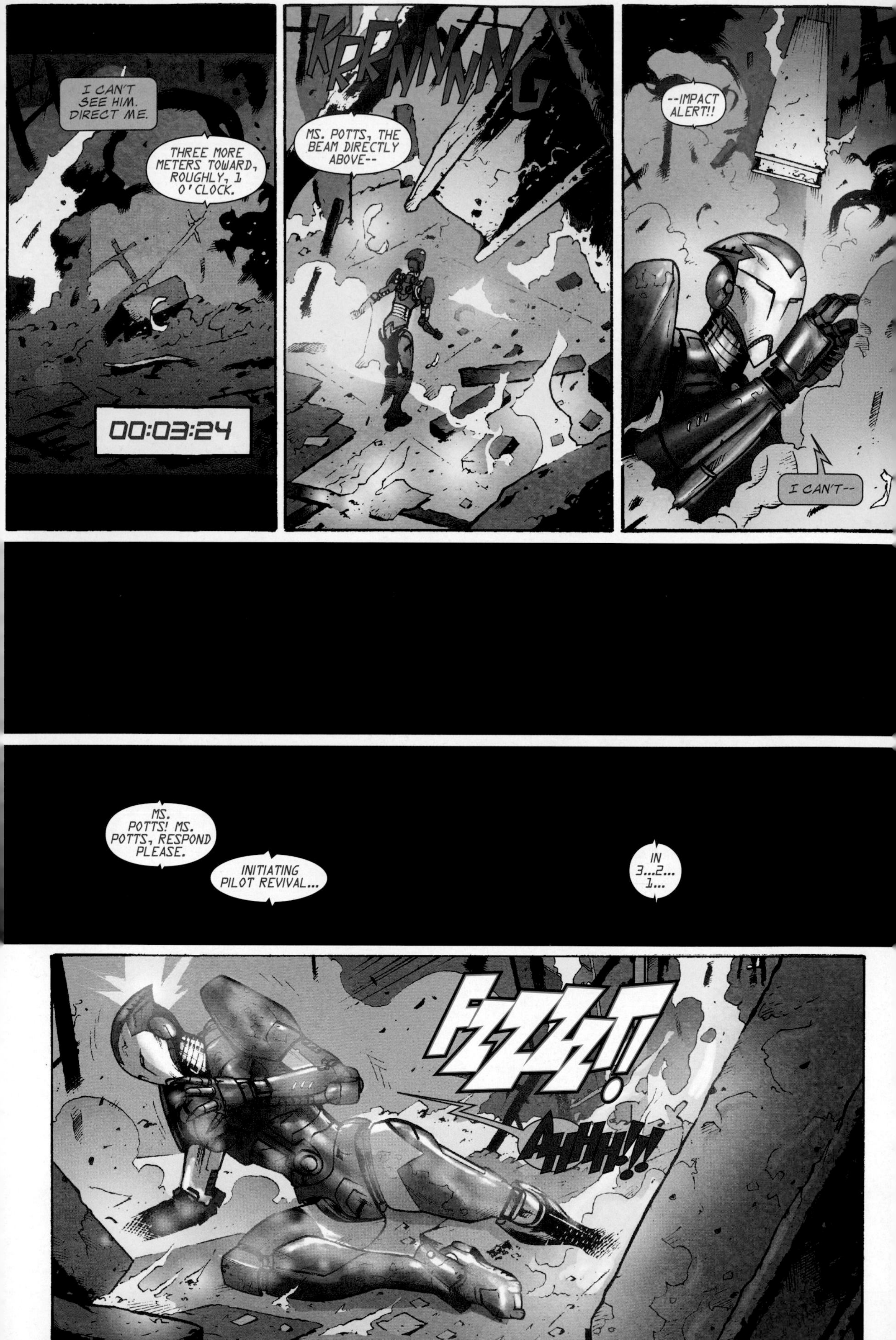
I CAN'T SEE HIM. DIRECT ME.
THREE MORE METERS TOWARD, ROUGHLY, 1 O'CLOCK.
00:03:24
KRRNNNNG
MS. POTTS, THE BEAM DIRECTLY ABOVE--
--IMPACT ALERT!!
I CAN'T--
MS. POTTS! MS. POTTS, RESPOND PLEASE.
INITIATING PILOT REVIVAL...
IN 3...2... 1...
FZZZT!!
AHHH!!

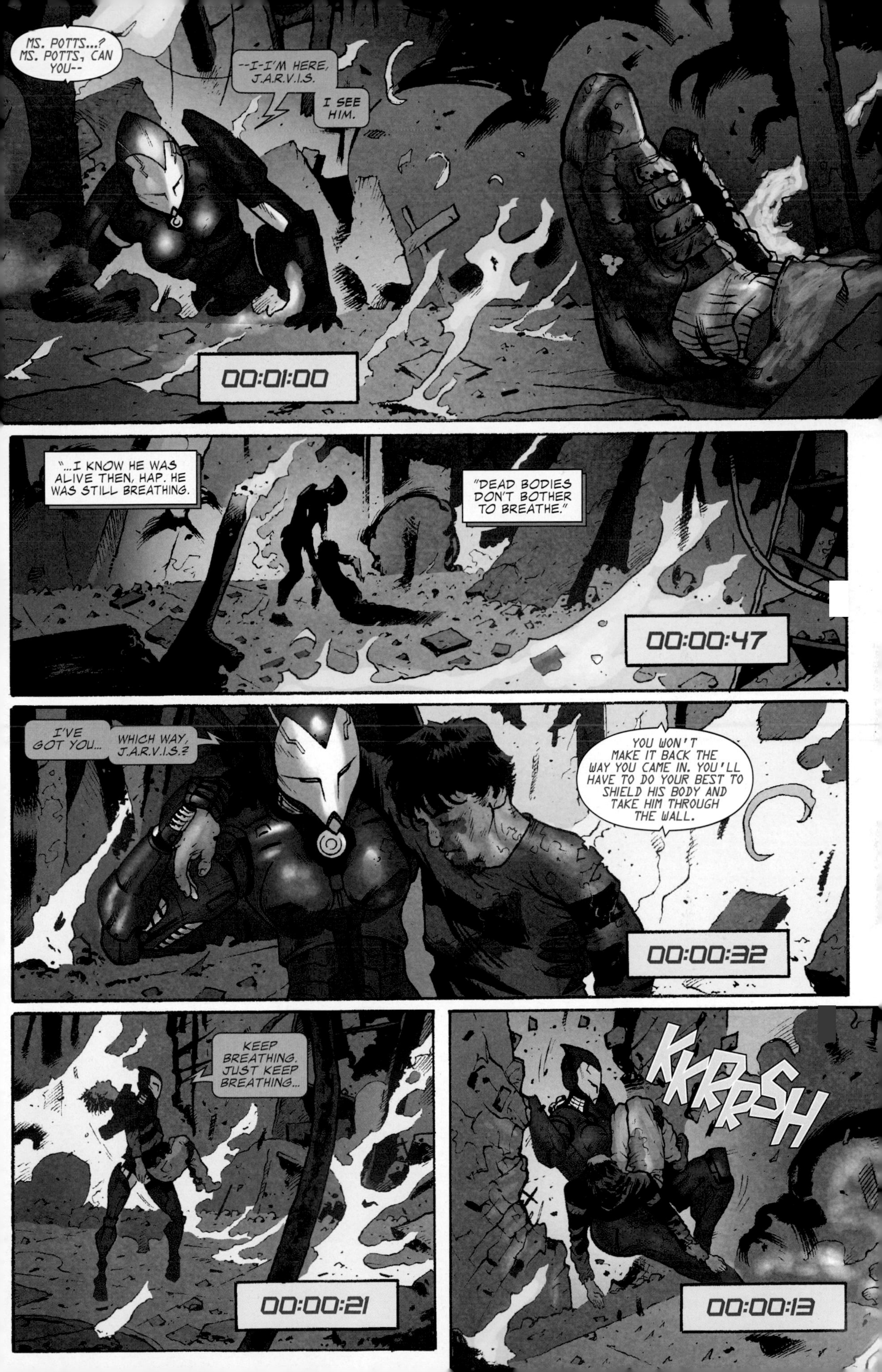

MS. POTTS...? MS. POTTS, CAN YOU--
--I-I'M HERE, J.A.R.V.I.S.
I SEE HIM.
00:01:00
"...I KNOW HE WAS ALIVE THEN, HAP. HE WAS STILL BREATHING.
"DEAD BODIES DON'T BOTHER TO BREATHE."
00:00:47
I'VE GOT YOU...
WHICH WAY, J.A.R.V.I.S.?
YOU WON'T MAKE IT BACK THE WAY YOU CAME IN. YOU'LL HAVE TO DO YOUR BEST TO SHIELD HIS BODY AND TAKE HIM THROUGH THE WALL.
00:00:32
KEEP BREATHING. JUST KEEP BREATHING...
00:00:21
KKRRSH
00:00:13

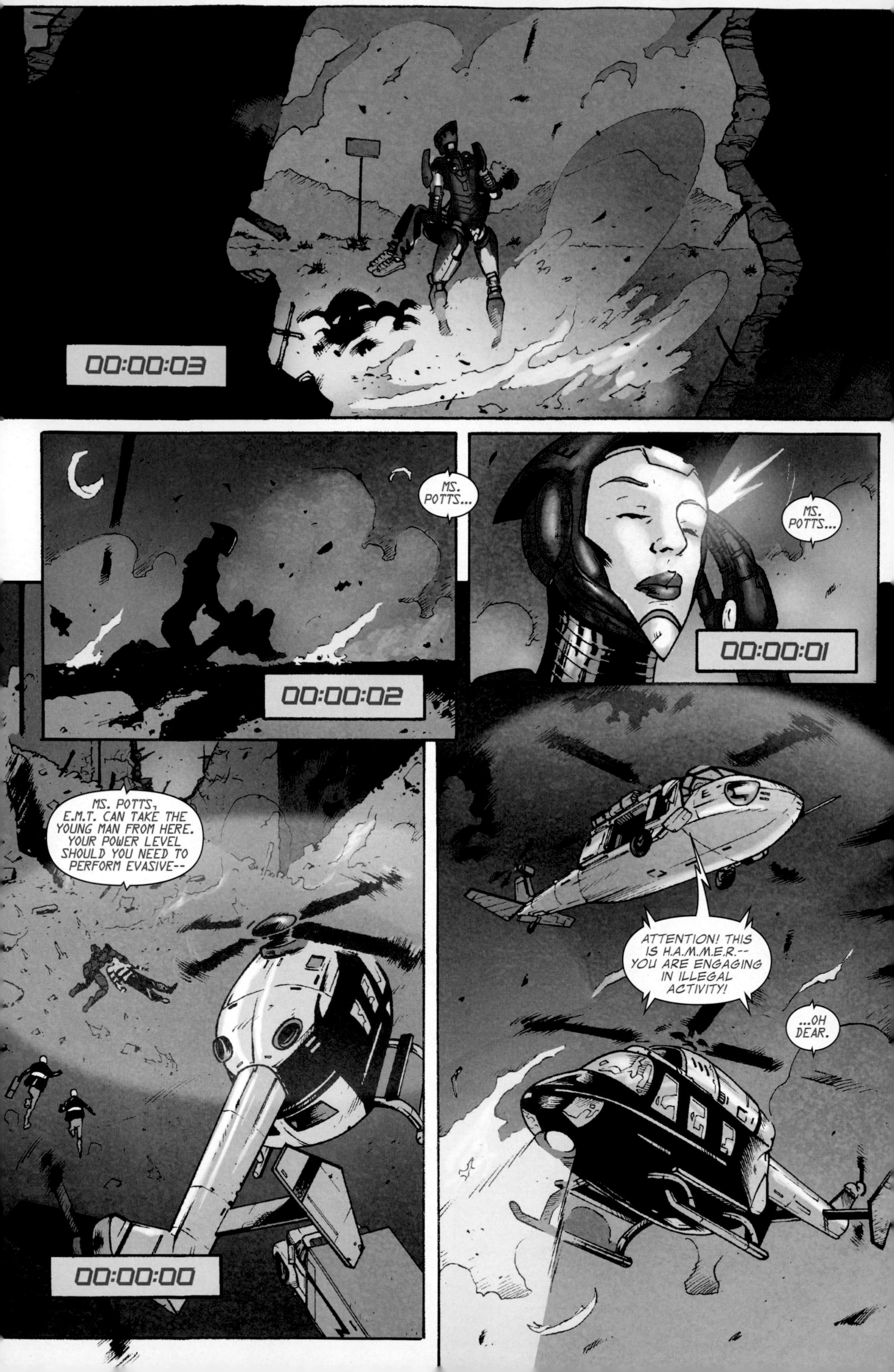
00:00:03
MS. POTTS...
00:00:02
MS. POTTS...
00:00:01
MS. POTTS, E.M.T. CAN TAKE THE YOUNG MAN FROM HERE. YOUR POWER LEVEL SHOULD YOU NEED TO PERFORM EVASIVE--
00:00:00
ATTENTION! THIS IS H.A.M.M.E.R.-- YOU ARE ENGAGING IN ILLEGAL ACTIVITY!
...OH DEAR.

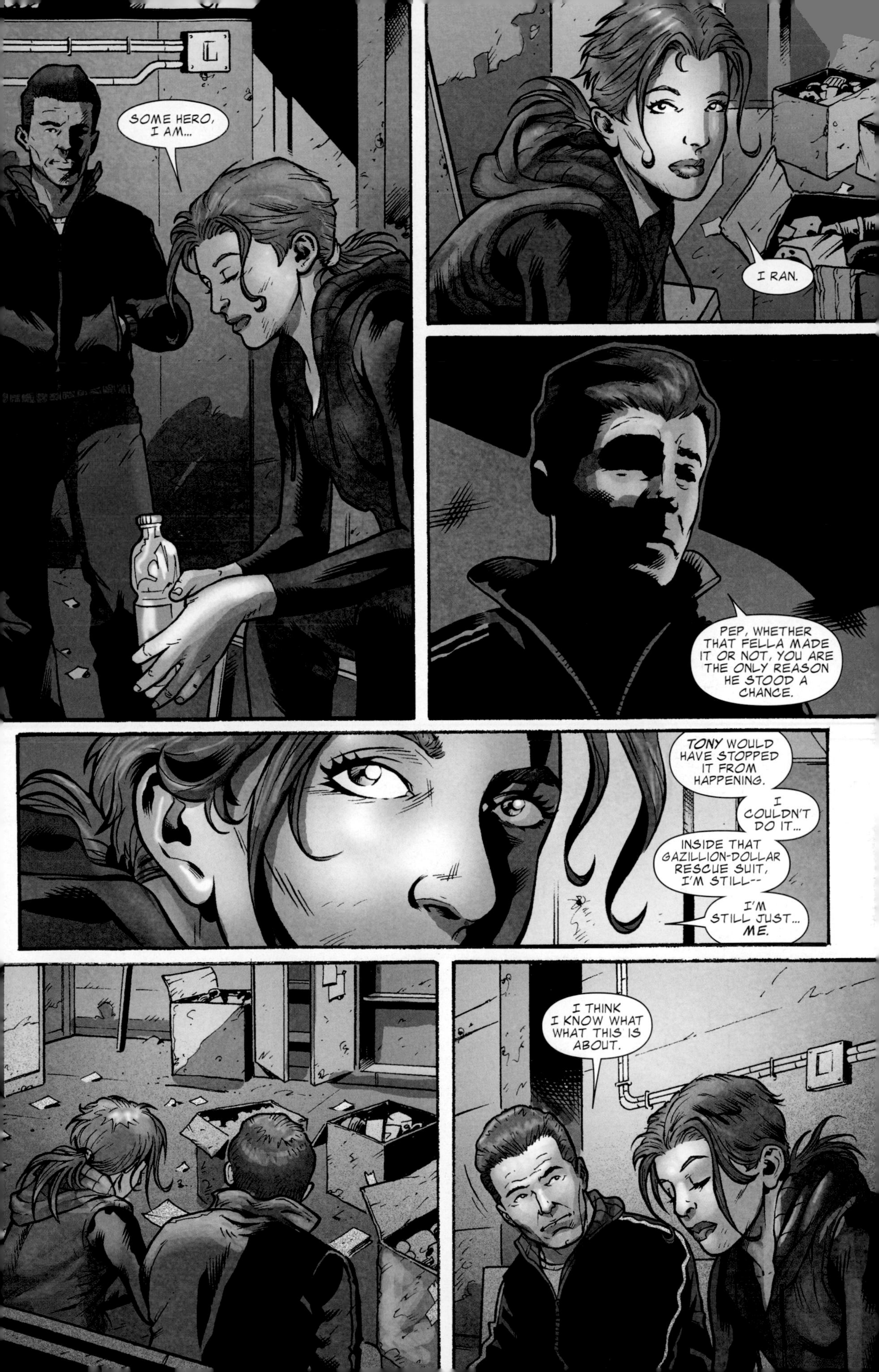
SOME HERO, I AM...
I RAN.
PEP, WHETHER THAT FELLA MADE IT OR NOT, YOU ARE THE ONLY REASON HE STOOD A CHANCE.
TONY WOULD HAVE STOPPED IT FROM HAPPENING.
I COULDN'T DO IT...
INSIDE THAT GAZILLION-DOLLAR RESCUE SUIT, I'M STILL--
I'M STILL JUST... ME.
I THINK I KNOW WHAT WHAT THIS IS ABOUT.

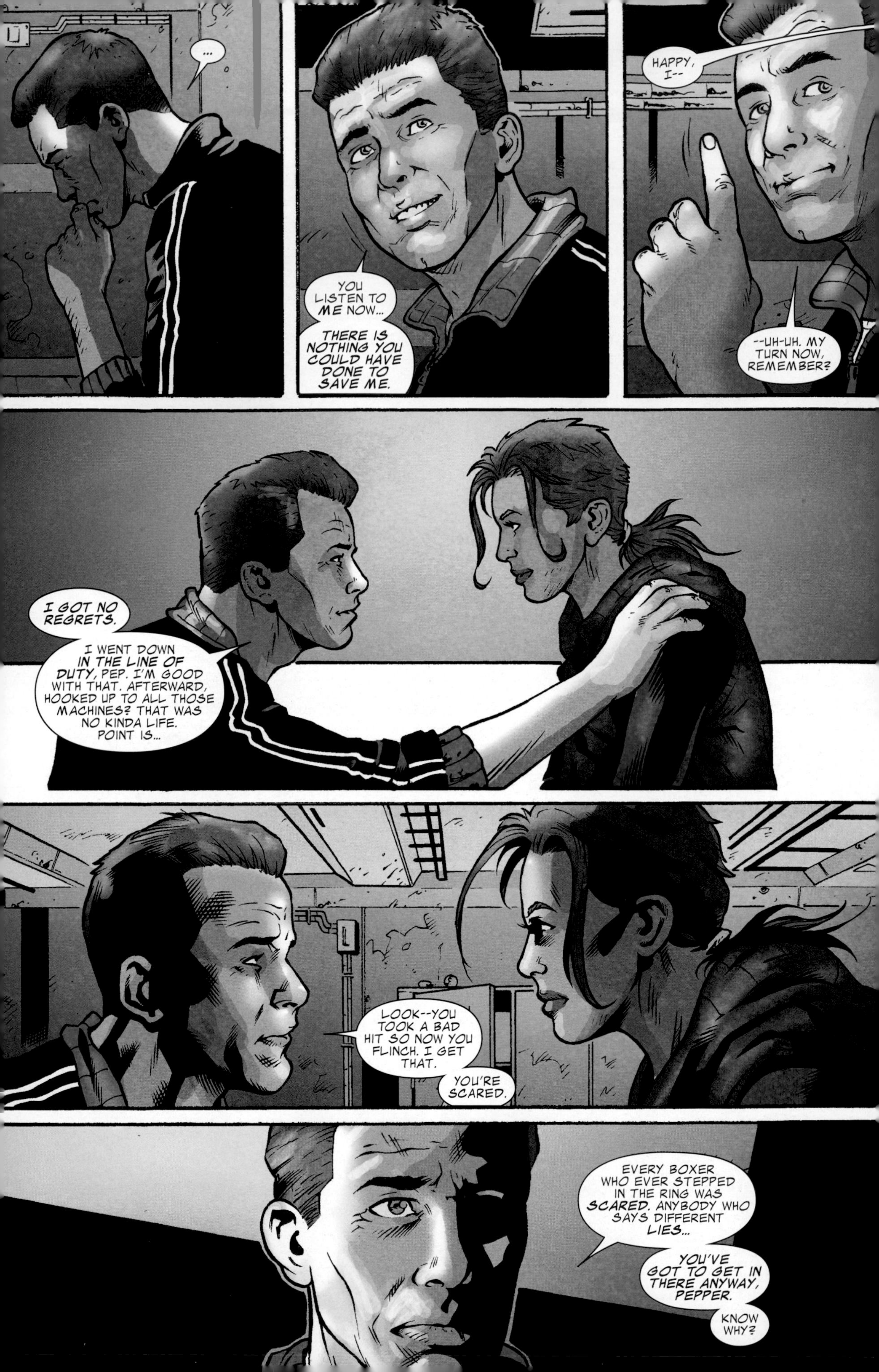
...
YOU LISTEN TO ME NOW...
THERE IS NOTHING YOU COULD HAVE DONE TO SAVE ME.
HAPPY, I--
--UH-UH. MY TURN NOW, REMEMBER?
I GOT NO REGRETS.
I WENT DOWN IN THE LINE OF DUTY, PEP. I'M GOOD WITH THAT. AFTERWARD, HOOKED UP TO ALL THOSE MACHINES? THAT WAS NO KINDA LIFE. POINT IS...
LOOK--YOU TOOK A BAD HIT SO NOW YOU FLINCH. I GET THAT.
YOU'RE SCARED.
EVERY BOXER WHO EVER STEPPED IN THE RING WAS SCARED. ANYBODY WHO SAYS DIFFERENT LIES...
YOU'VE GOT TO GET IN THERE ANYWAY, PEPPER.
KNOW WHY?

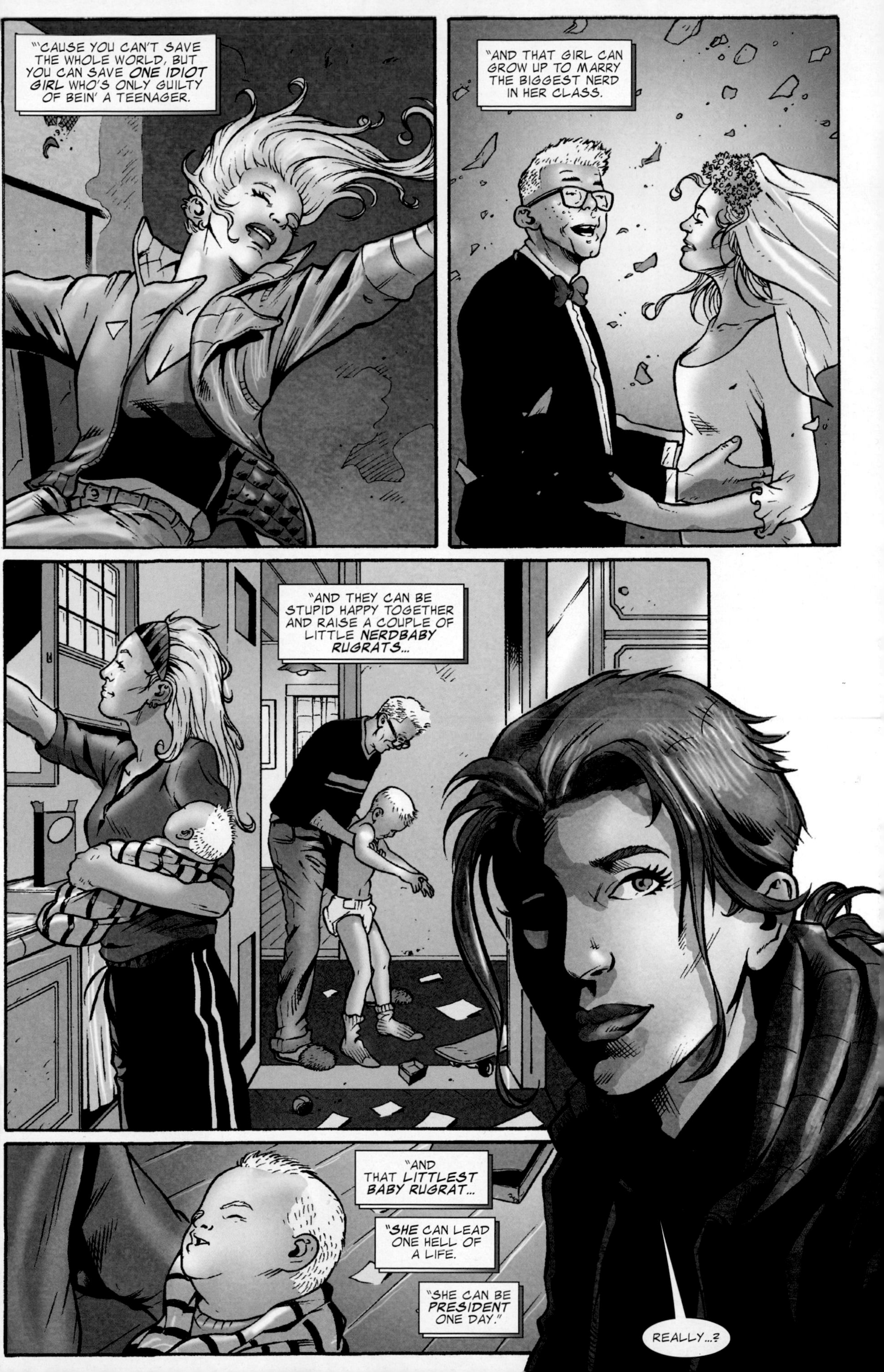
"'CAUSE YOU CAN'T SAVE THE WHOLE WORLD, BUT YOU CAN SAVE ONE IDIOT GIRL WHO'S ONLY GUILTY OF BEIN' A TEENAGER.
"AND THAT GIRL CAN GROW UP TO MARRY THE BIGGEST NERD IN HER CLASS.
"AND THEY CAN BE STUPID HAPPY TOGETHER AND RAISE A COUPLE OF LITTLE NERDBABY RUGRATS...
"AND THAT LITTLEST BABY RUGRAT...
"SHE CAN LEAD ONE HELL OF A LIFE.
"SHE CAN BE PRESIDENT ONE DAY."
REALLY...?

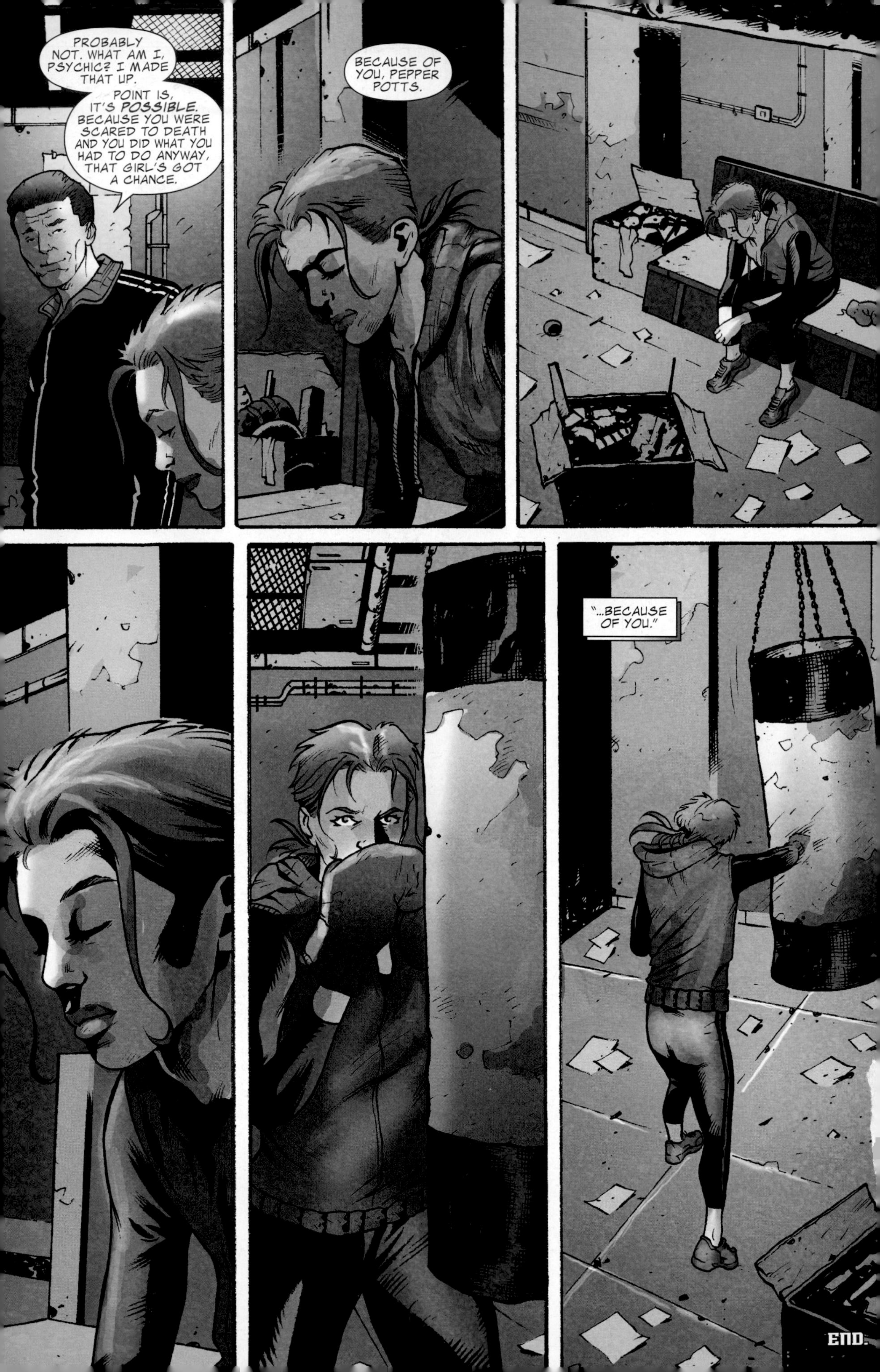
PROBABLY NOT. WHAT AM I, PSYCHIC? I MADE THAT UP.
POINT IS, IT'S *POSSIBLE*. BECAUSE YOU WERE SCARED TO DEATH AND YOU DID WHAT YOU HAD TO DO ANYWAY, THAT GIRL'S GOT A CHANCE.
BECAUSE OF YOU, PEPPER POTTS.
"...BECAUSE OF YOU."
END.

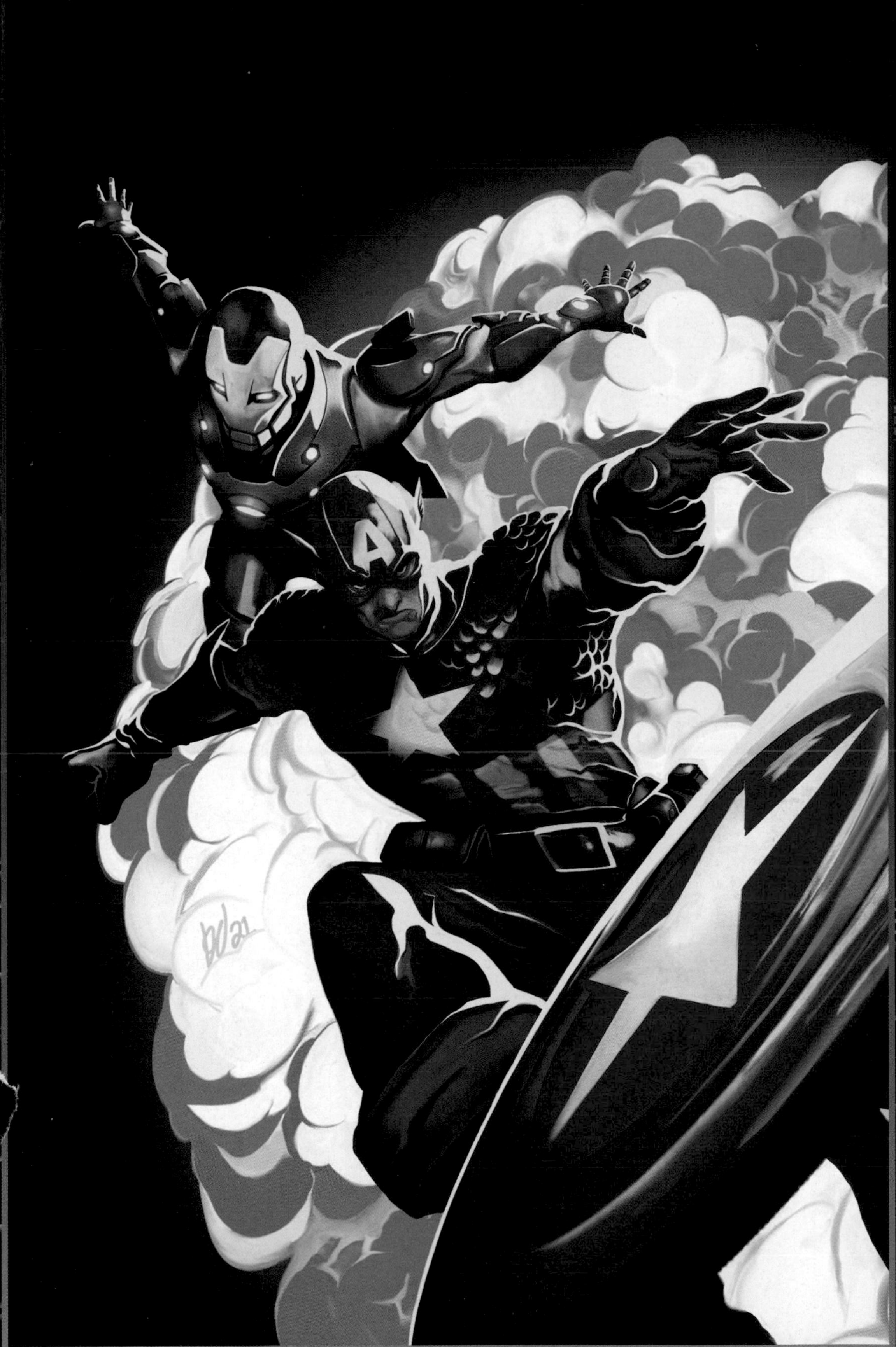

#502 CAPTAIN AMERICA 70TH ANNIVERSARY VARIANT
BY MICHAEL DEL MUNDO

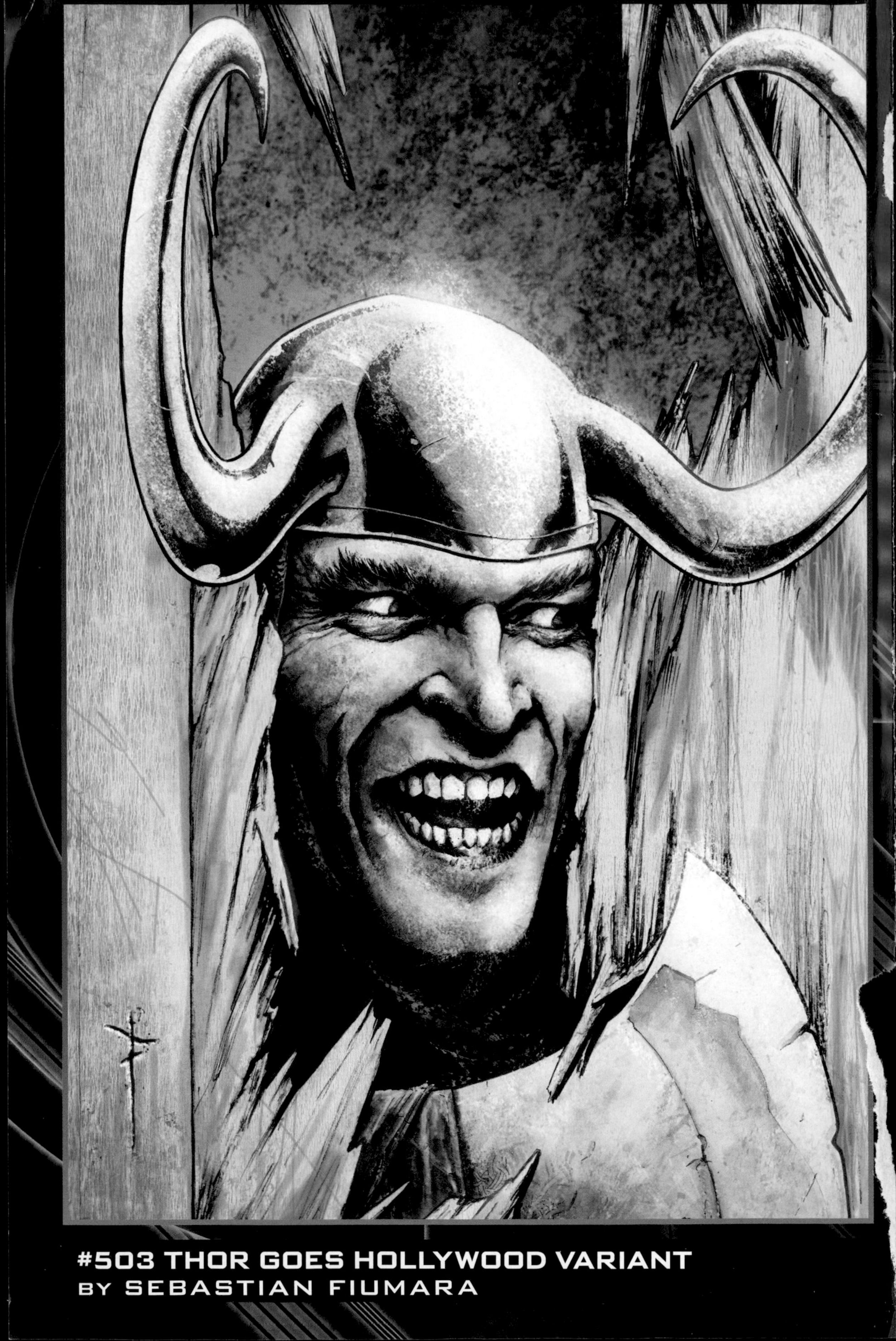

#503 THOR GOES HOLLYWOOD VARIANT
BY SEBASTIAN FIUMARA